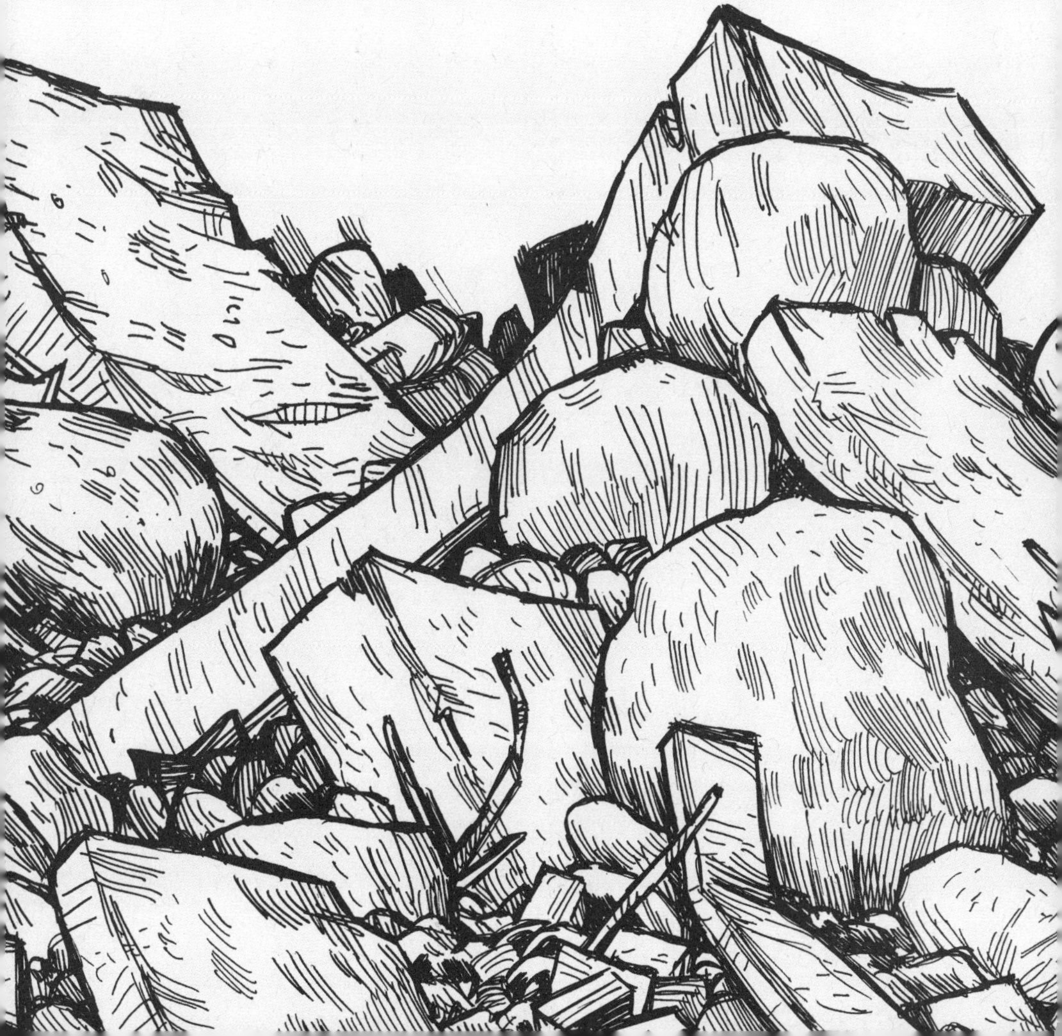

DAYBREAK

BRIAN RALPH

DRAWN & QUARTERLY

MOST OF THIS BOOK WAS PRINTED IN PAMPHLET FORM
(DAYBREAK 1, 2, AND 3) BY BODEGA.
PRODUCTION BY RANDY CHANG WITH ASSISTANCE
BY RAY SOHN, ANDREW ARNOLD, AND SHANNON TIEN.

FIRST HARDCOVER EDITION: AUGUST 2011
FIRST PAPERBACK EDITION: FEBRUARY 2013
PRINTED IN CANADA

10 9 8 7 6 5 4 3 2 1
LIBRARY AND ARCHIVES CANADA
CATALOGUING IN PUBLICATION

RALPH, BRIAN, 1973 -
DAYBREAK/ BRIAN RALPH.

ISBN 978-1-77046-124-6
     1. GRAPHIC NOVELS. I. TITLE.
PN6727. R35D38 2013   741.5'973
     C2012-907129-3

PUBLISHED IN THE USA BY DRAWN AND QUARTERLY, A CLIENT
PUBLISHER OF FARRAR, STRAUS AND GIROUX
18 WEST 18TH ST. NEW YORK, NY 10011 ORDERS: 888.330.8477

PUBLISHED IN CANADA BY DRAWN AND QUARTERLY, A CLIENT
PUBLISHER OF RAINCOAST BOOKS
2440 VIKING WAY, RICHMOND, BC V6V 1N2
ORDERS: 800.663.5714

DISTRIBUTED IN THE UK BY:
PUBLISHERS GROUP UK
63-66 HATTON GARDEN
LONDON EC1N 8LE UNITED KINGDOM
ORDERS: INFO@PGUK.CO.UK

WWW.DRAWNANDQUARTERLY.COM

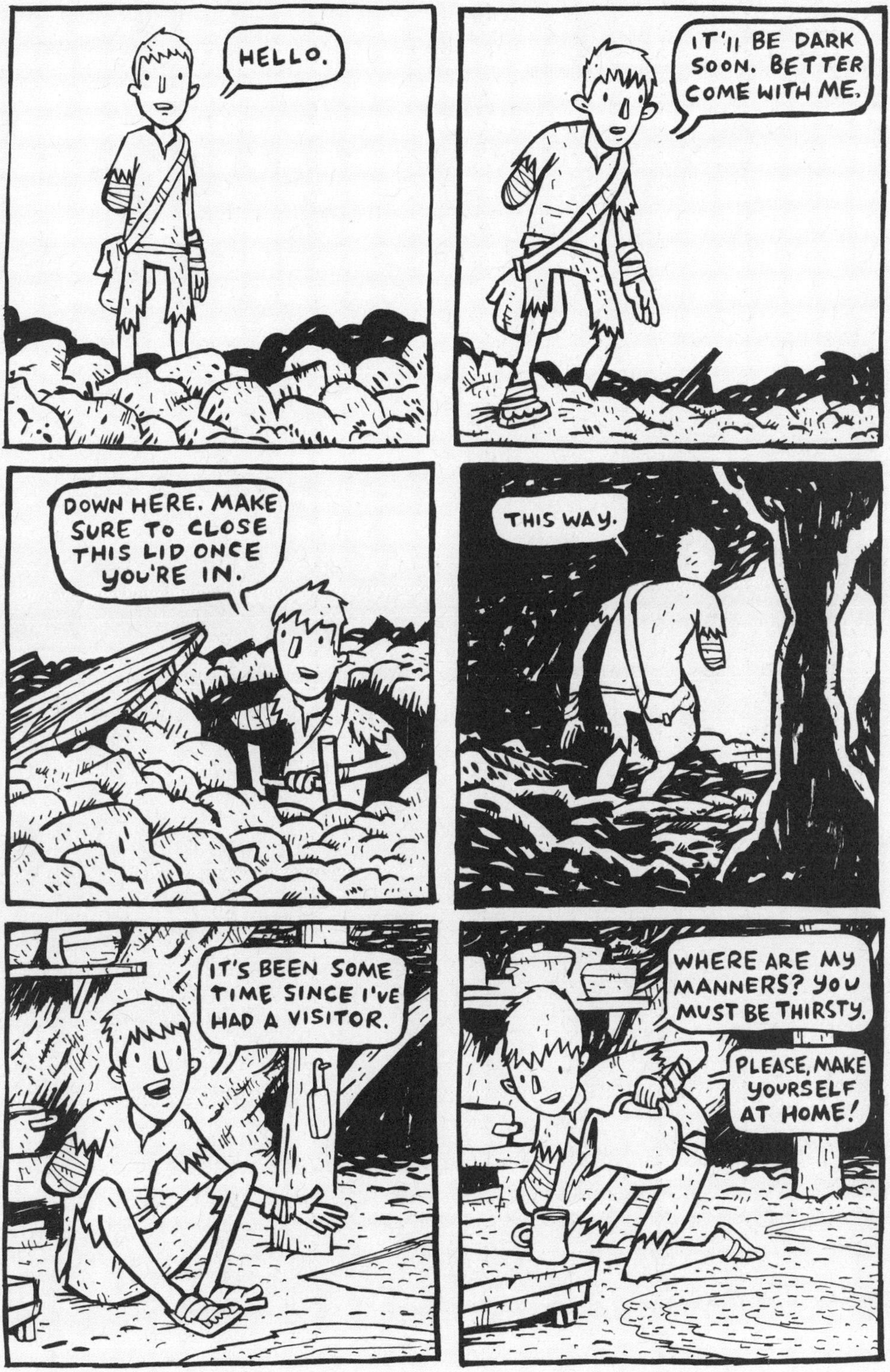
HELLO.
IT'll BE DARK SOON. BETTER COME WITH ME.
DOWN HERE. MAKE SURE TO CLOSE THIS LID ONCE YOU'RE IN.
THIS WAY.
IT'S BEEN SOME TIME SINCE I'VE HAD A VISITOR.
WHERE ARE MY MANNERS? YOU MUST BE THIRSTY.
PLEASE, MAKE YOURSELF AT HOME!

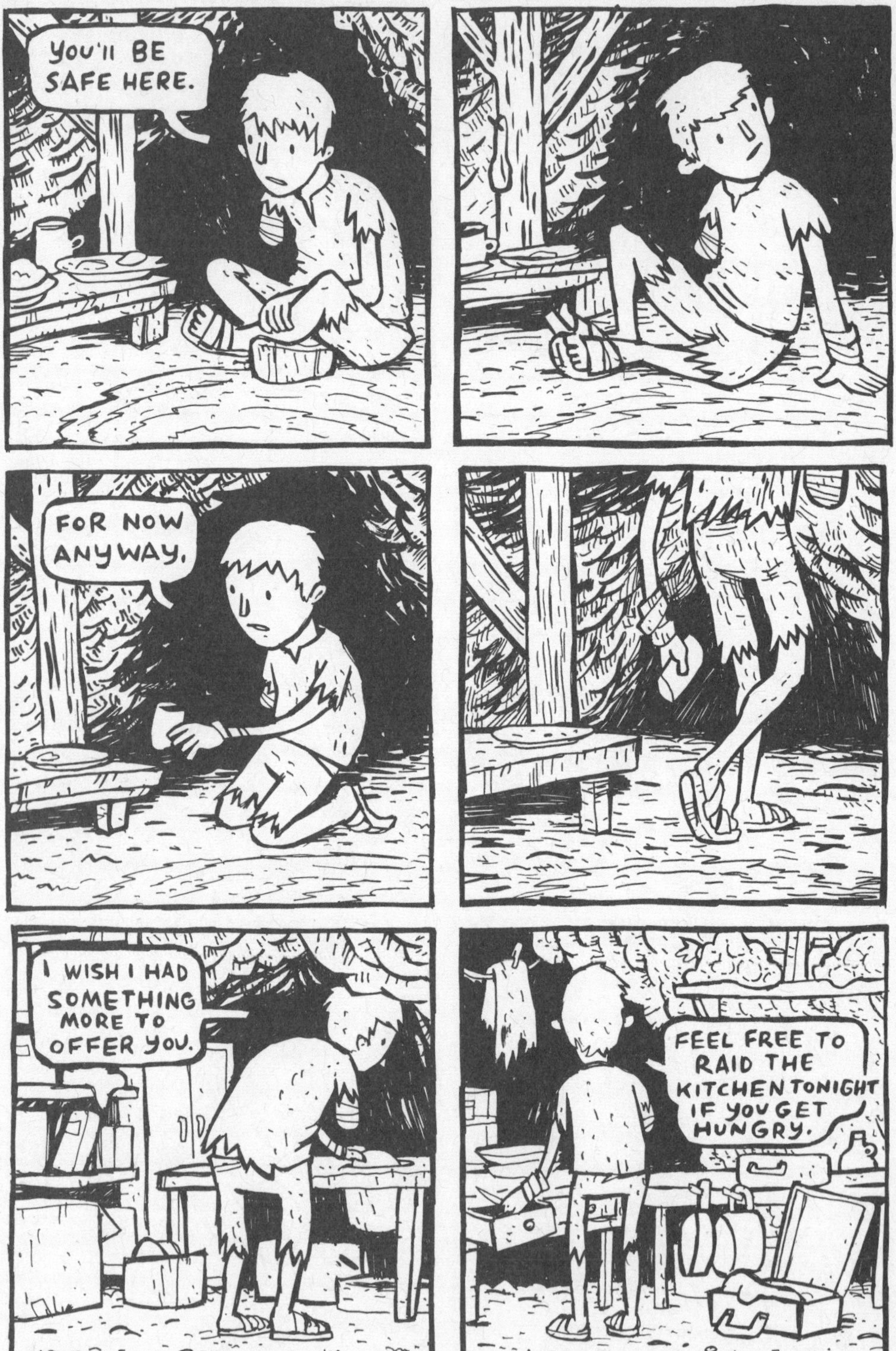
YOU'll BE SAFE HERE.
FOR NOW ANYWAY.
I WISH I HAD SOMETHING MORE TO OFFER YOU.
FEEL FREE TO RAID THE KITCHEN TONIGHT IF YOU GET HUNGRY.

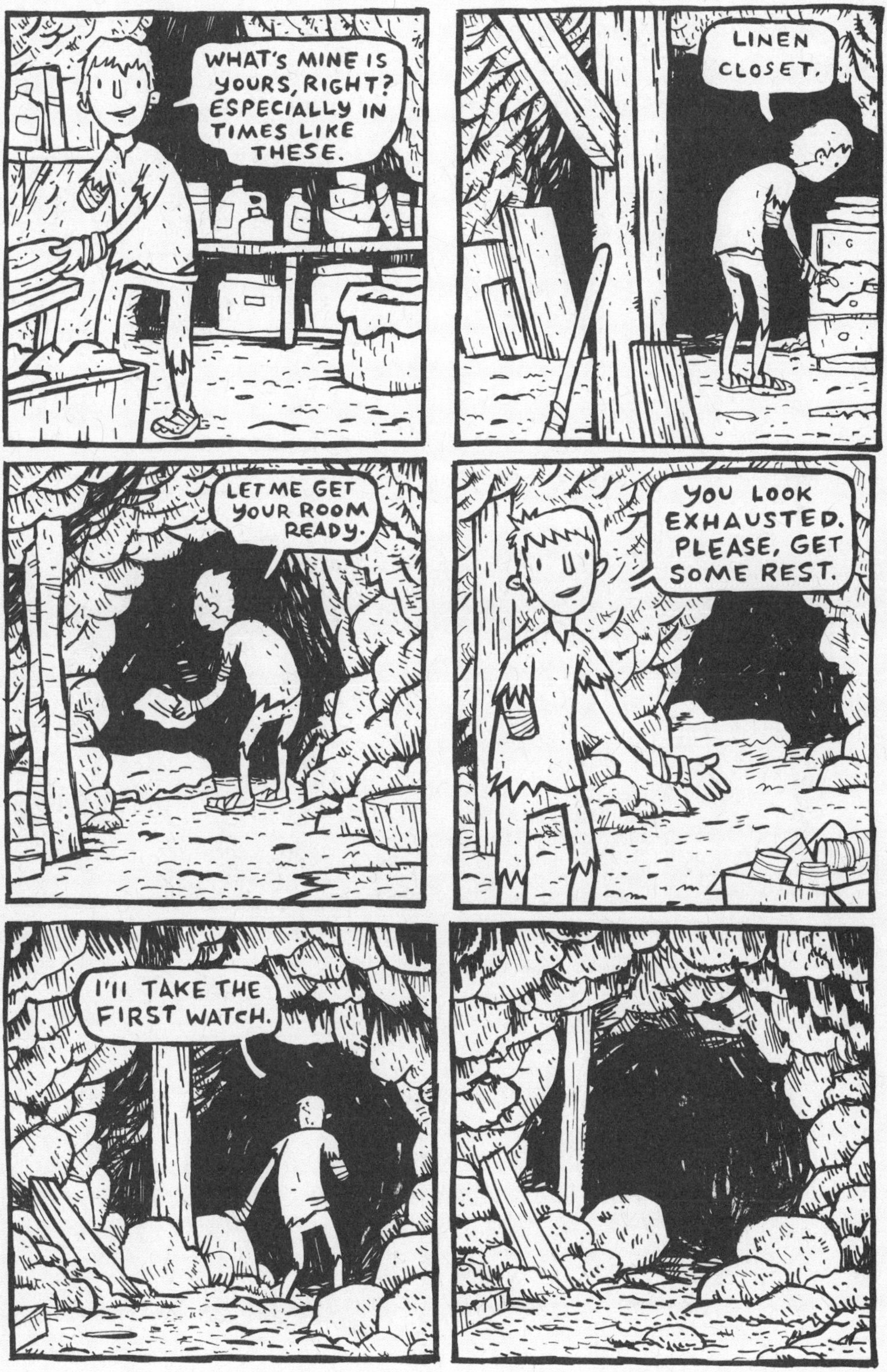
WHAT'S MINE IS YOURS, RIGHT? ESPECIALLY IN TIMES LIKE THESE.
LINEN CLOSET.
LET ME GET YOUR ROOM READY.
YOU LOOK EXHAUSTED. PLEASE, GET SOME REST.
I'll TAKE THE FIRST WATCH.

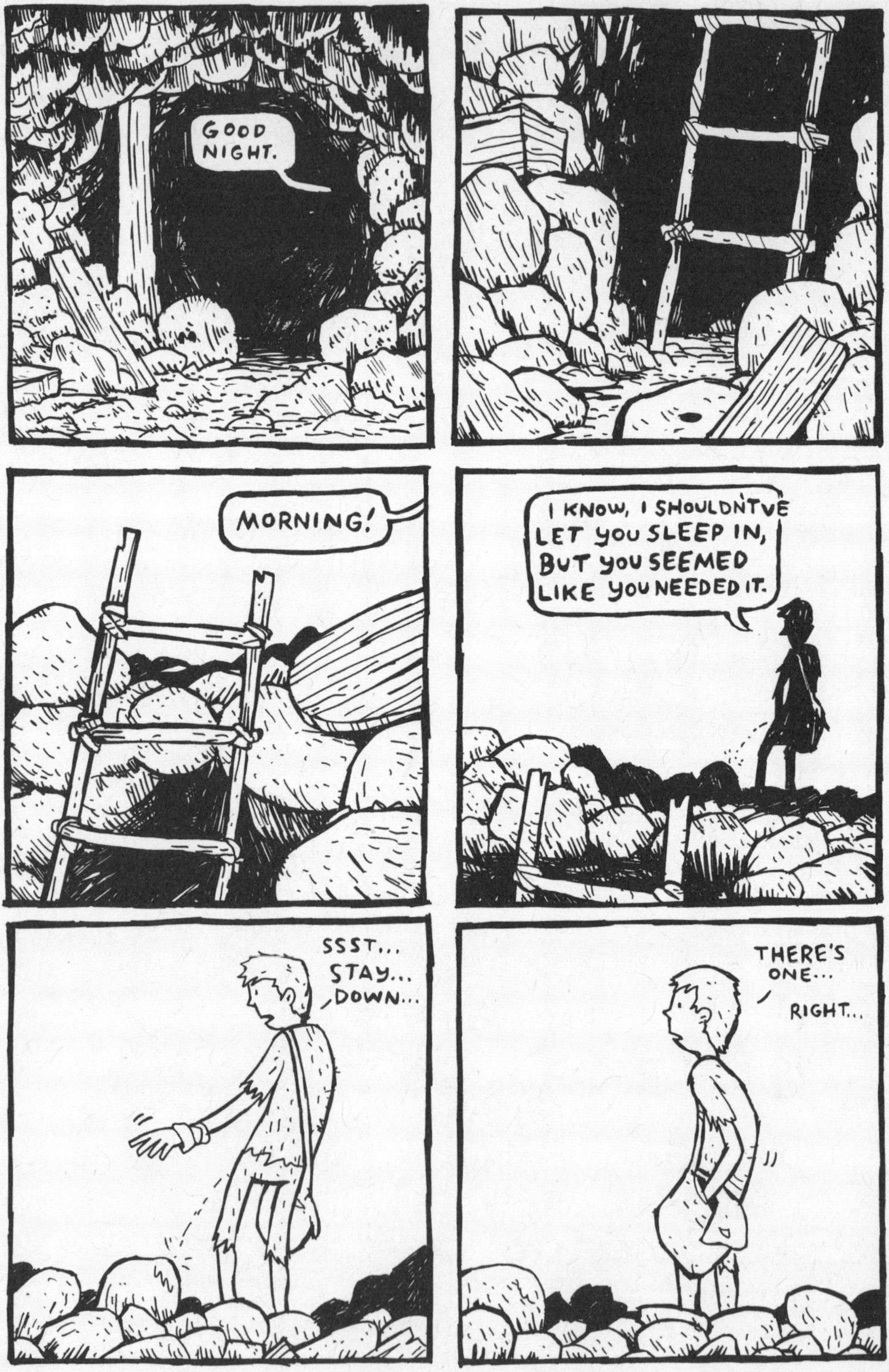
GOOD NIGHT.
MORNING!
I KNOW, I SHOULDN'T'VE LET YOU SLEEP IN, BUT YOU SEEMED LIKE YOU NEEDED IT.
SSST... STAY... DOWN...
THERE'S ONE...
RIGHT...

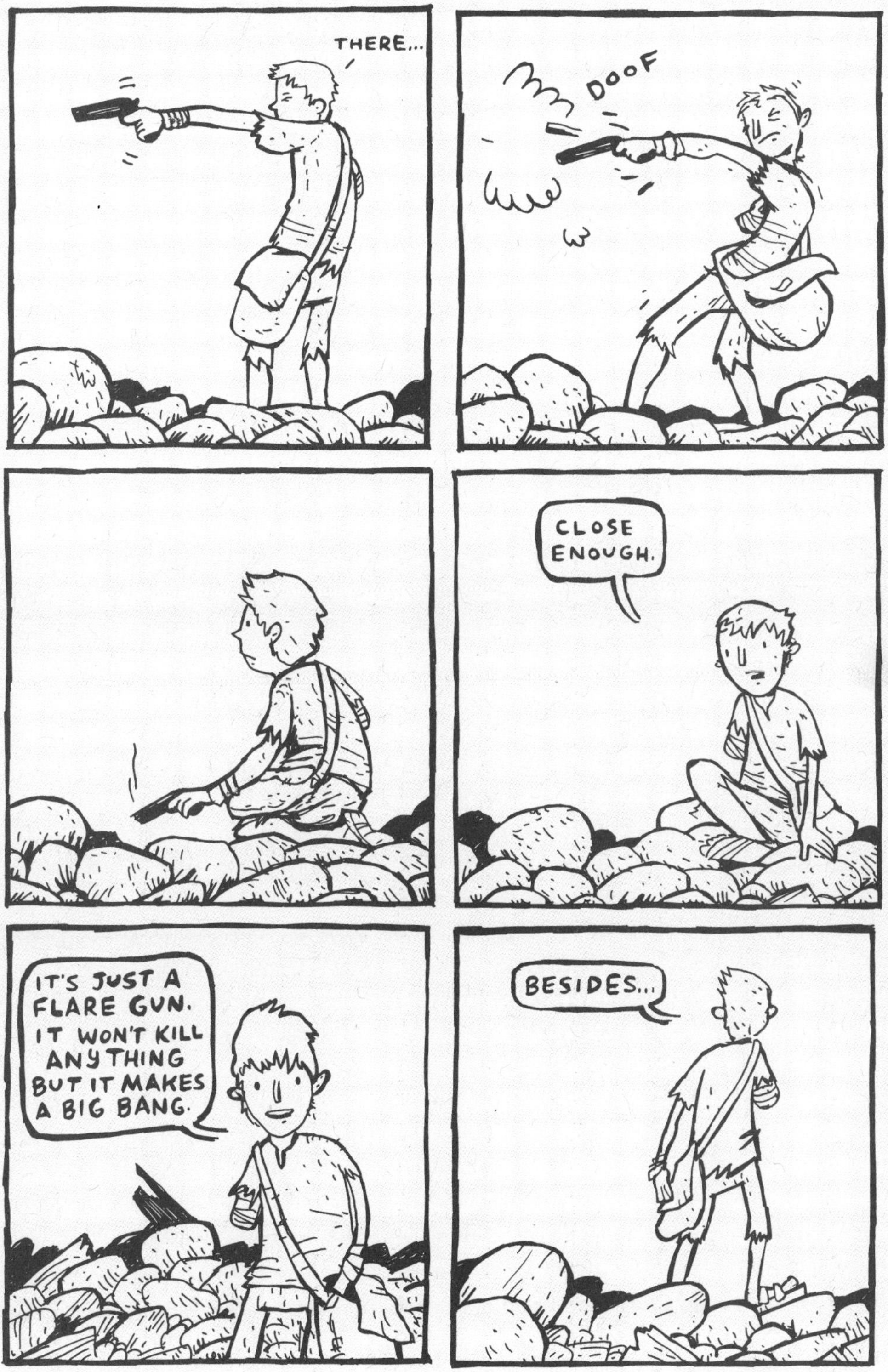
THERE...
DOOF
CLOSE ENOUGH.
IT'S JUST A FLARE GUN. IT WON'T KILL ANYTHING BUT IT MAKES A BIG BANG.
BESIDES...

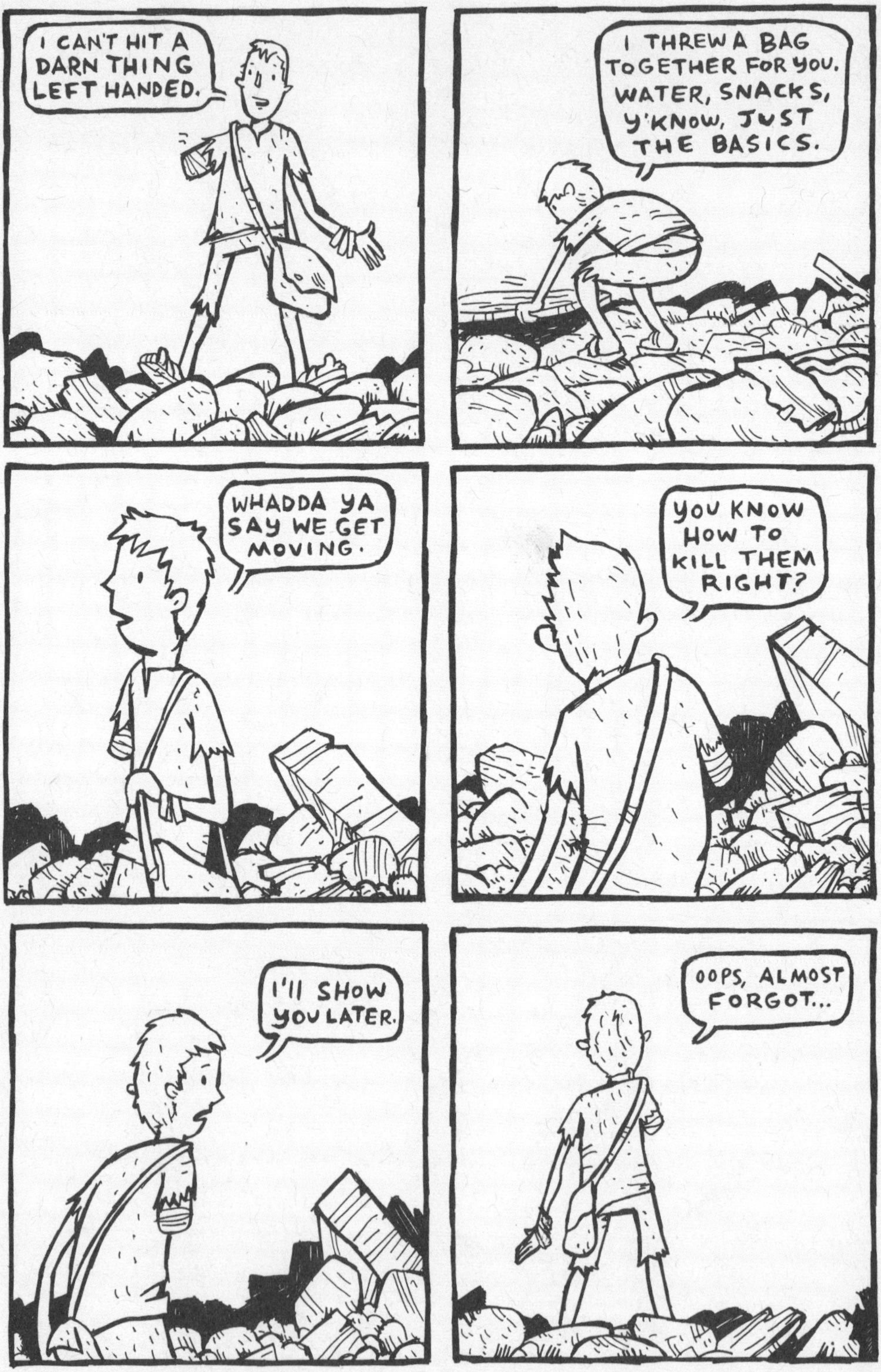
I CAN'T HIT A DARN THING LEFT HANDED.
I THREW A BAG TOGETHER FOR YOU. WATER, SNACKS, Y'KNOW, JUST THE BASICS.
WHADDA YA SAY WE GET MOVING.
YOU KNOW HOW TO KILL THEM RIGHT?
I'LL SHOW YOU LATER.
OOPS, ALMOST FORGOT...

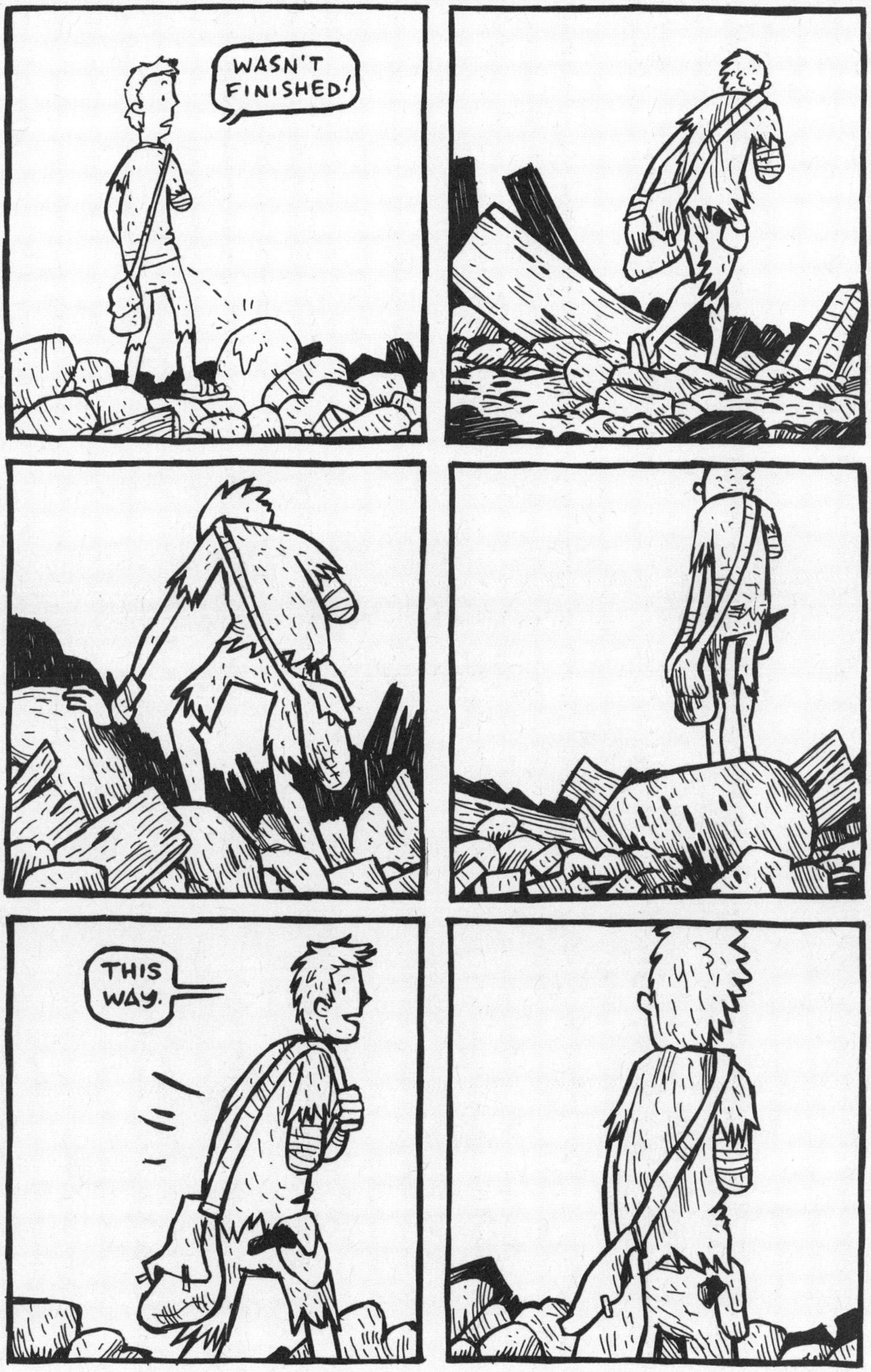
WASN'T FINISHED!
THIS WAY.

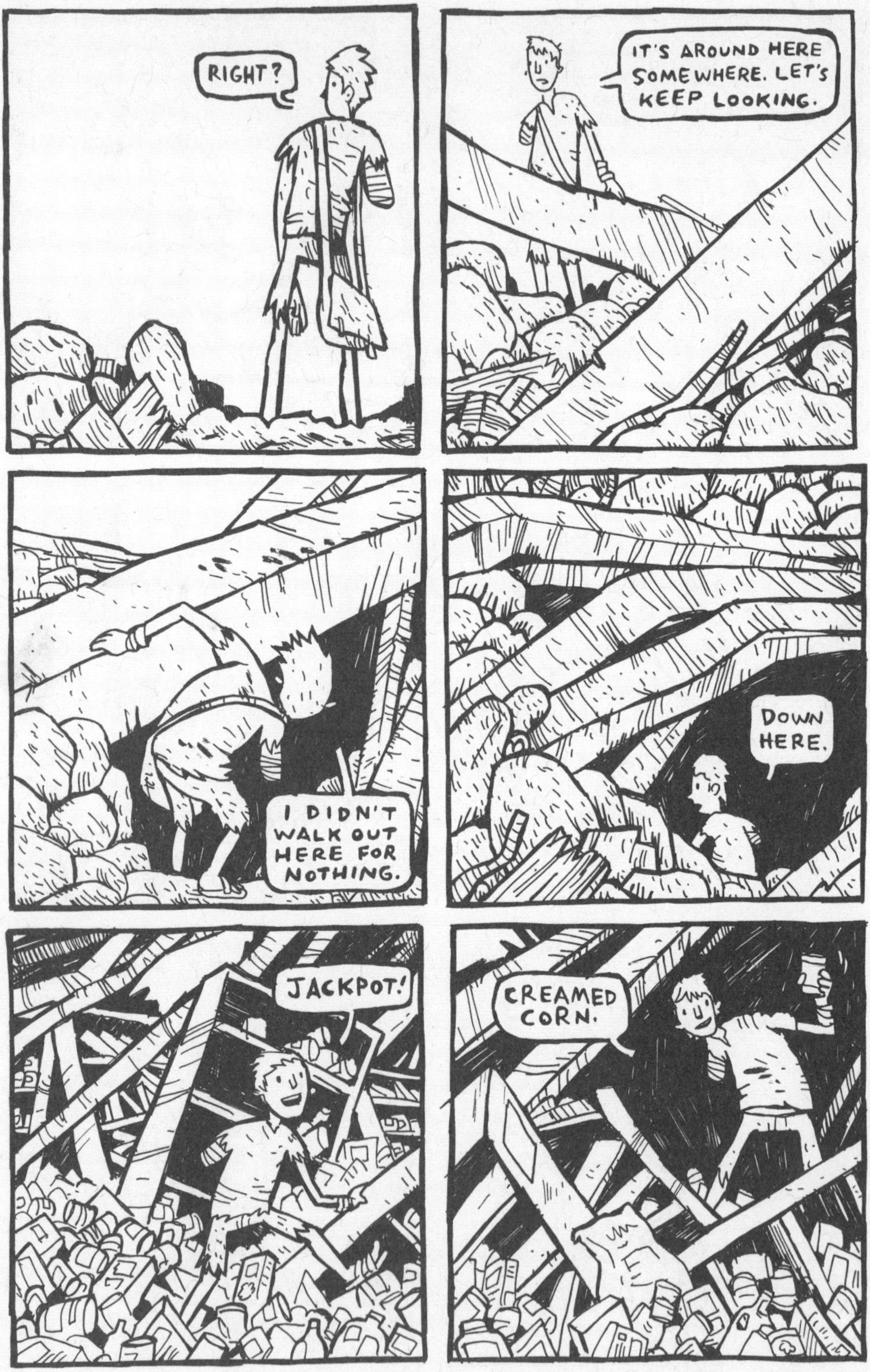
RIGHT?
IT'S AROUND HERE SOMEWHERE. LET'S KEEP LOOKING.
I DIDN'T WALK OUT HERE FOR NOTHING.
DOWN HERE.
JACKPOT!
CREAMED CORN.

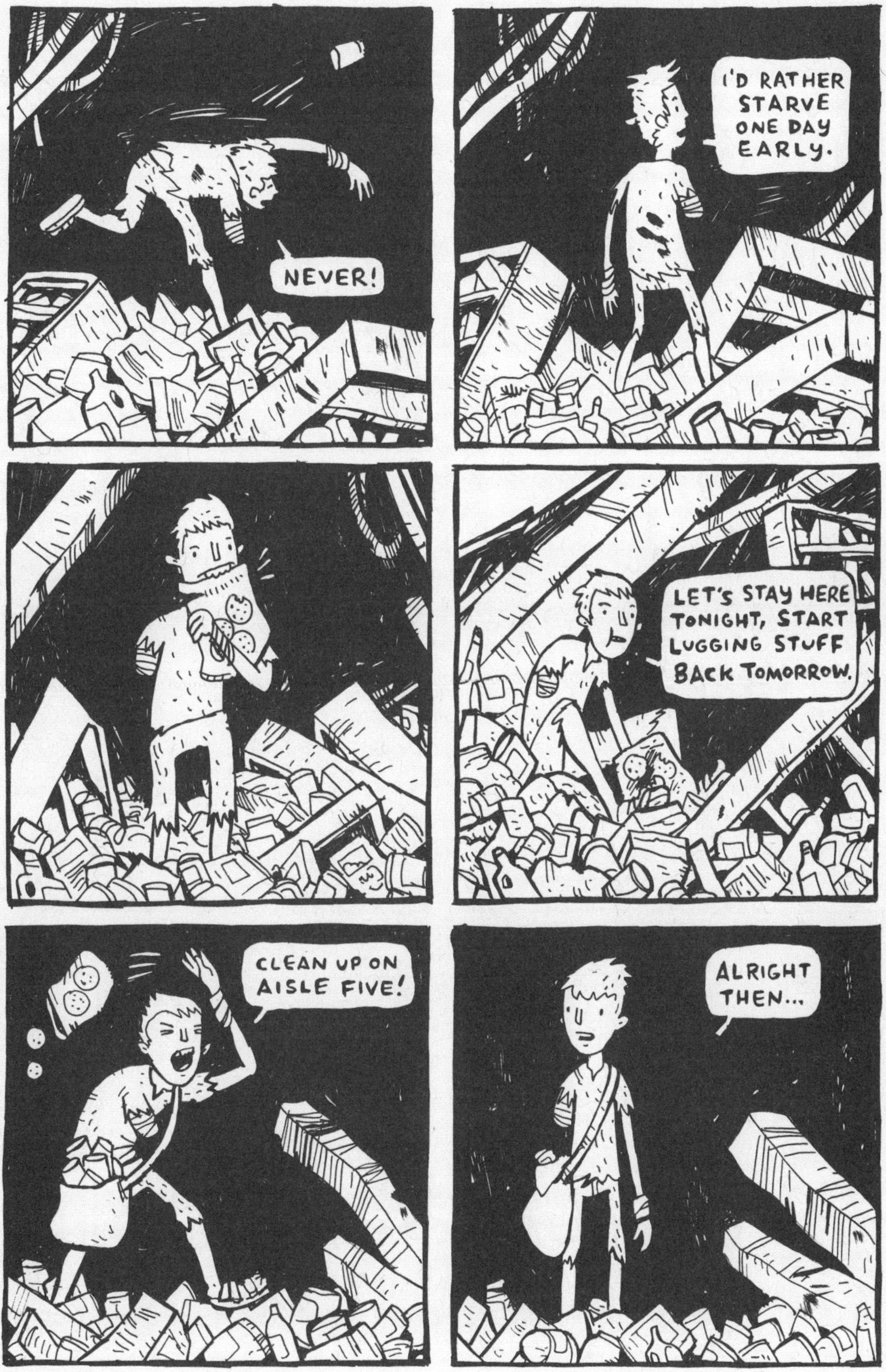
NEVER!
I'D RATHER STARVE ONE DAY EARLY.
LET'S STAY HERE TONIGHT, START LUGGING STUFF BACK TOMORROW.
CLEAN UP ON AISLE FIVE!
ALRIGHT THEN...

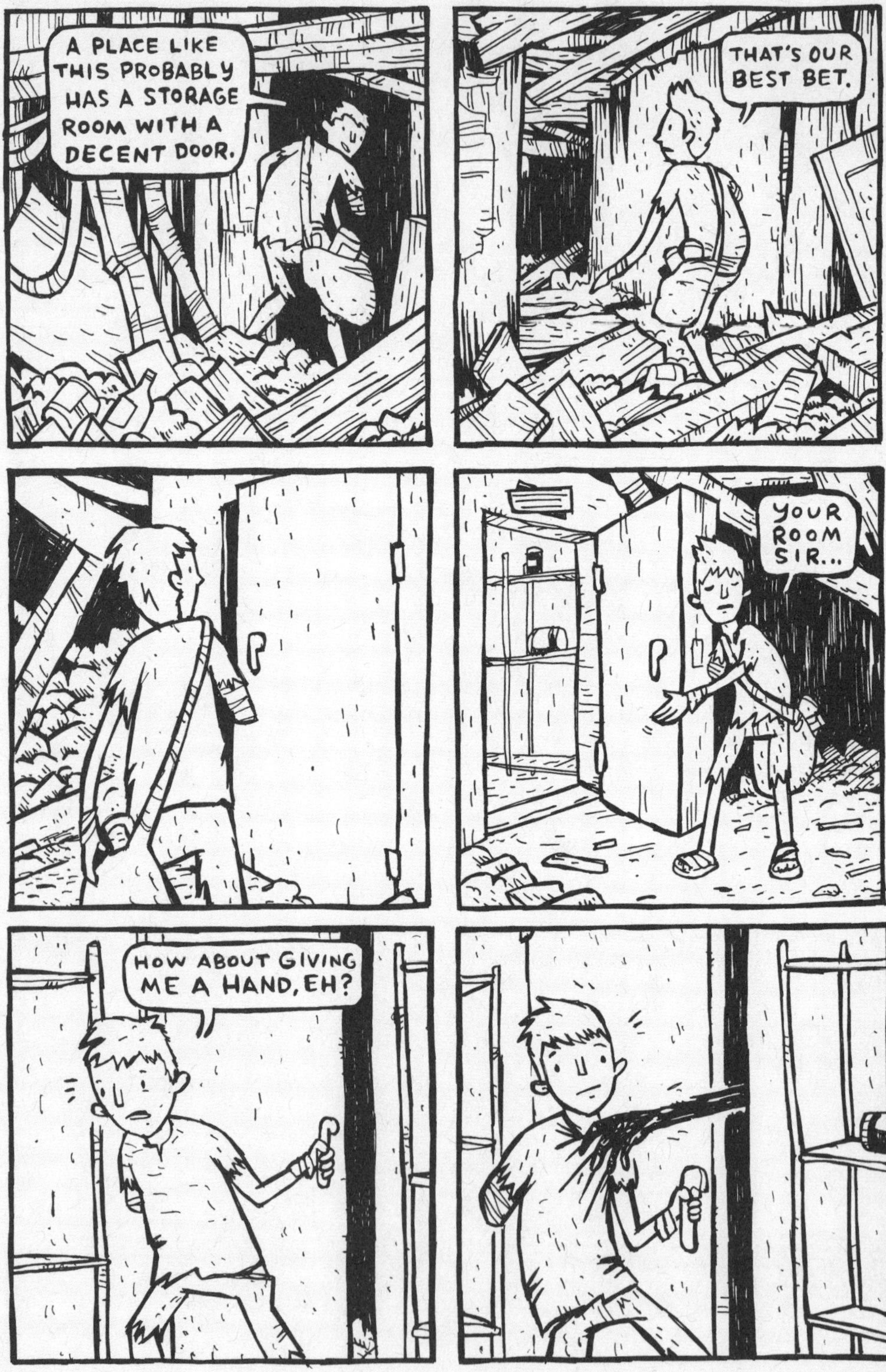
A PLACE LIKE THIS PROBABLY HAS A STORAGE ROOM WITH A DECENT DOOR.
THAT'S OUR BEST BET.
YOUR ROOM SIR...
HOW ABOUT GIVING ME A HAND, EH?

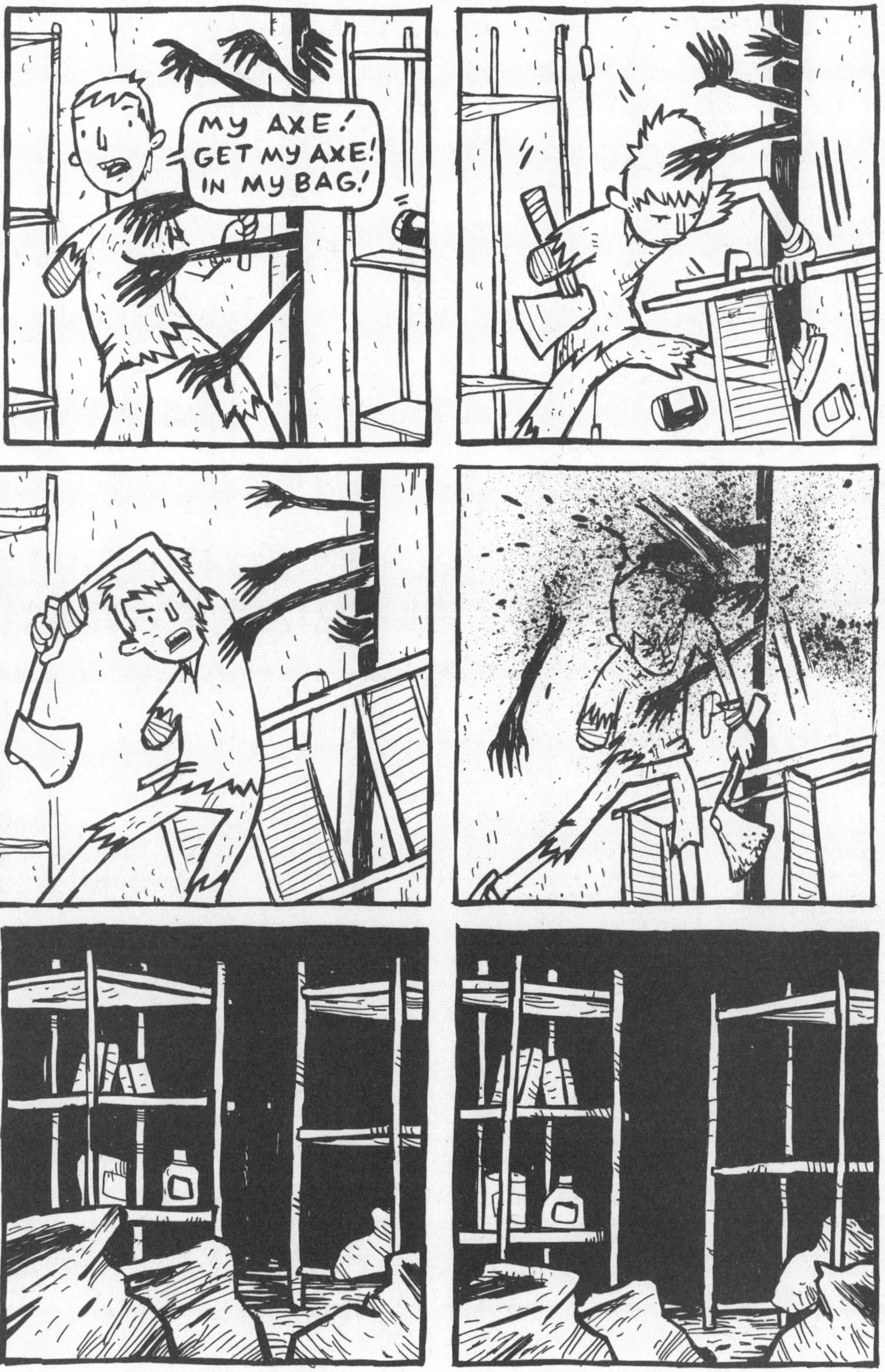
MY AXE! GET MY AXE! IN MY BAG!

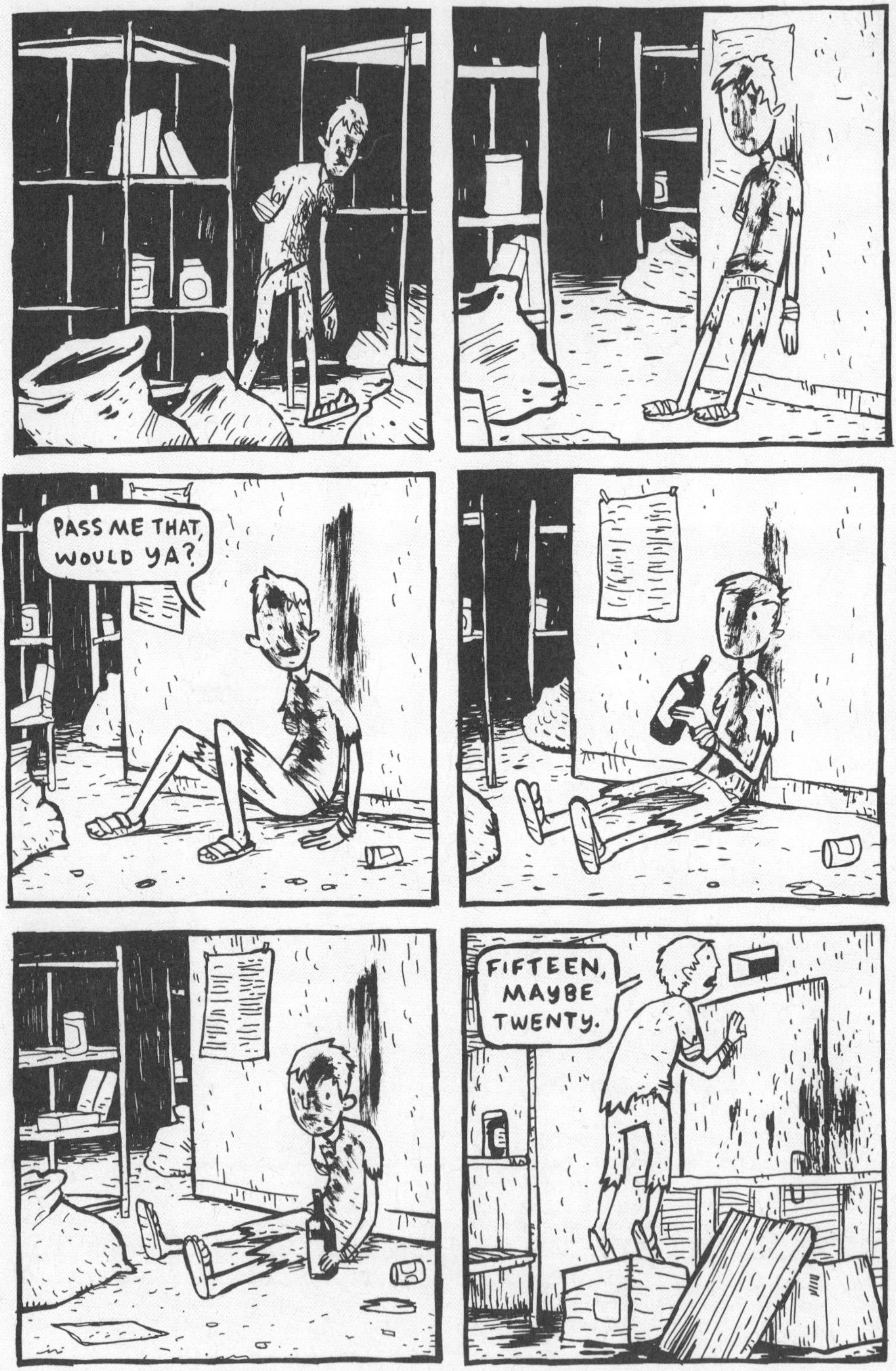
PASS ME THAT, WOULD YA?
FIFTEEN, MAYBE TWENTY.

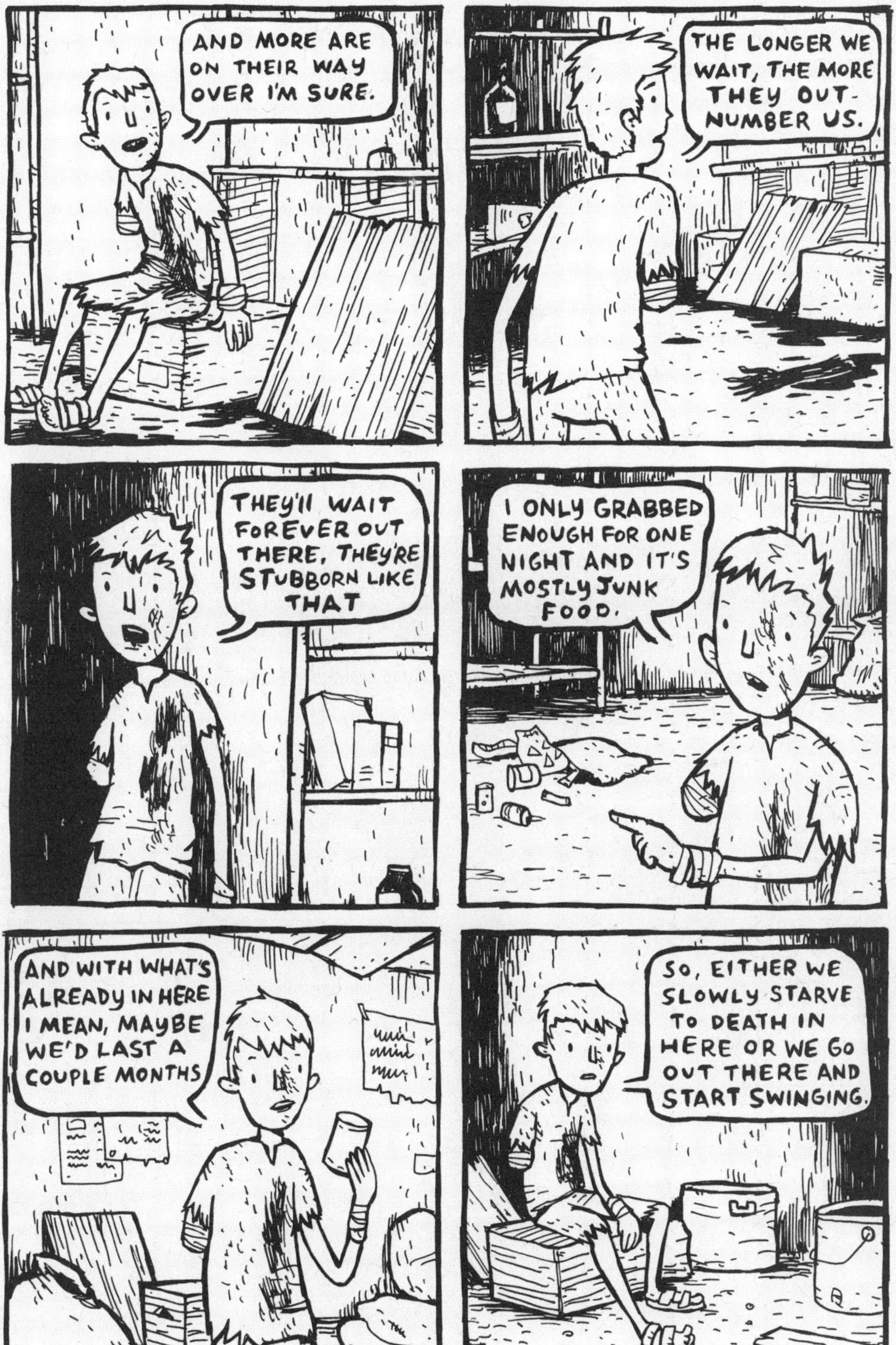
AND MORE ARE ON THEIR WAY OVER I'M SURE.
THE LONGER WE WAIT, THE MORE THEY OUT-NUMBER US.
THEY'll WAIT FOREVER OUT THERE. THEY'RE STUBBORN LIKE THAT
I ONLY GRABBED ENOUGH FOR ONE NIGHT AND IT'S MOSTLY JUNK FOOD.
AND WITH WHAT'S ALREADY IN HERE I MEAN, MAYBE WE'D LAST A COUPLE MONTHS
So, EITHER WE SLOWLY STARVE TO DEATH IN HERE OR WE GO OUT THERE AND START SWINGING.

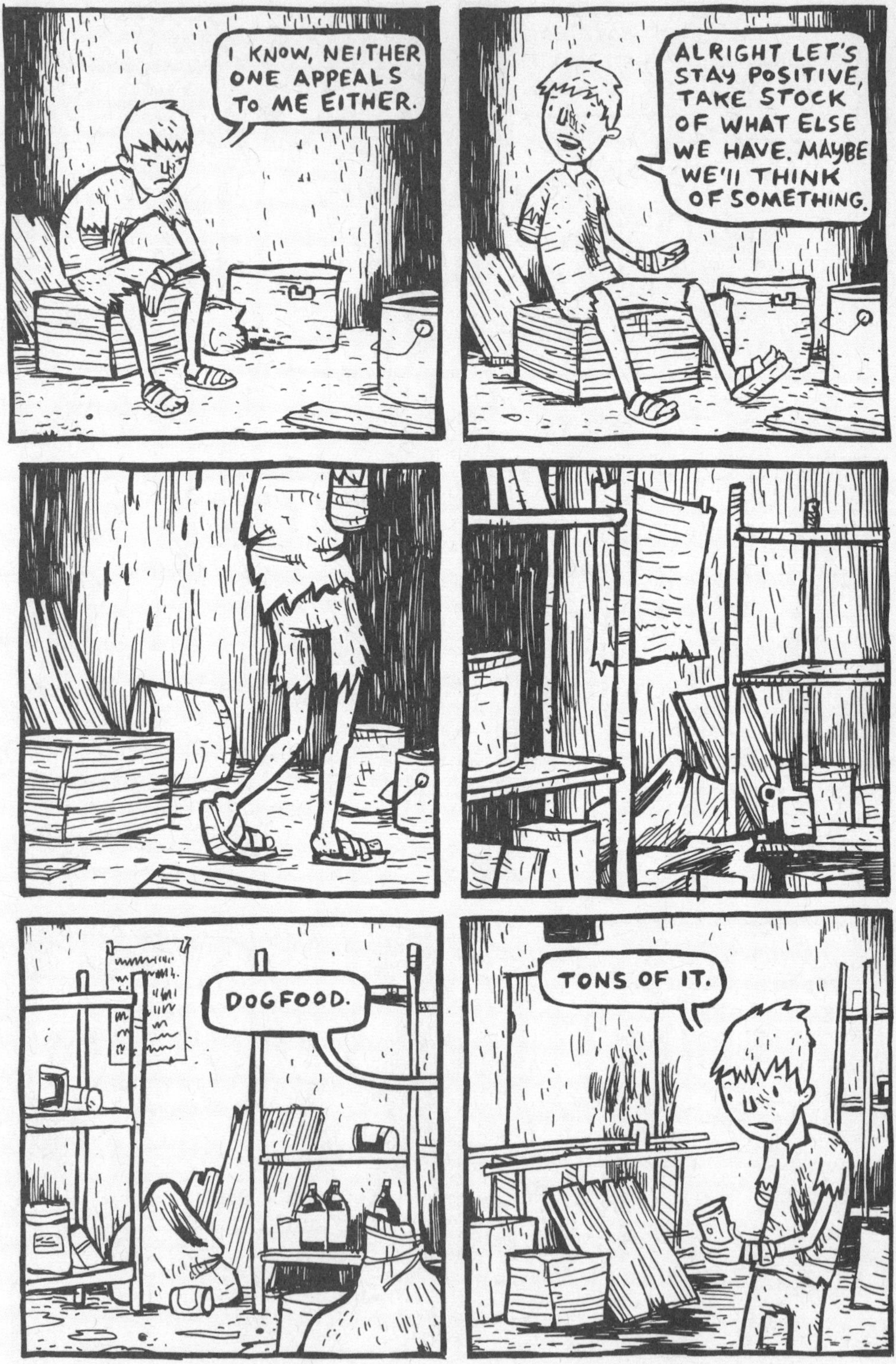
I KNOW, NEITHER ONE APPEALS TO ME EITHER.
ALRIGHT LET'S STAY POSITIVE, TAKE STOCK OF WHAT ELSE WE HAVE. MAYBE WE'll THINK OF SOMETHING.
DOGFOOD.
TONS OF IT.

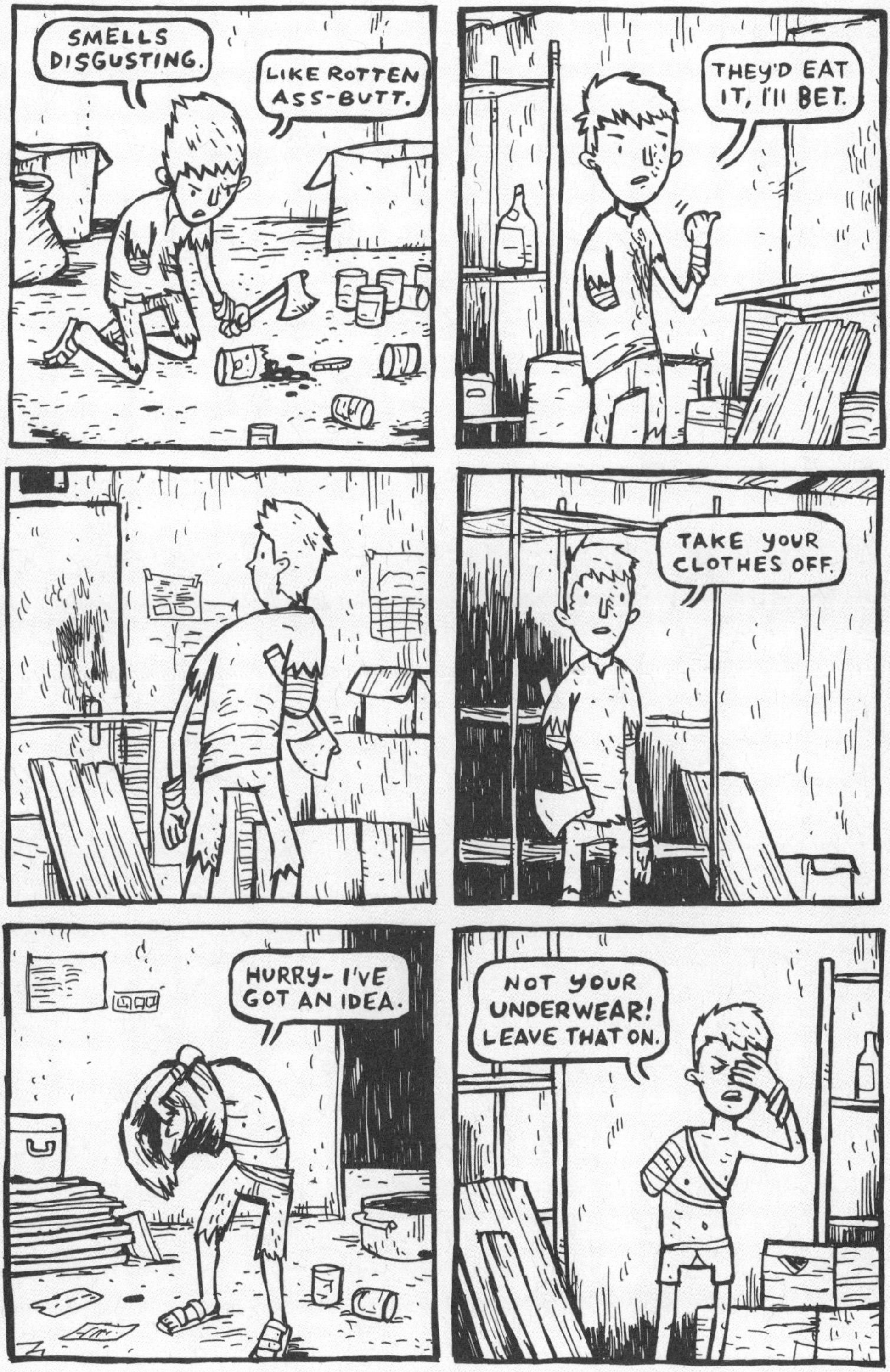
SMELLS DISGUSTING.
LIKE ROTTEN ASS-BUTT.
THEY'D EAT IT, I'll BET.
TAKE YOUR CLOTHES OFF.
HURRY- I'VE GOT AN IDEA.
NOT YOUR UNDERWEAR! LEAVE THAT ON.

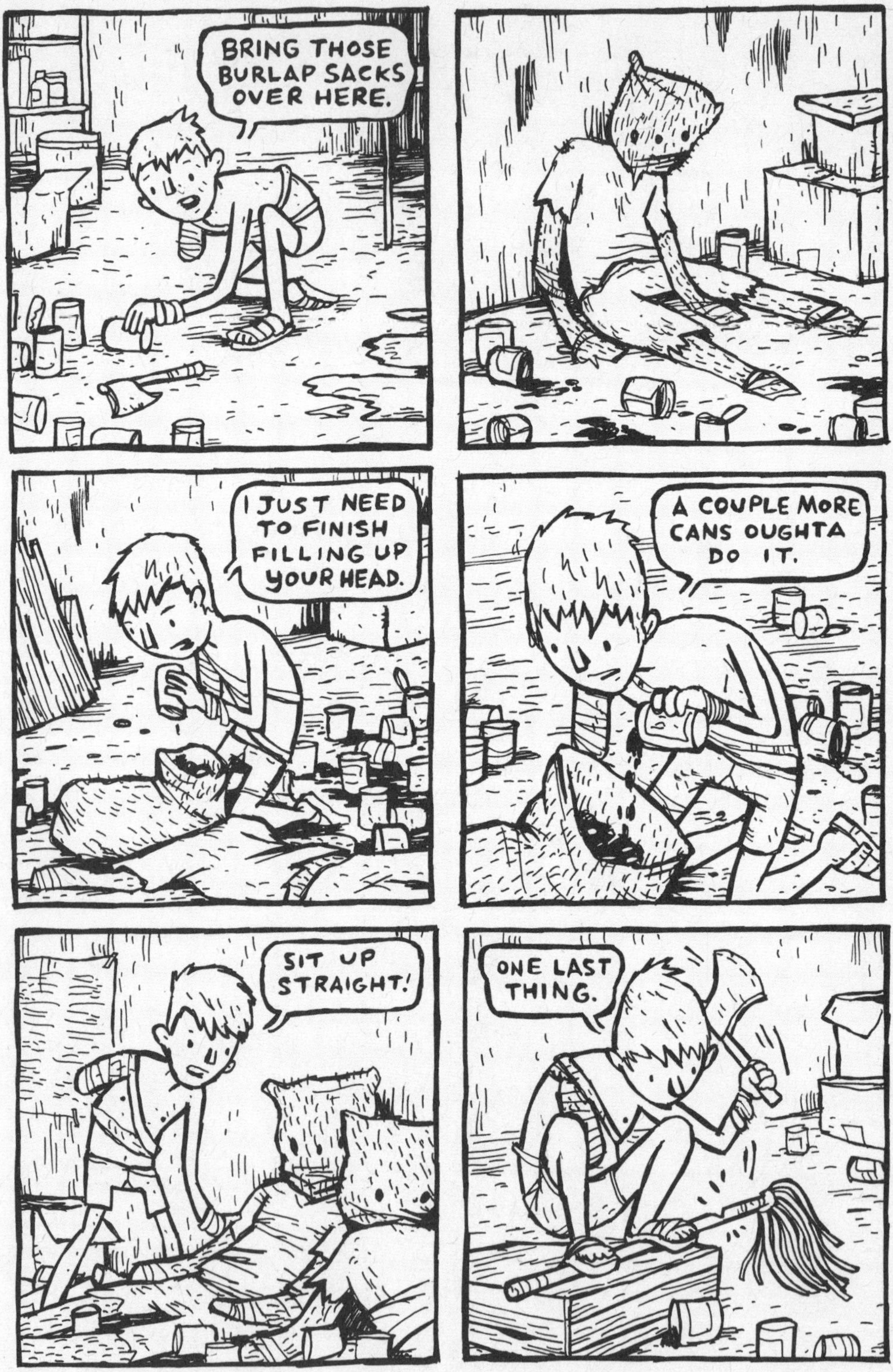
BRING THOSE BURLAP SACKS OVER HERE.
I JUST NEED TO FINISH FILLING UP YOUR HEAD.
A COUPLE MORE CANS OUGHTA DO IT.
SIT UP STRAIGHT!
ONE LAST THING.

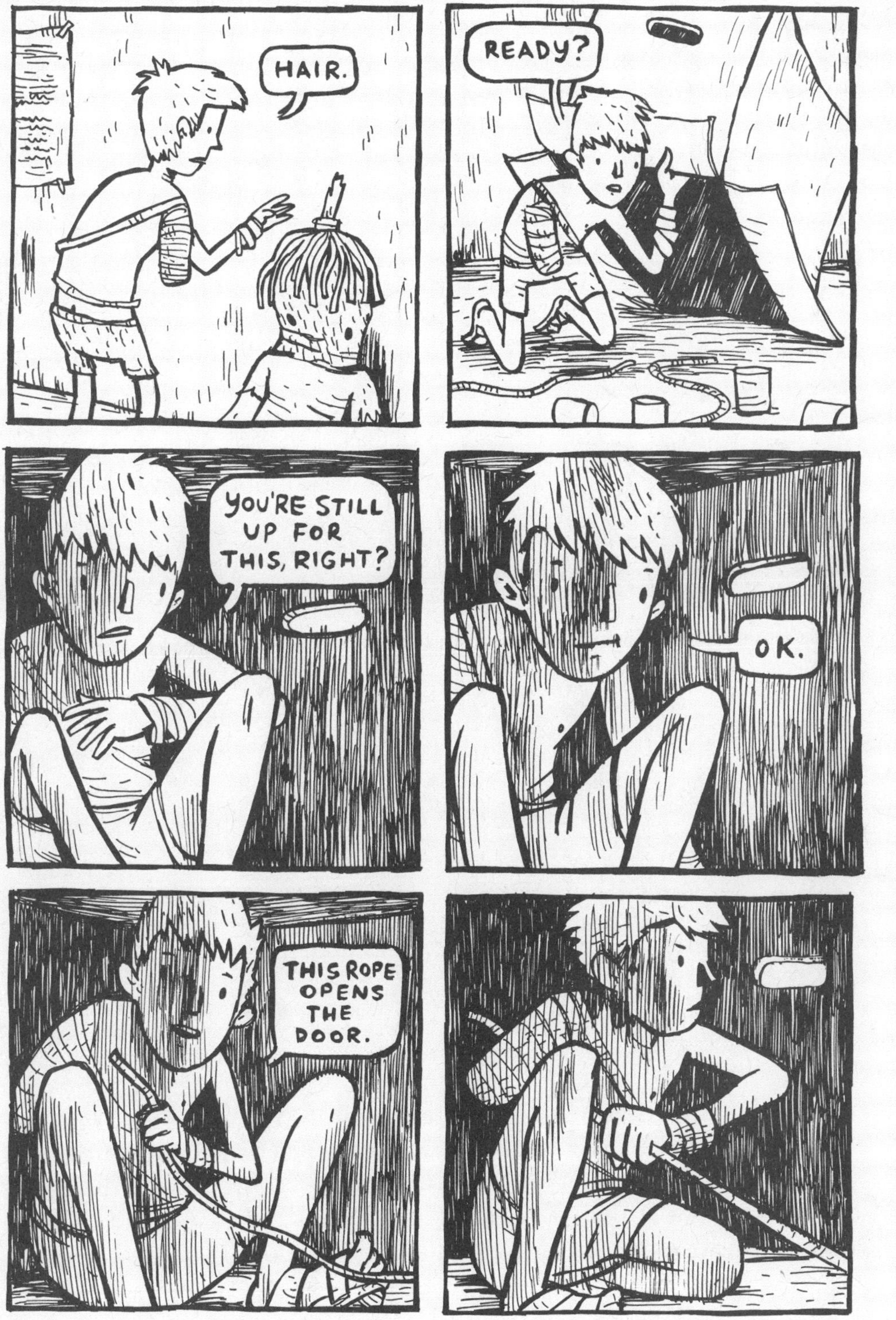
HAIR.
READY?
YOU'RE STILL UP FOR THIS, RIGHT?
OK.
THIS ROPE OPENS THE DOOR.

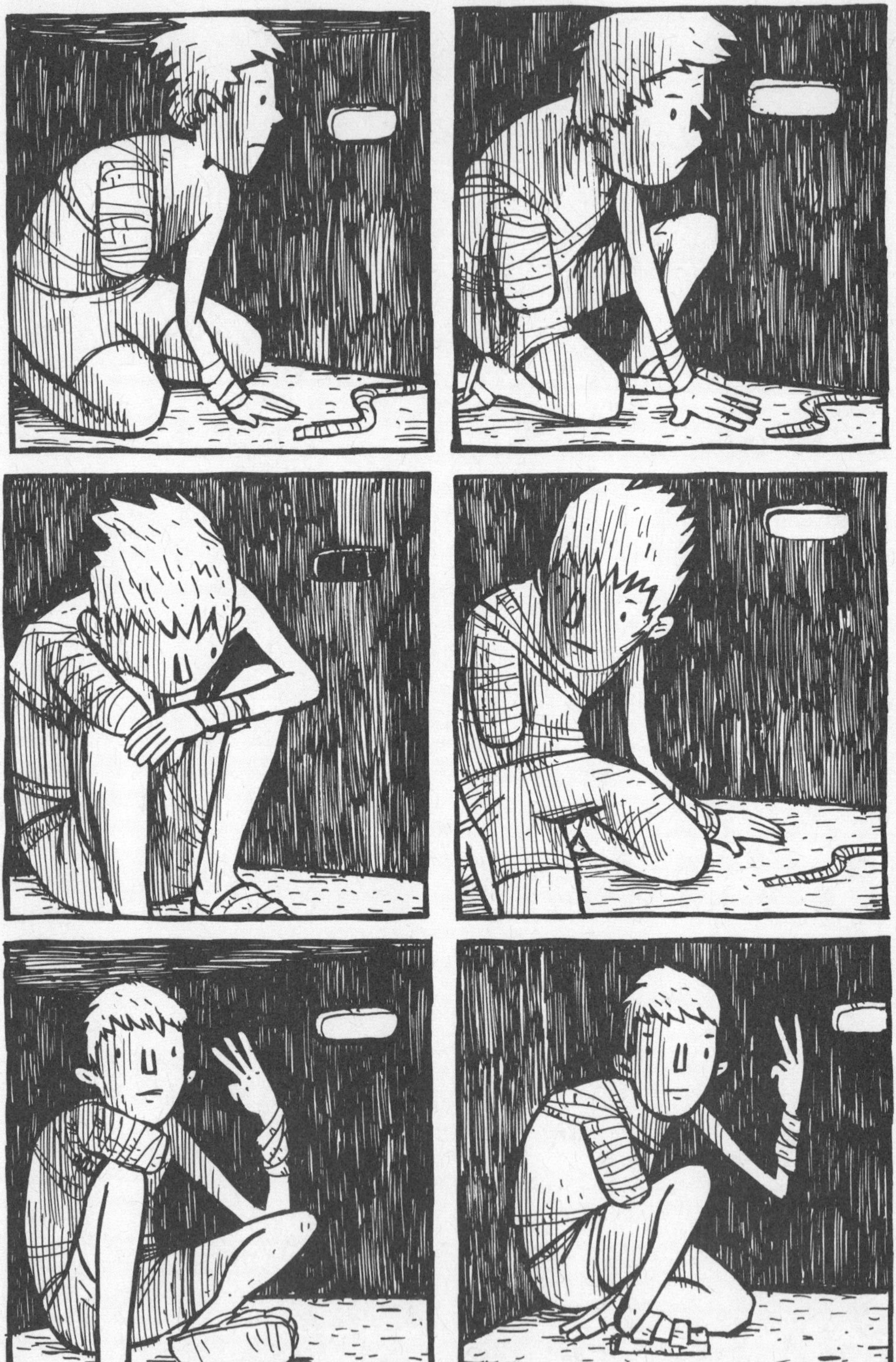

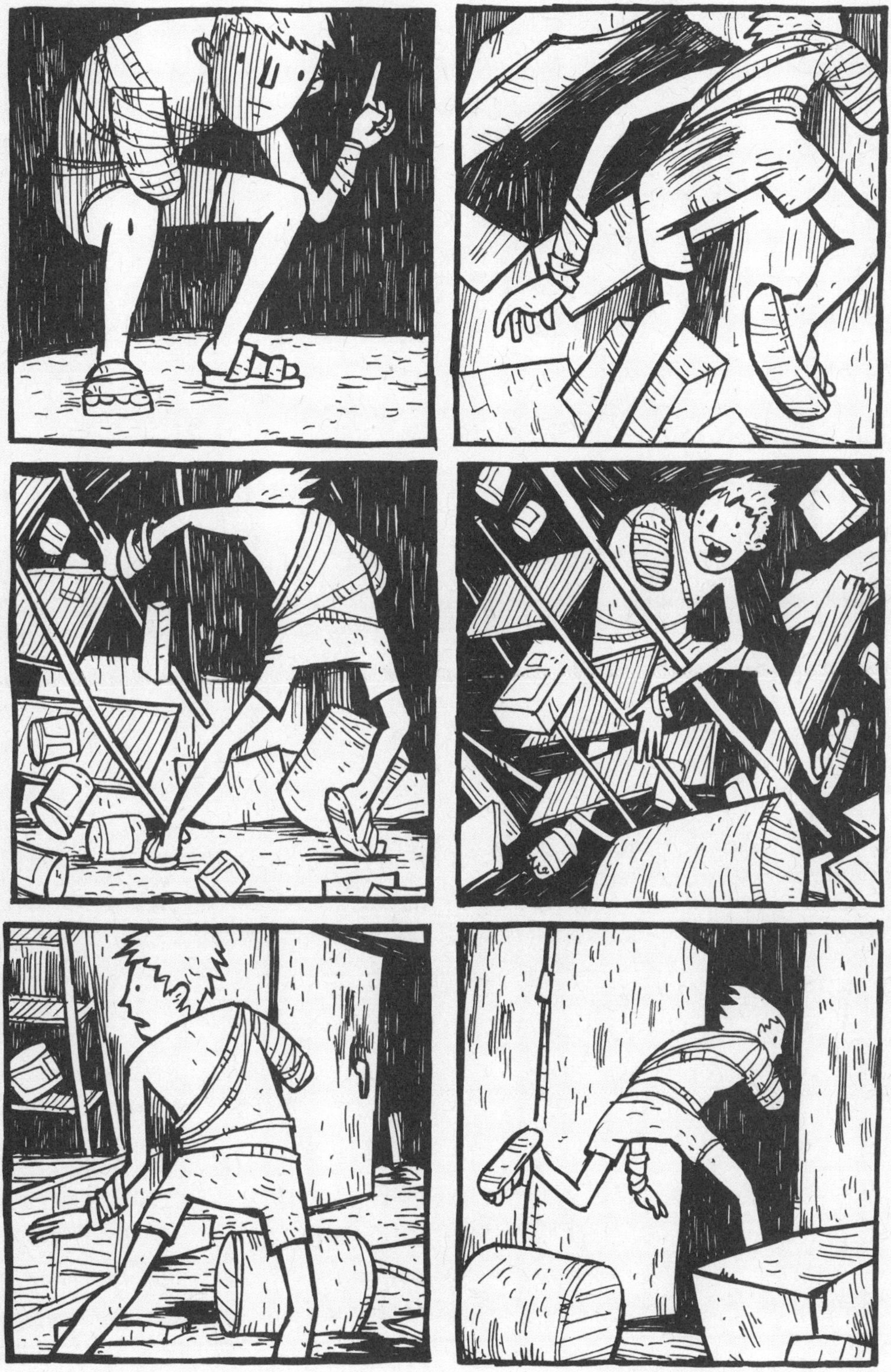

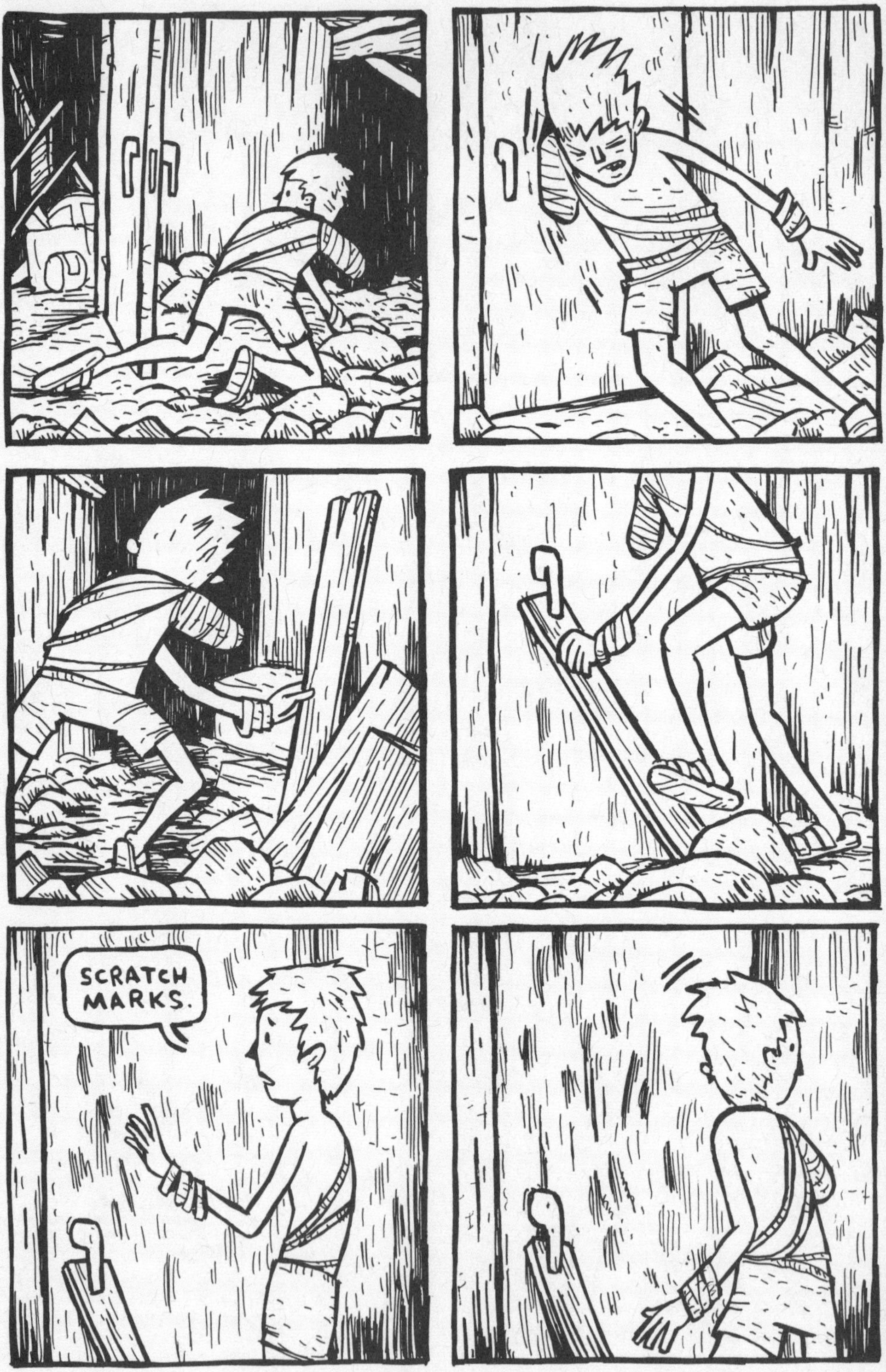
SCRATCH MARKS.

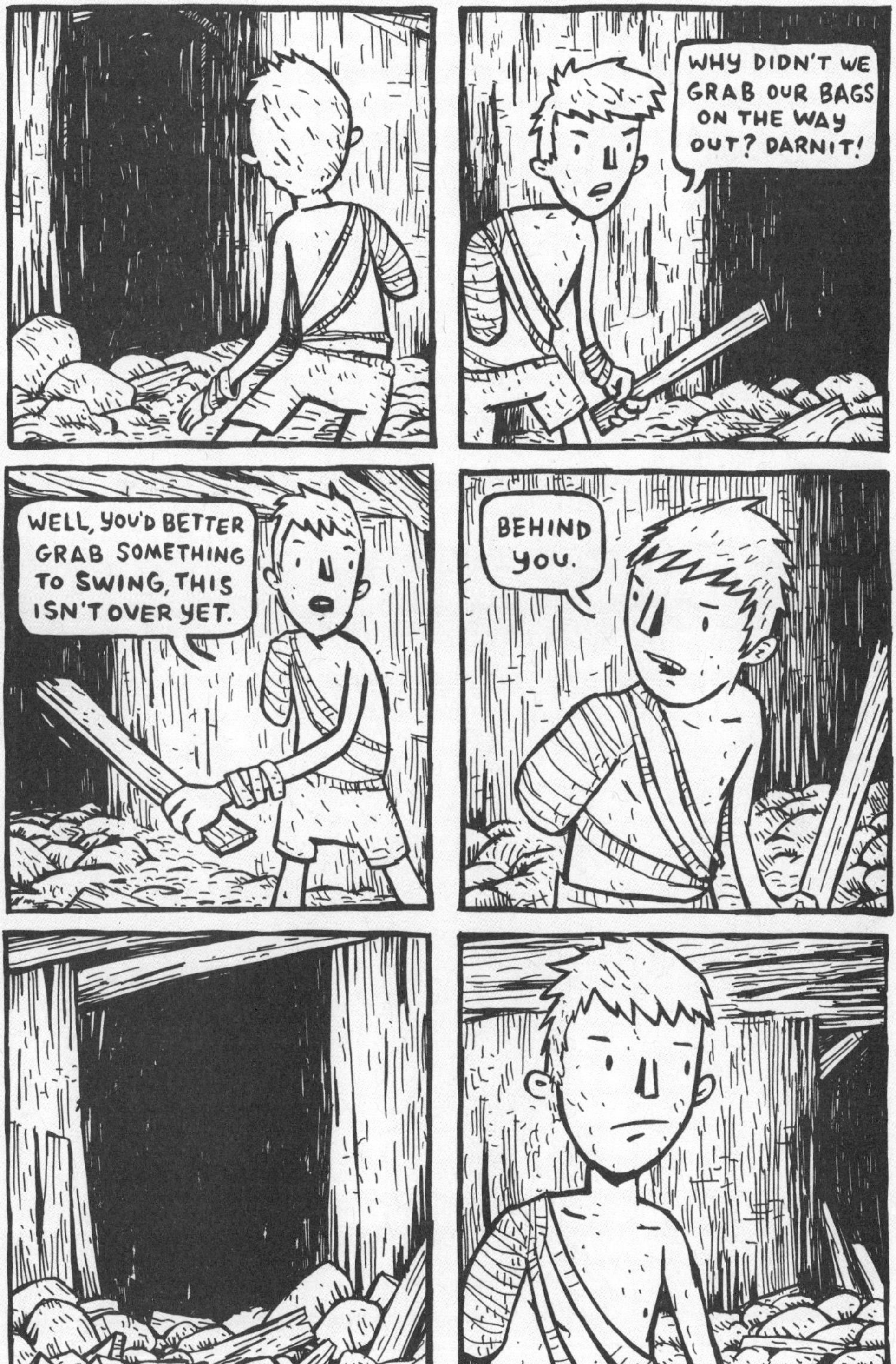
WHY DIDN'T WE GRAB OUR BAGS ON THE WAY OUT? DARNIT!
WELL, YOU'D BETTER GRAB SOMETHING TO SWING, THIS ISN'T OVER YET.
BEHIND YOU.

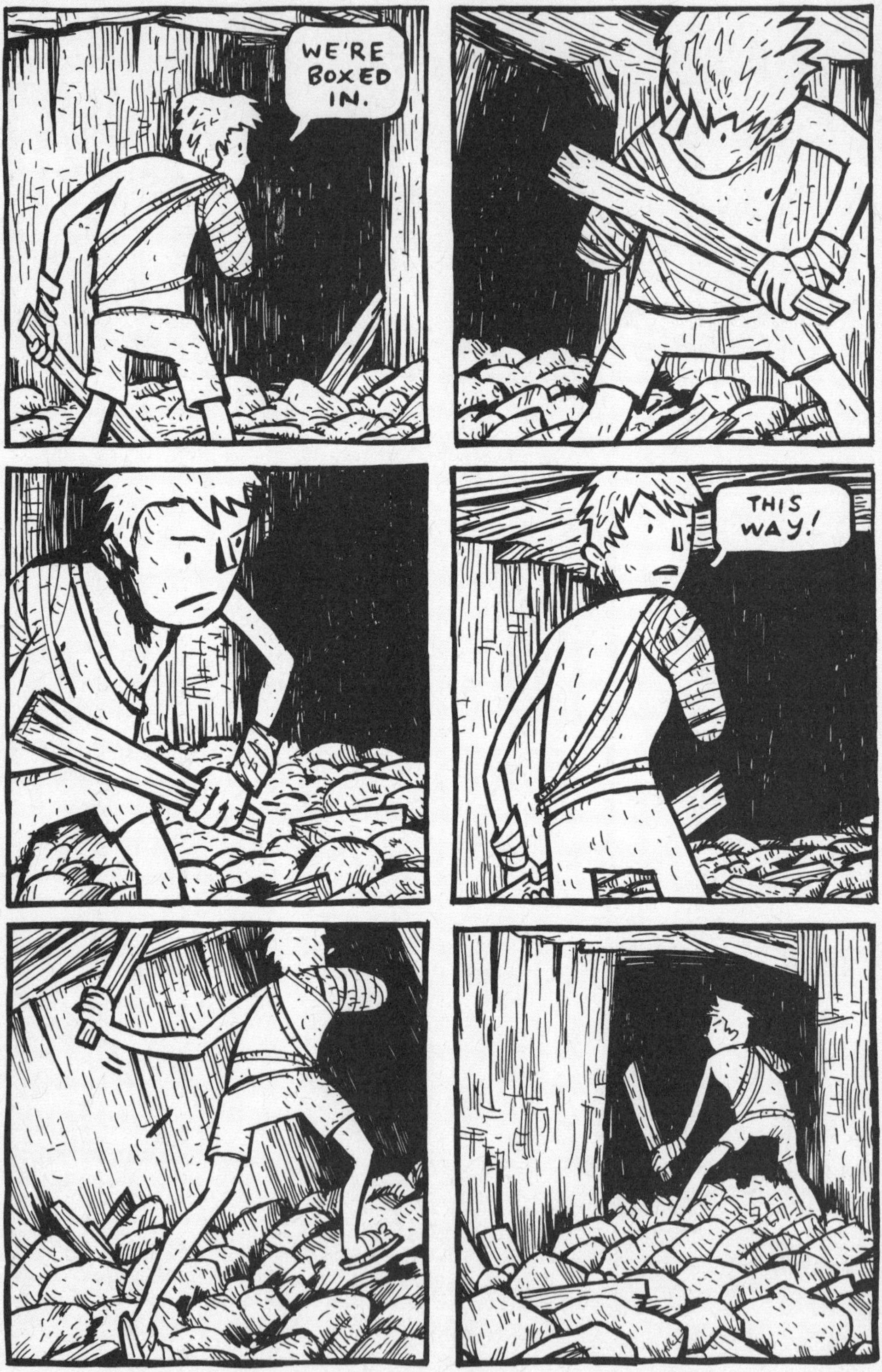
WE'RE BOXED IN.
THIS WAY!

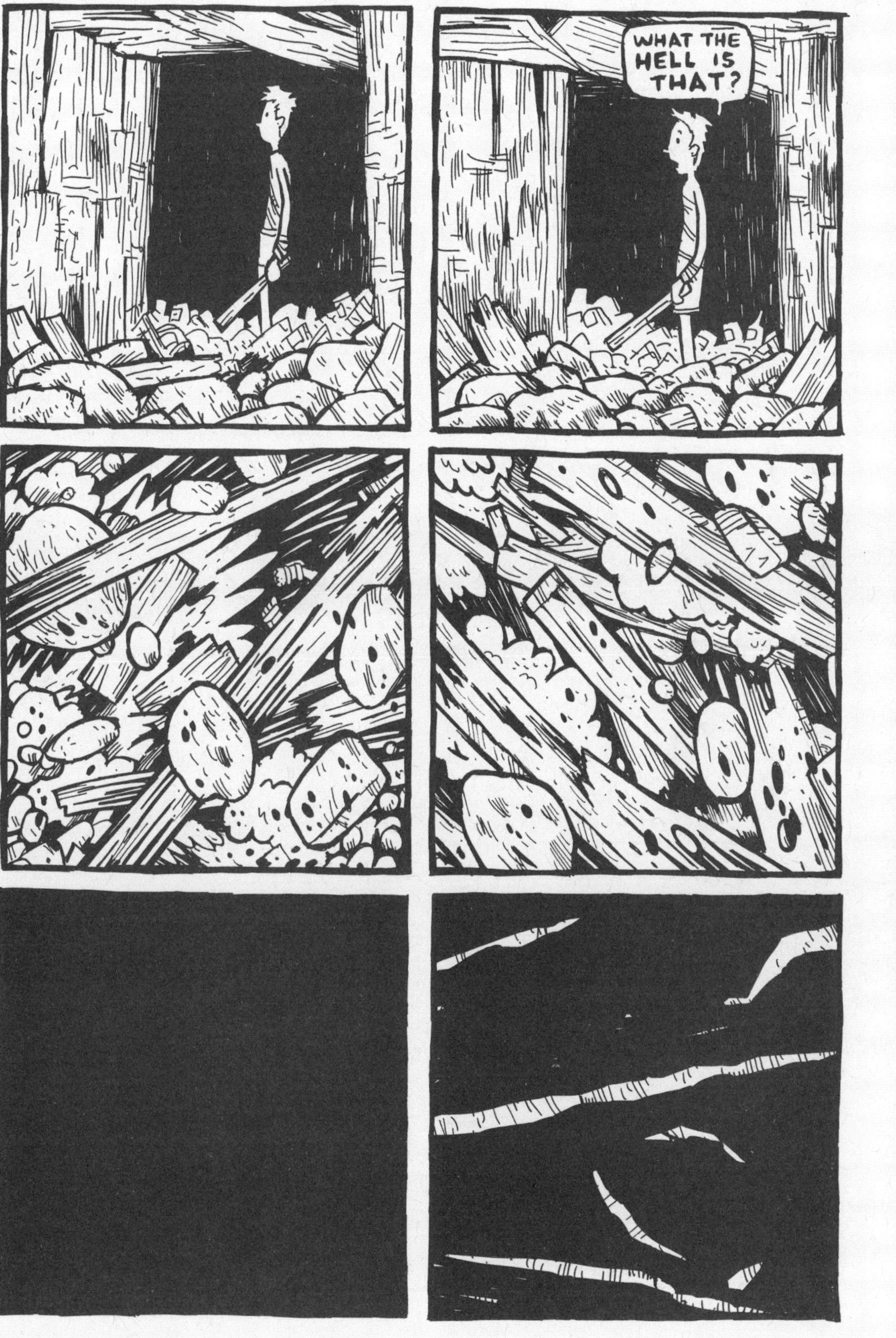
WHAT THE HELL IS THAT?

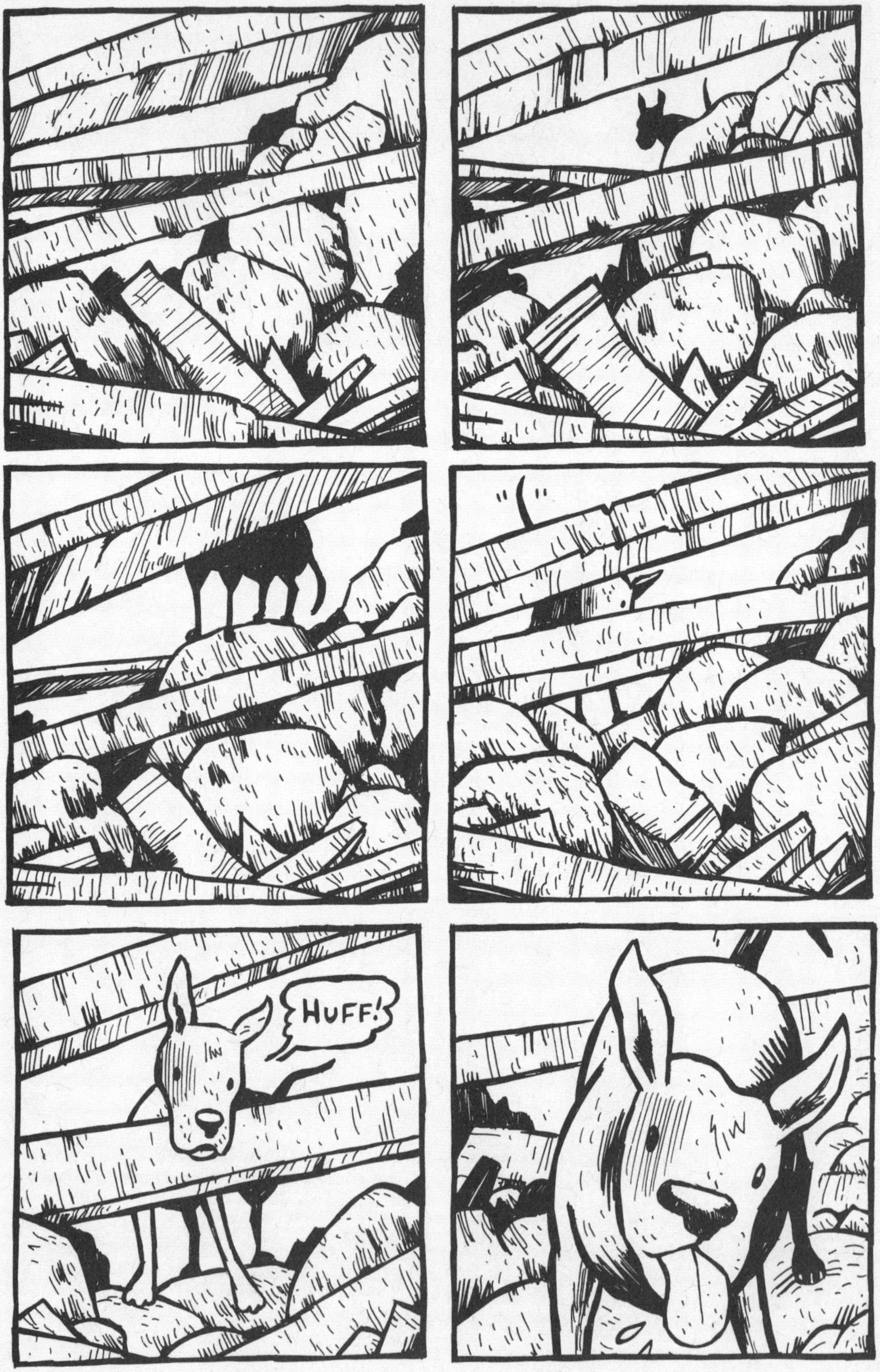
HUFF!

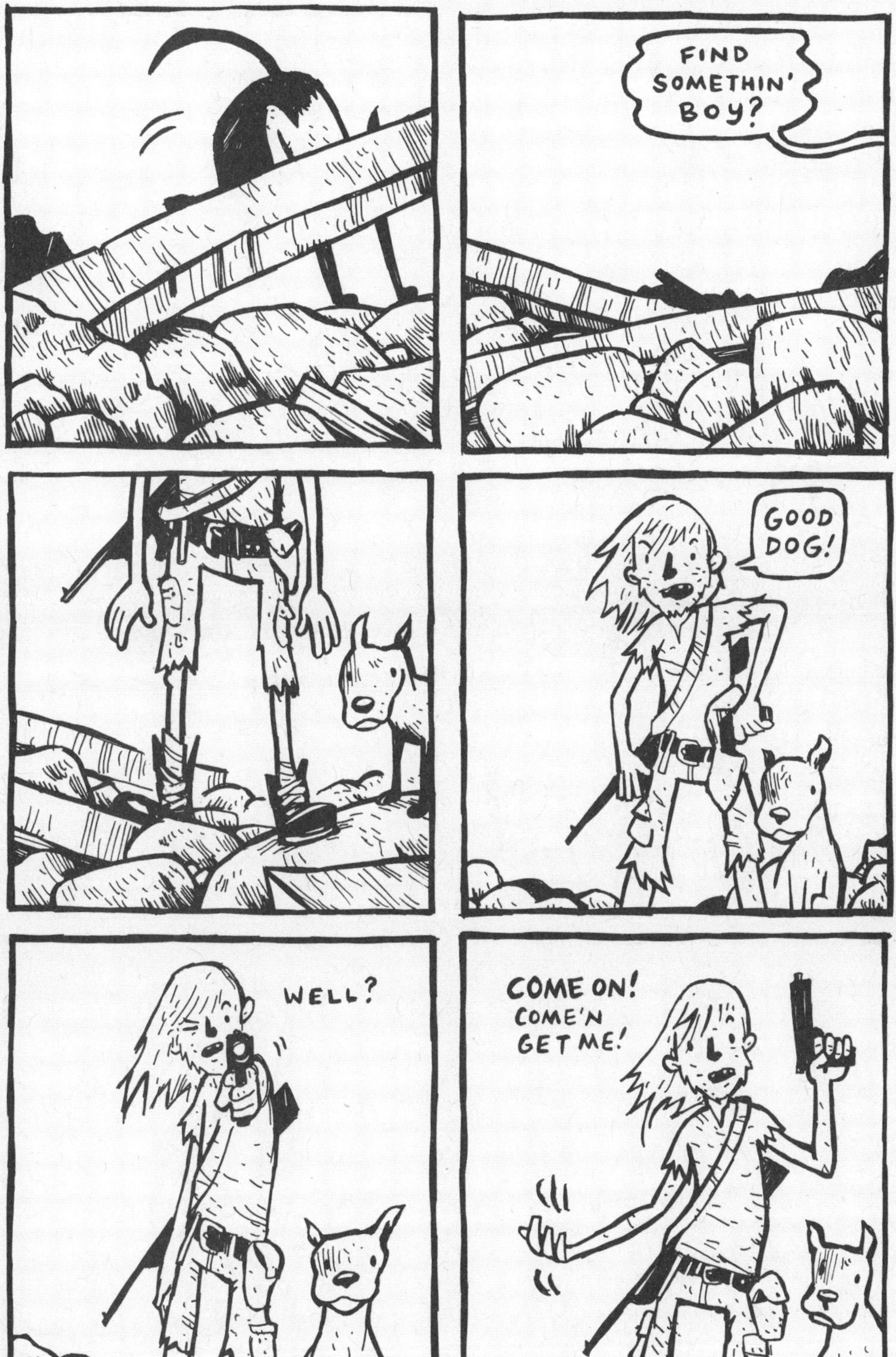
FIND SOMETHIN' BOY?
GOOD DOG!
WELL?
COME ON!
COME'N GET ME!

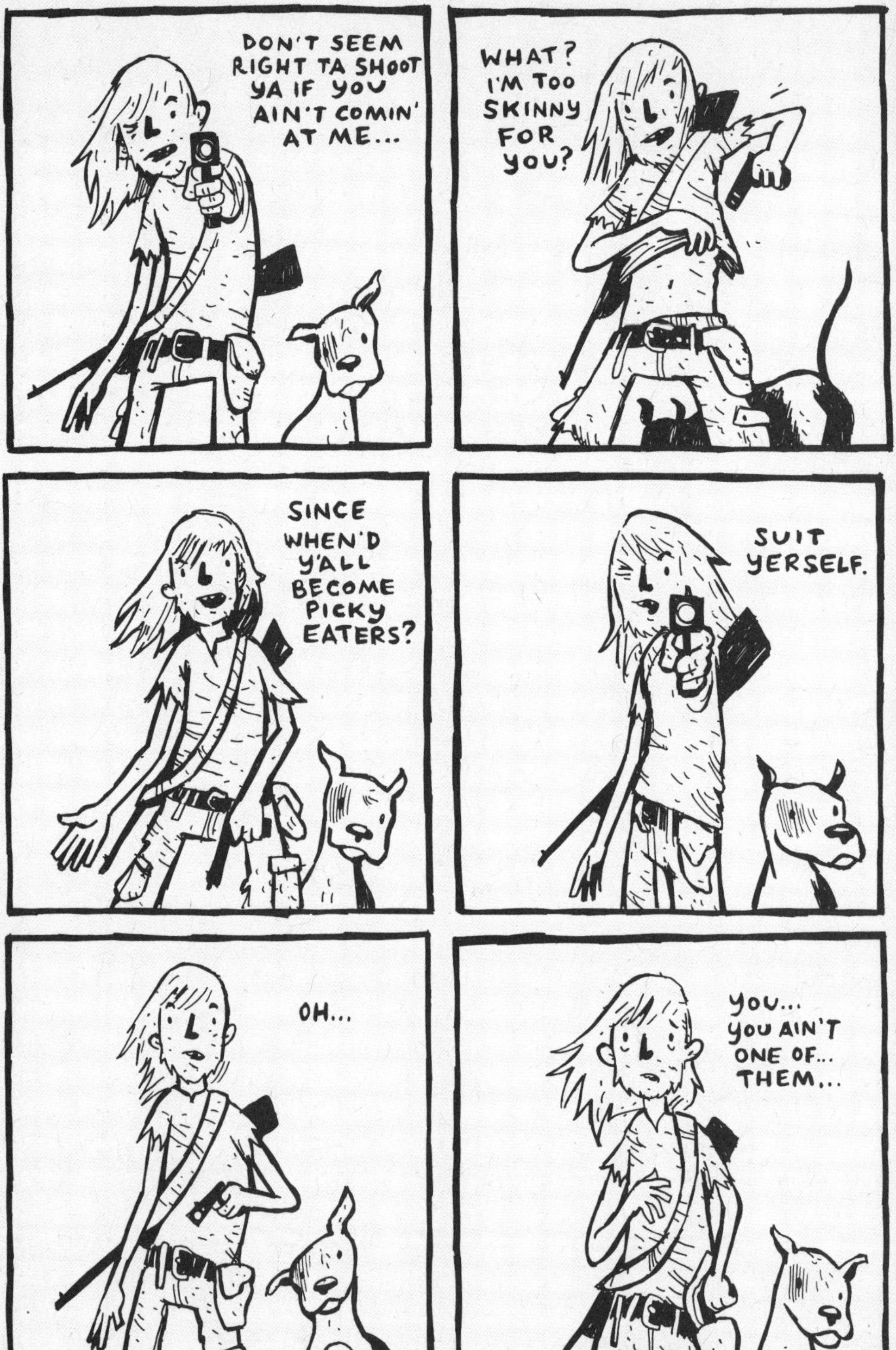
DON'T SEEM RIGHT TA SHOOT YA IF YOU AIN'T COMIN' AT ME...
WHAT? I'M TOO SKINNY FOR YOU?
SINCE WHEN'D Y'ALL BECOME PICKY EATERS?
SUIT YERSELF.
OH...
YOU... YOU AIN'T ONE OF... THEM...

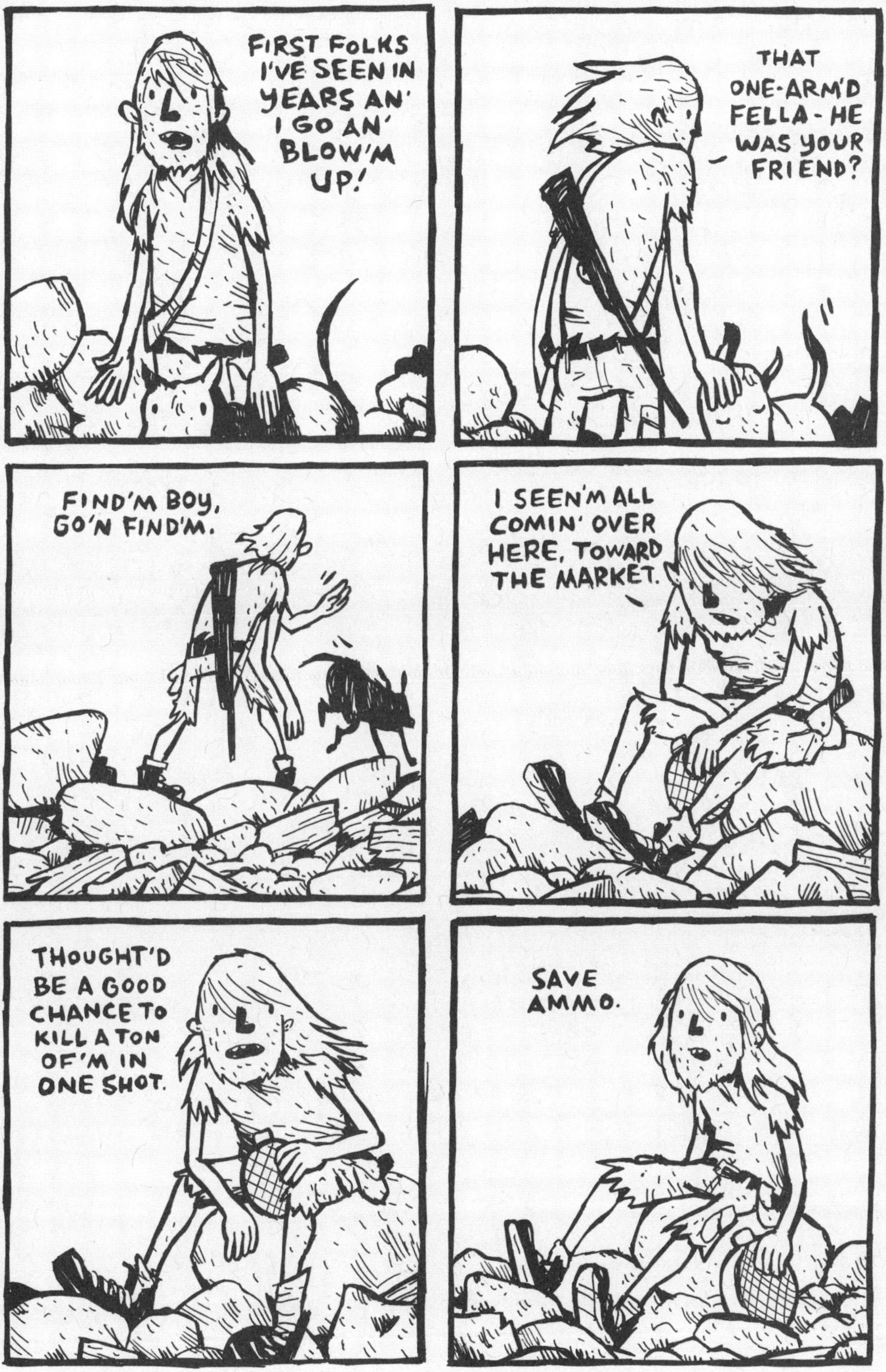
FIRST FOLKS I'VE SEEN IN YEARS AN' I GO AN' BLOW'M UP!
THAT ONE-ARM'D FELLA - HE WAS YOUR FRIEND?
FIND'M BOY, GO'N FIND'M.
I SEEN'M ALL COMIN' OVER HERE, TOWARD THE MARKET.
THOUGHT'D BE A GOOD CHANCE TO KILL A TON OF'M IN ONE SHOT.
SAVE AMMO.

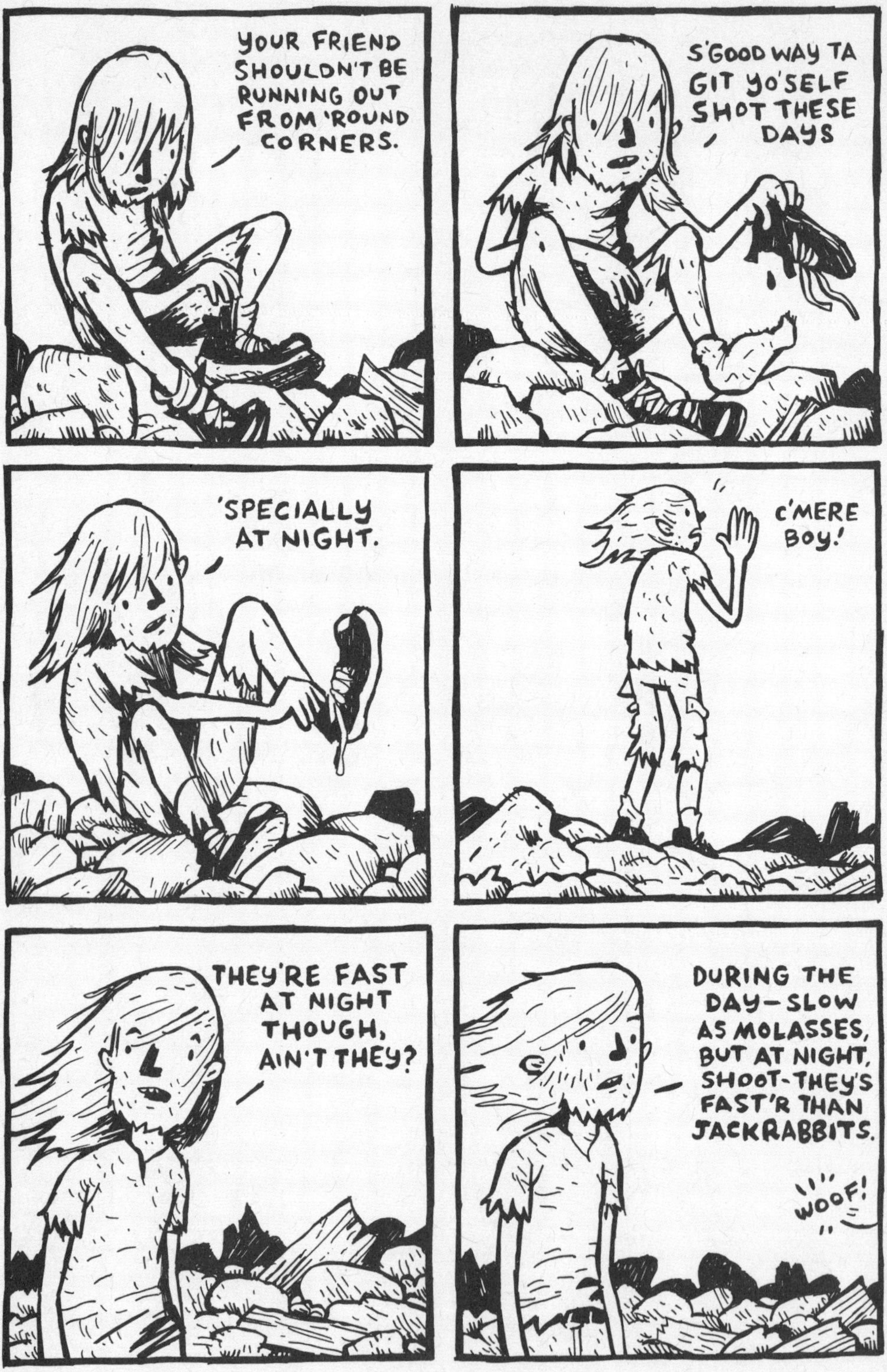
YOUR FRIEND SHOULDN'T BE RUNNING OUT FROM 'ROUND CORNERS.
S'GOOD WAY TA GIT YO'SELF SHOT THESE DAYS
'SPECIALLY AT NIGHT.
C'MERE BOY!
THEY'RE FAST AT NIGHT THOUGH, AIN'T THEY?
DURING THE DAY—SLOW AS MOLASSES, BUT AT NIGHT, SHOOT-THEY'S FAST'R THAN JACKRABBITS.
WOOF!

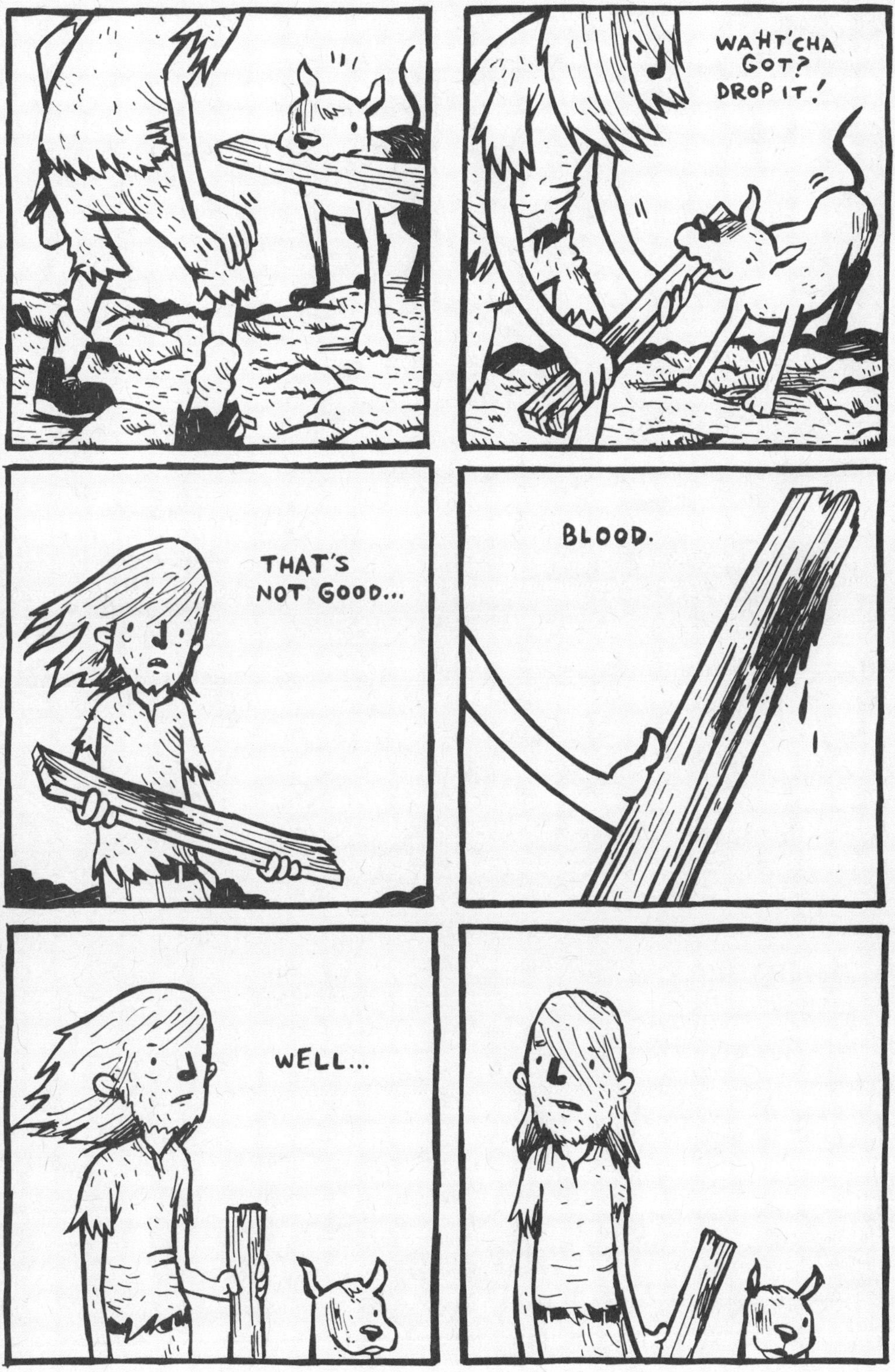
WAHT'CHA GOT? DROP IT!
THAT'S NOT GOOD...
BLOOD.
WELL...

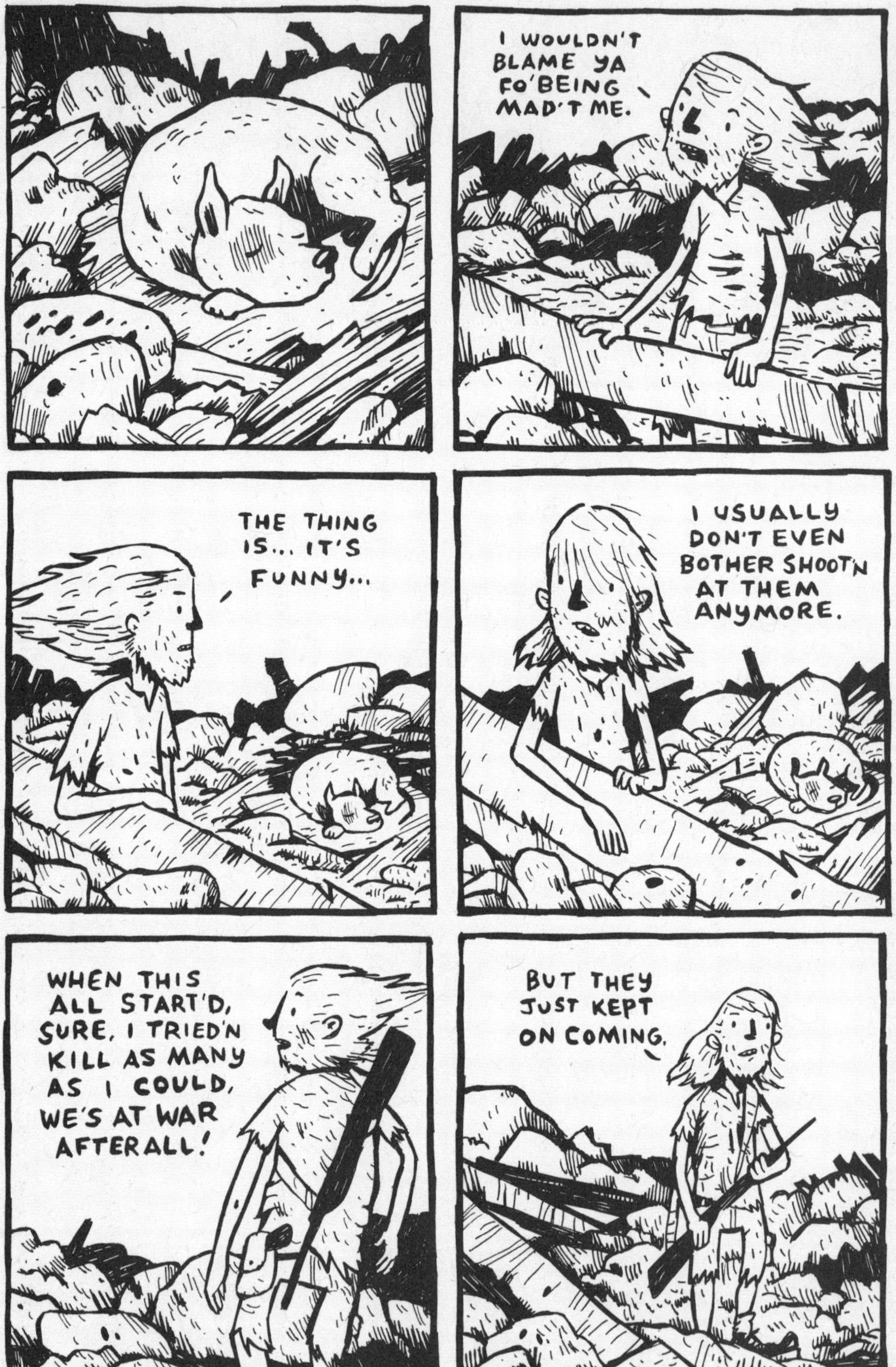
I WOULDN'T BLAME YA FO'BEING MAD'T ME.
THE THING IS... IT'S FUNNY...
I USUALLY DON'T EVEN BOTHER SHOOT'N AT THEM ANYMORE.
WHEN THIS ALL START'D, SURE, I TRIED'N KILL AS MANY AS I COULD, WE'S AT WAR AFTERALL!
BUT THEY JUST KEPT ON COMING.

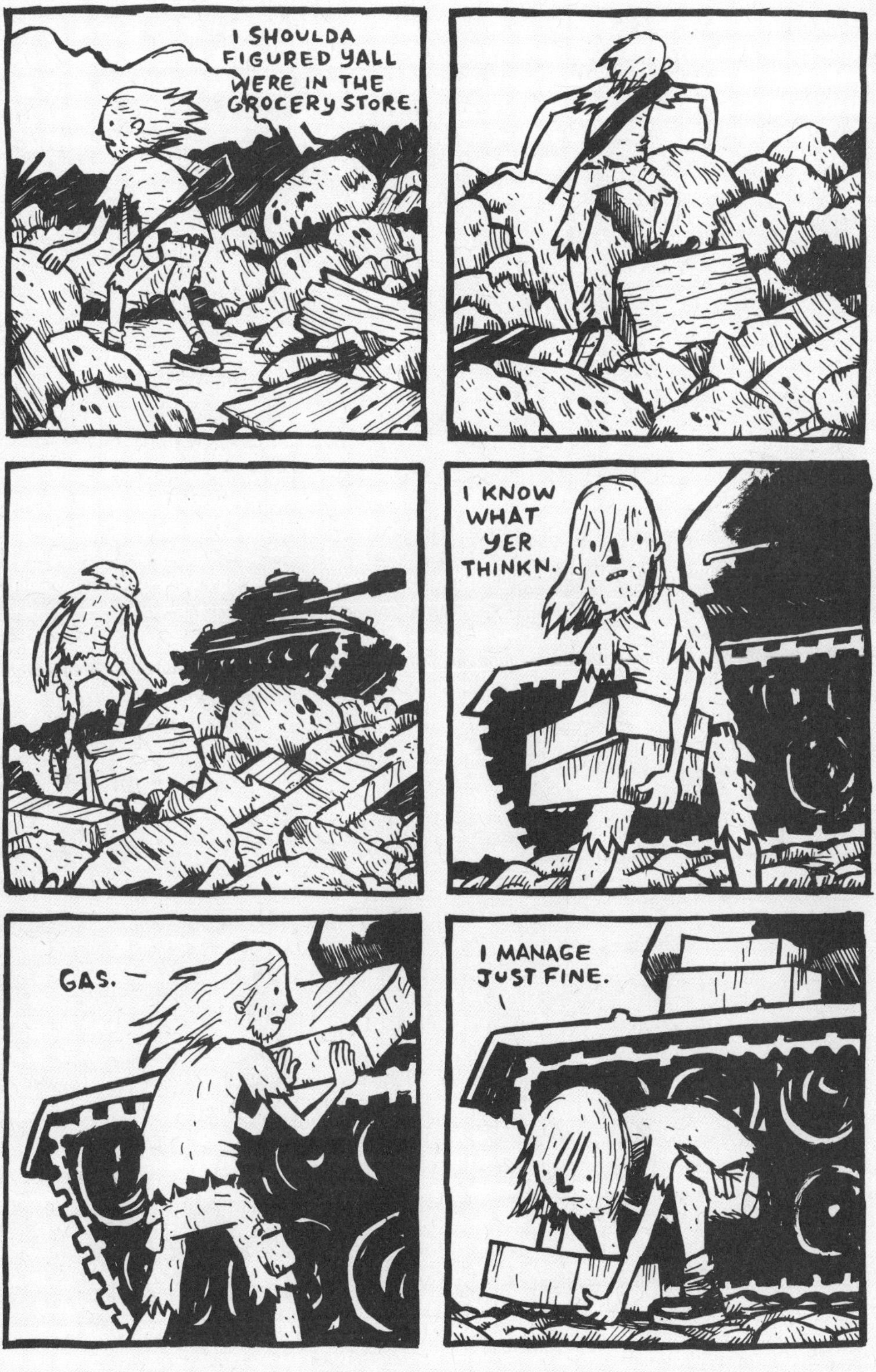
I SHOULDA FIGURED YALL WERE IN THE GROCERY STORE.
I KNOW WHAT YER THINKN.
GAS.
I MANAGE JUST FINE.

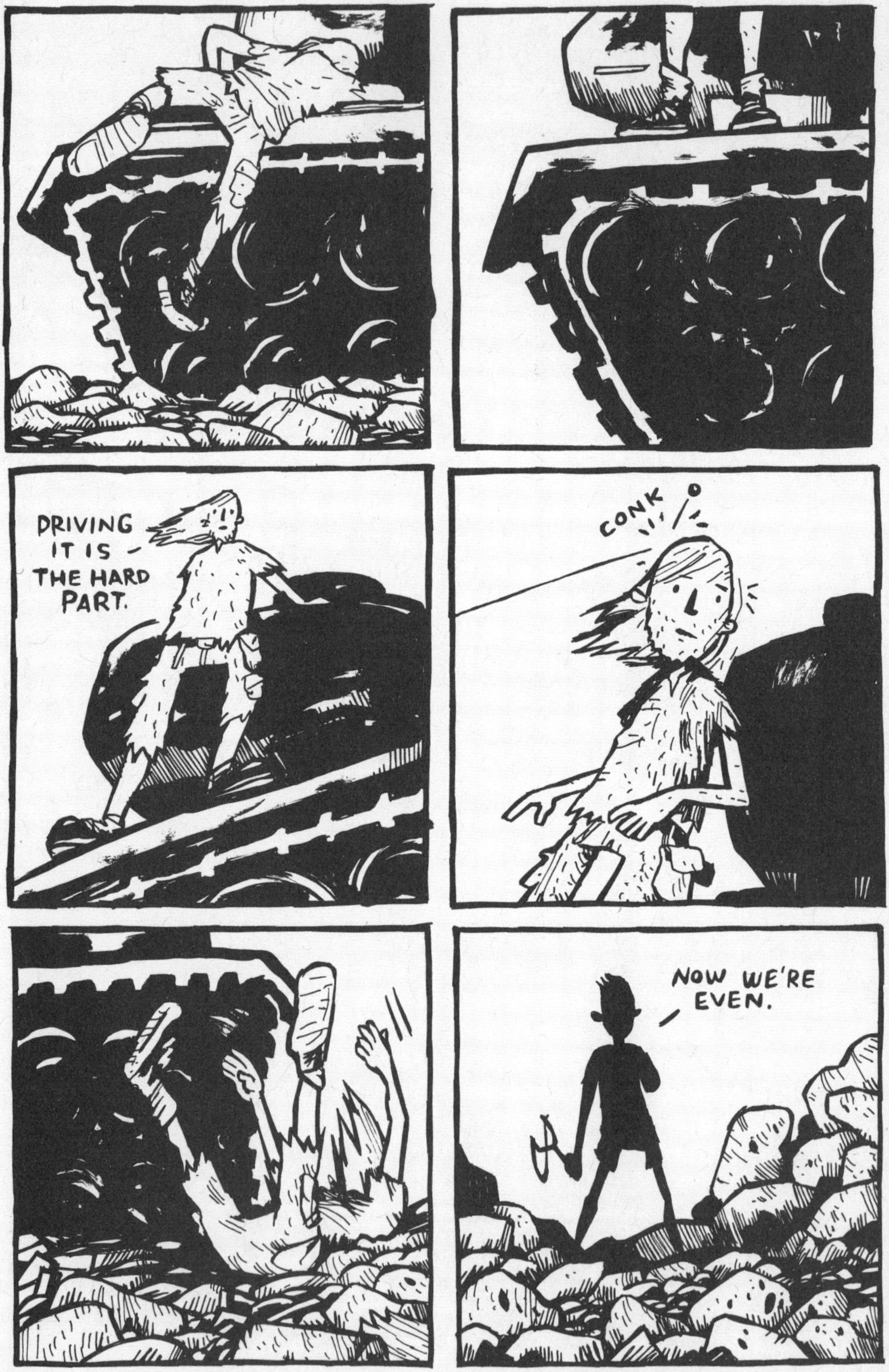
DRIVING IT IS THE HARD PART.
CONK
NOW WE'RE EVEN.

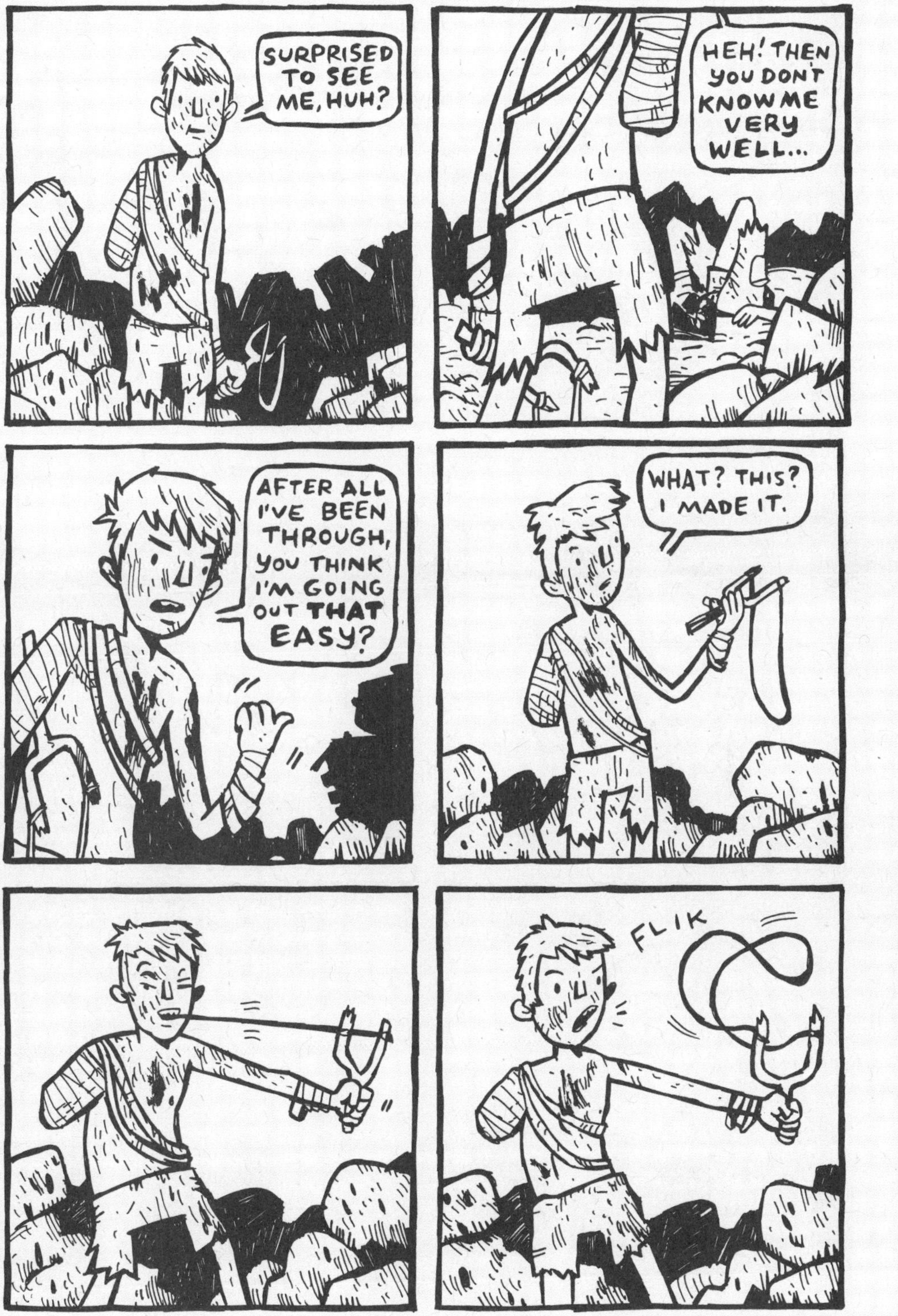
SURPRISED TO SEE ME, HUH?
HEH! THEN YOU DON'T KNOW ME VERY WELL...
AFTER ALL I'VE BEEN THROUGH, YOU THINK I'M GOING OUT THAT EASY?
WHAT? THIS? I MADE IT.
FLIK

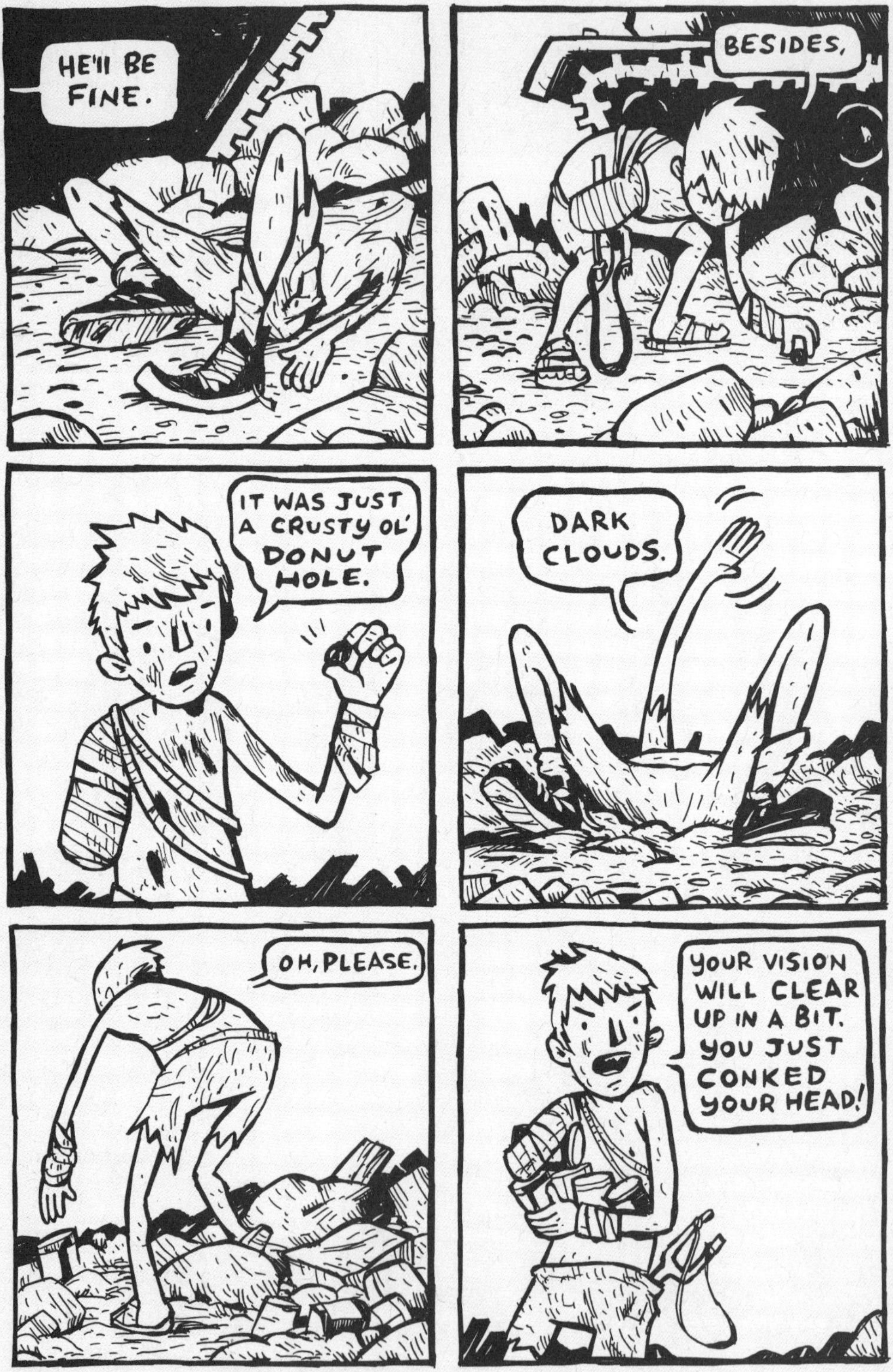
HE'll BE FINE.
BESIDES,
IT WAS JUST A CRUSTY OL' DONUT HOLE.
DARK CLOUDS.
OH, PLEASE.
YOUR VISION WILL CLEAR UP IN A BIT. YOU JUST CONKED YOUR HEAD!

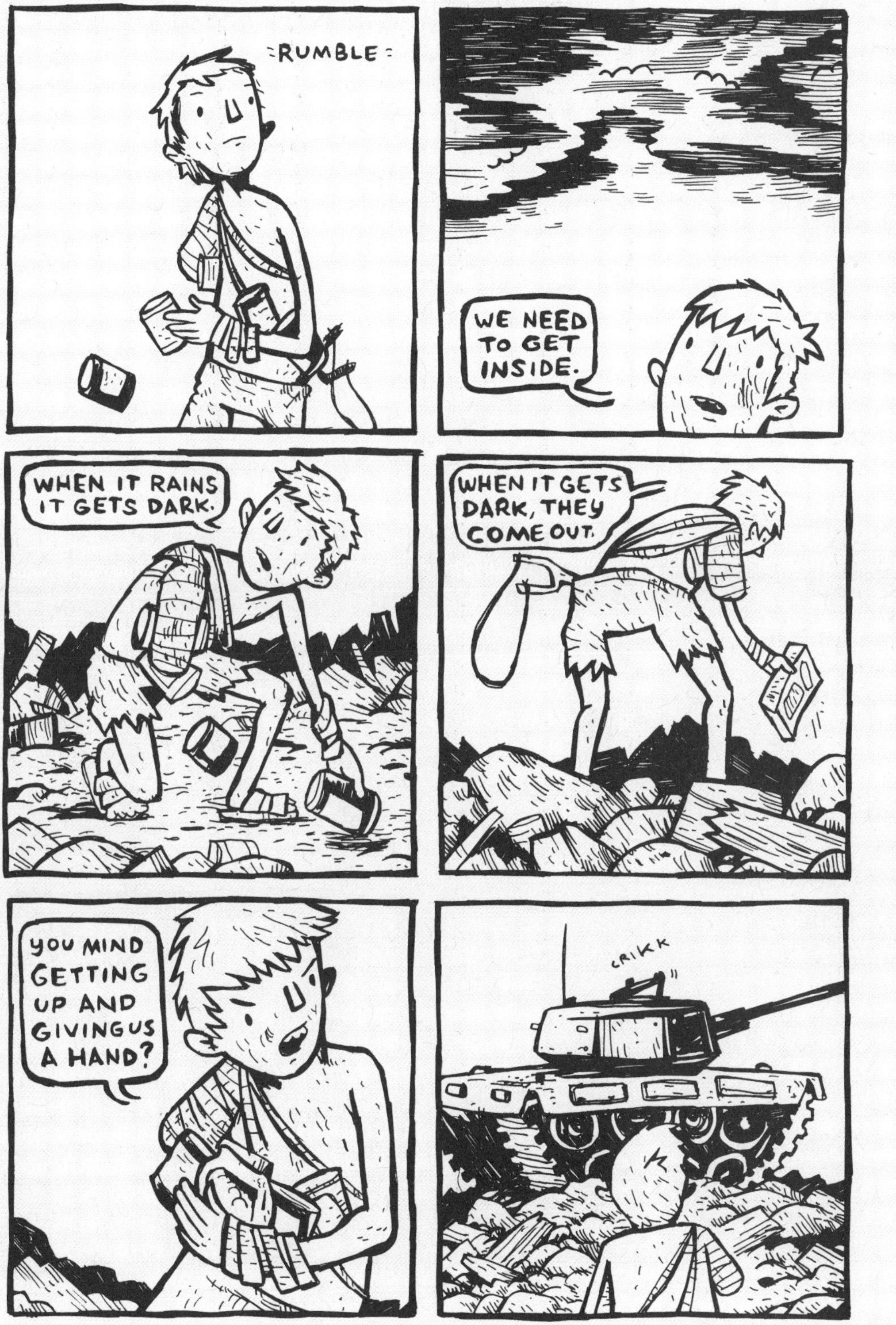

RUMBLE
WE NEED TO GET INSIDE.
WHEN IT RAINS IT GETS DARK.
WHEN IT GETS DARK, THEY COME OUT.
YOU MIND GETTING UP AND GIVINGUS A HAND?
CRIKK

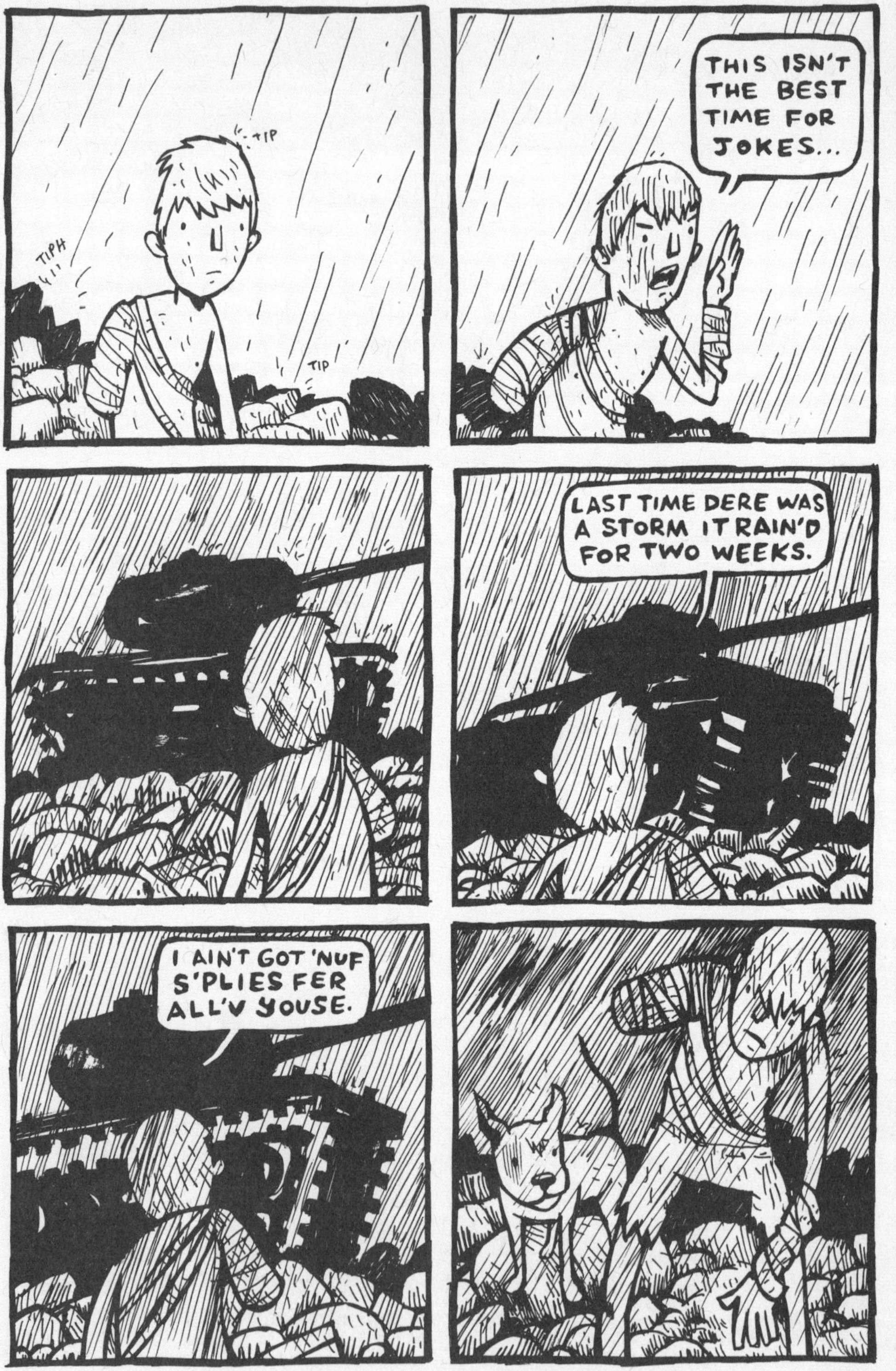
TIP
TIPH
TIP
THIS ISN'T THE BEST TIME FOR JOKES...
LAST TIME DERE WAS A STORM IT RAIN'D FOR TWO WEEKS.
I AIN'T GOT 'NUF S'PLIES FER ALL'V YOUSE.

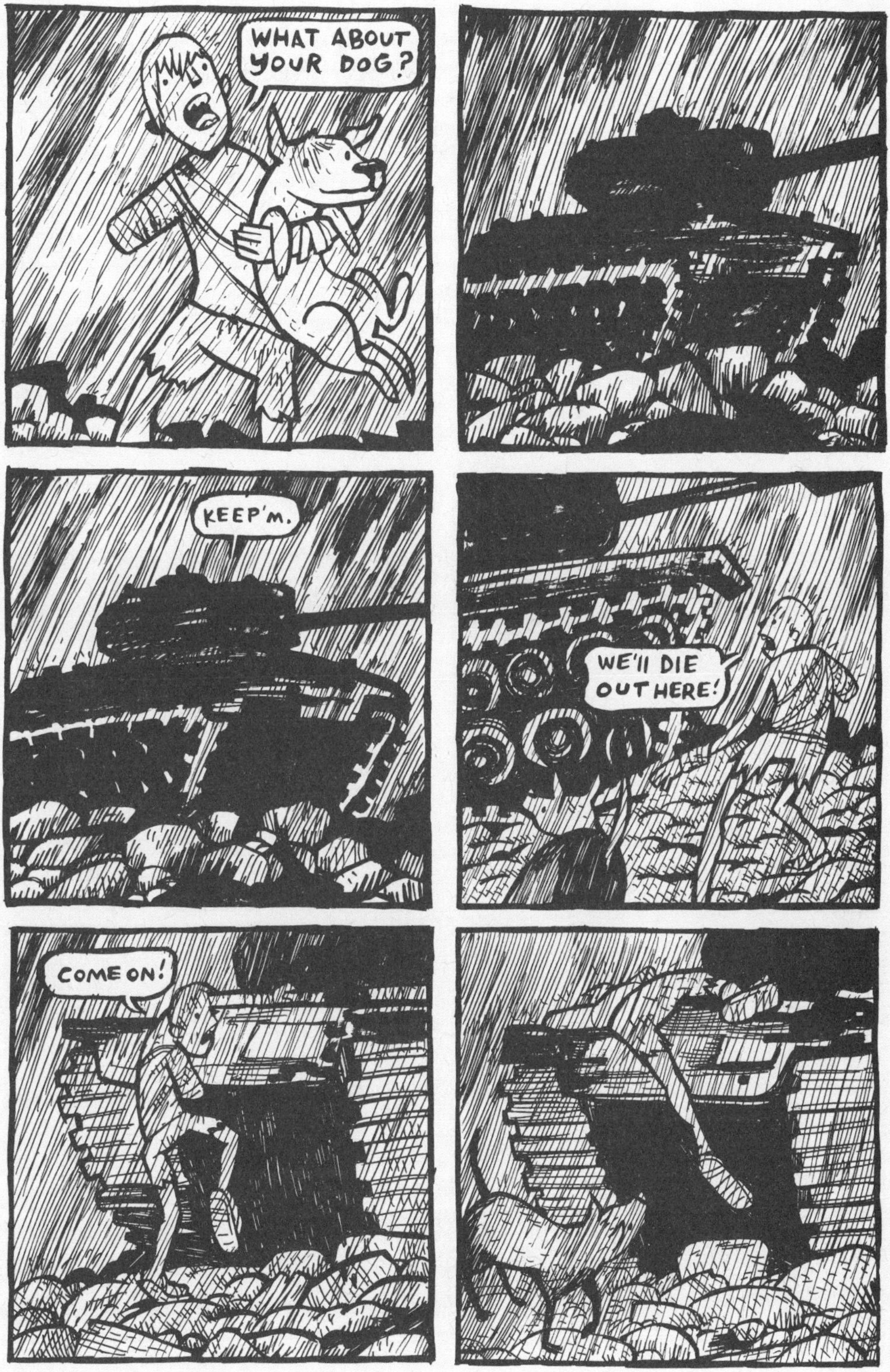

WHAT ABOUT YOUR DOG?
KEEP'M.
WE'll DIE OUT HERE!
COME ON!

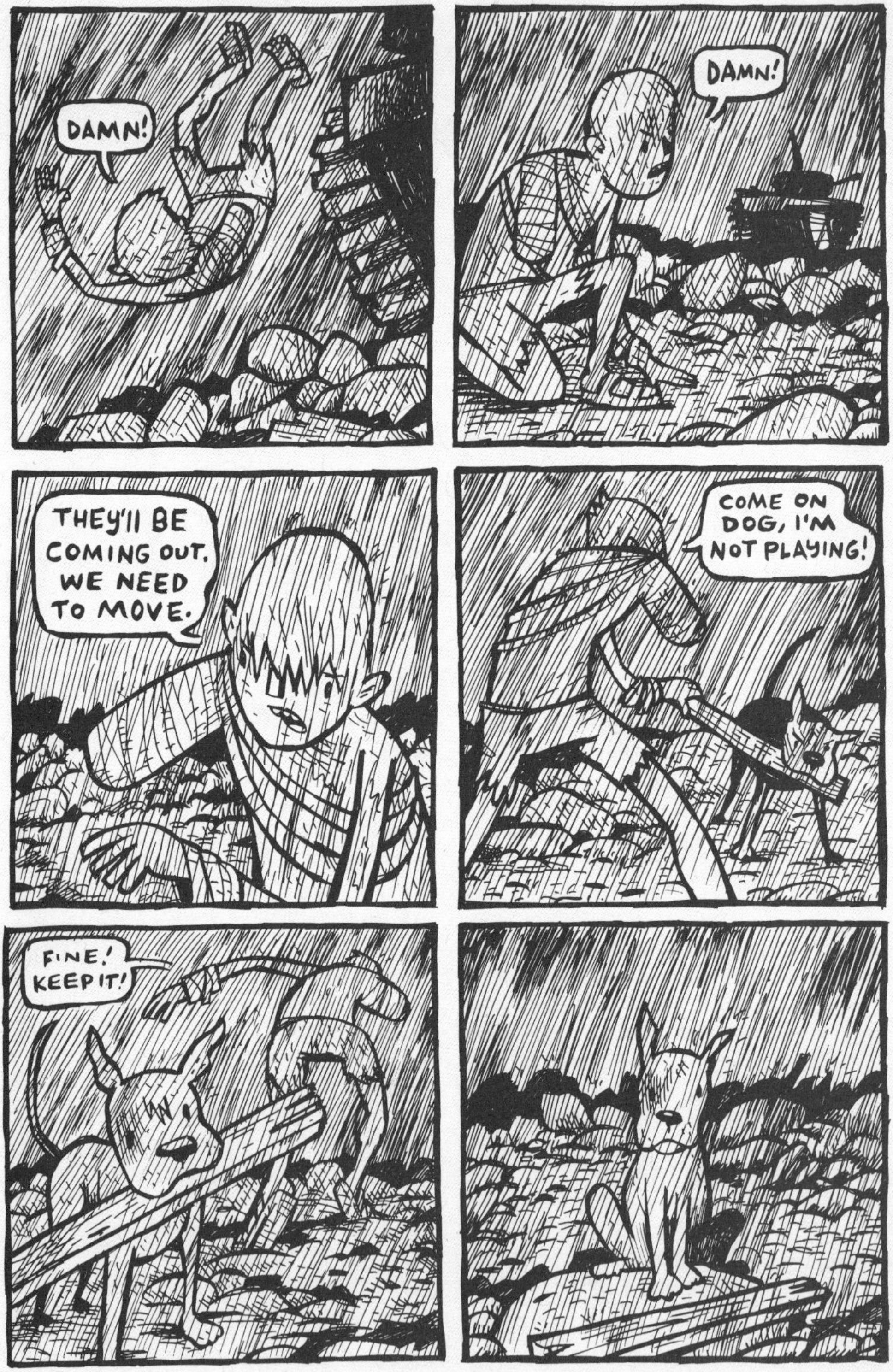
DAMN!
DAMN!
THEY'll BE COMING OUT. WE NEED TO MOVE.
COME ON DOG, I'M NOT PLAYING!
FINE! KEEP IT!

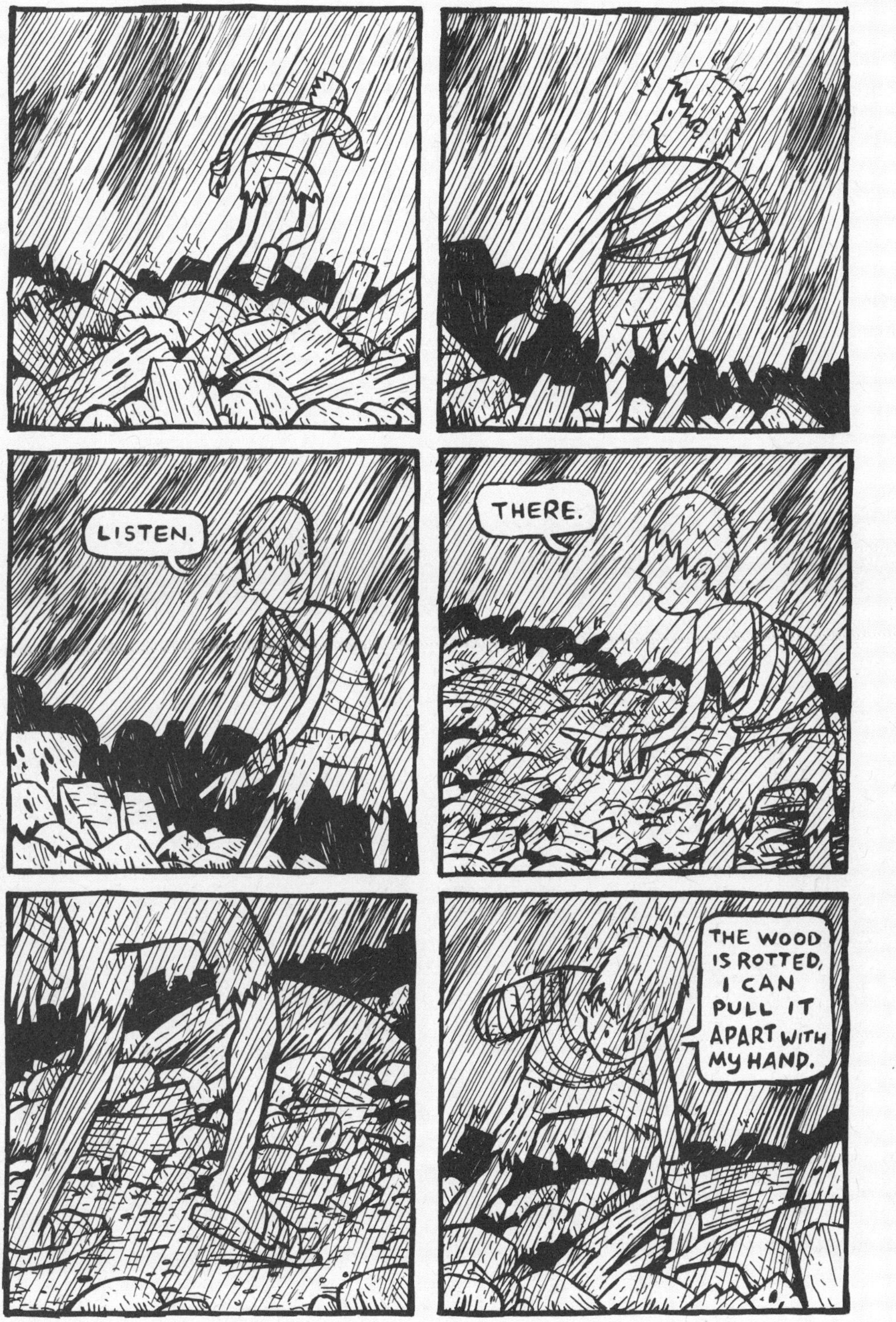
LISTEN.
THERE.
THE WOOD IS ROTTED, I CAN PULL IT APART WITH MY HAND.

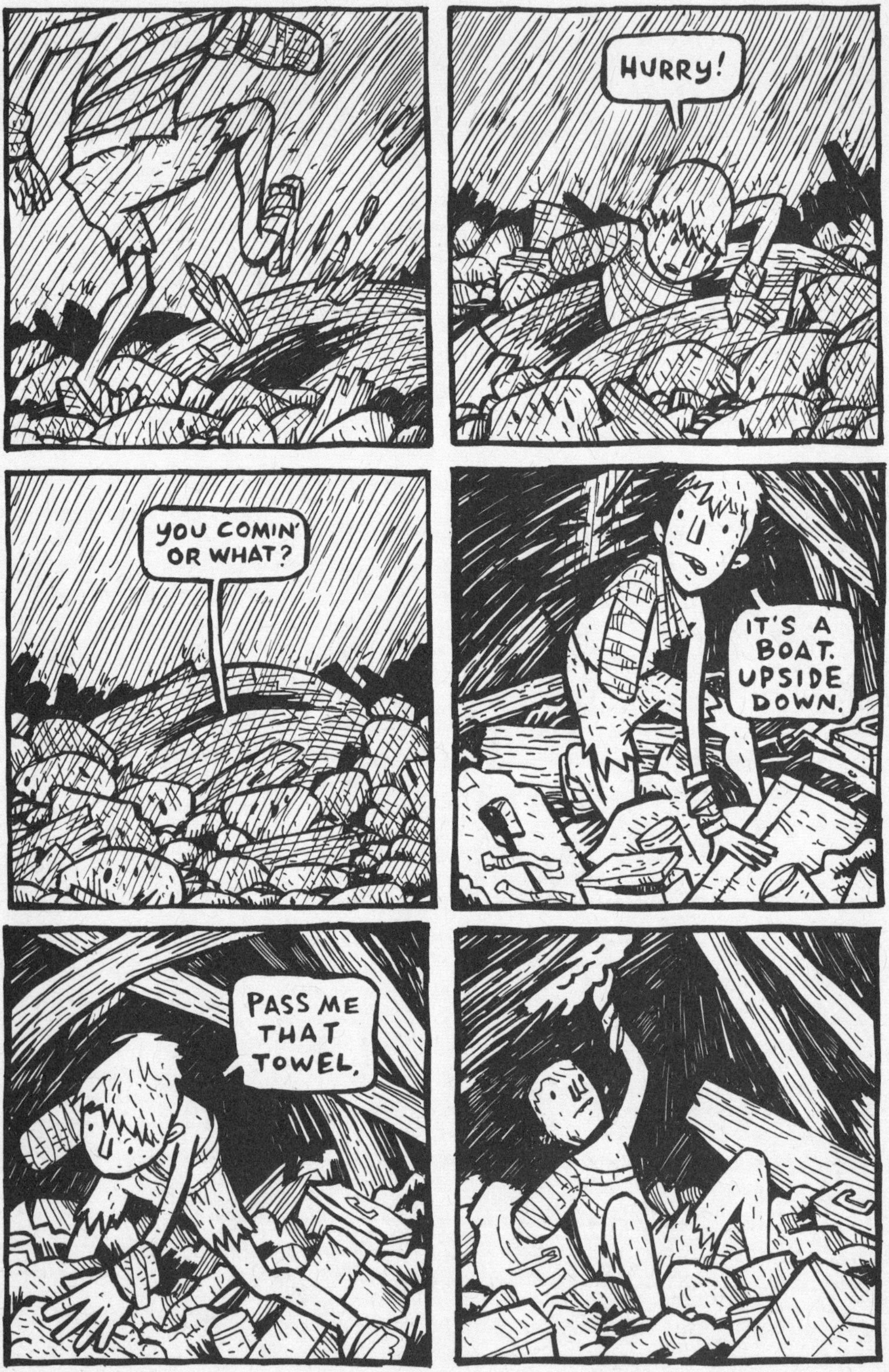
HURRY!
YOU COMIN' OR WHAT?
IT'S A BOAT. UPSIDE DOWN.
PASS ME THAT TOWEL.

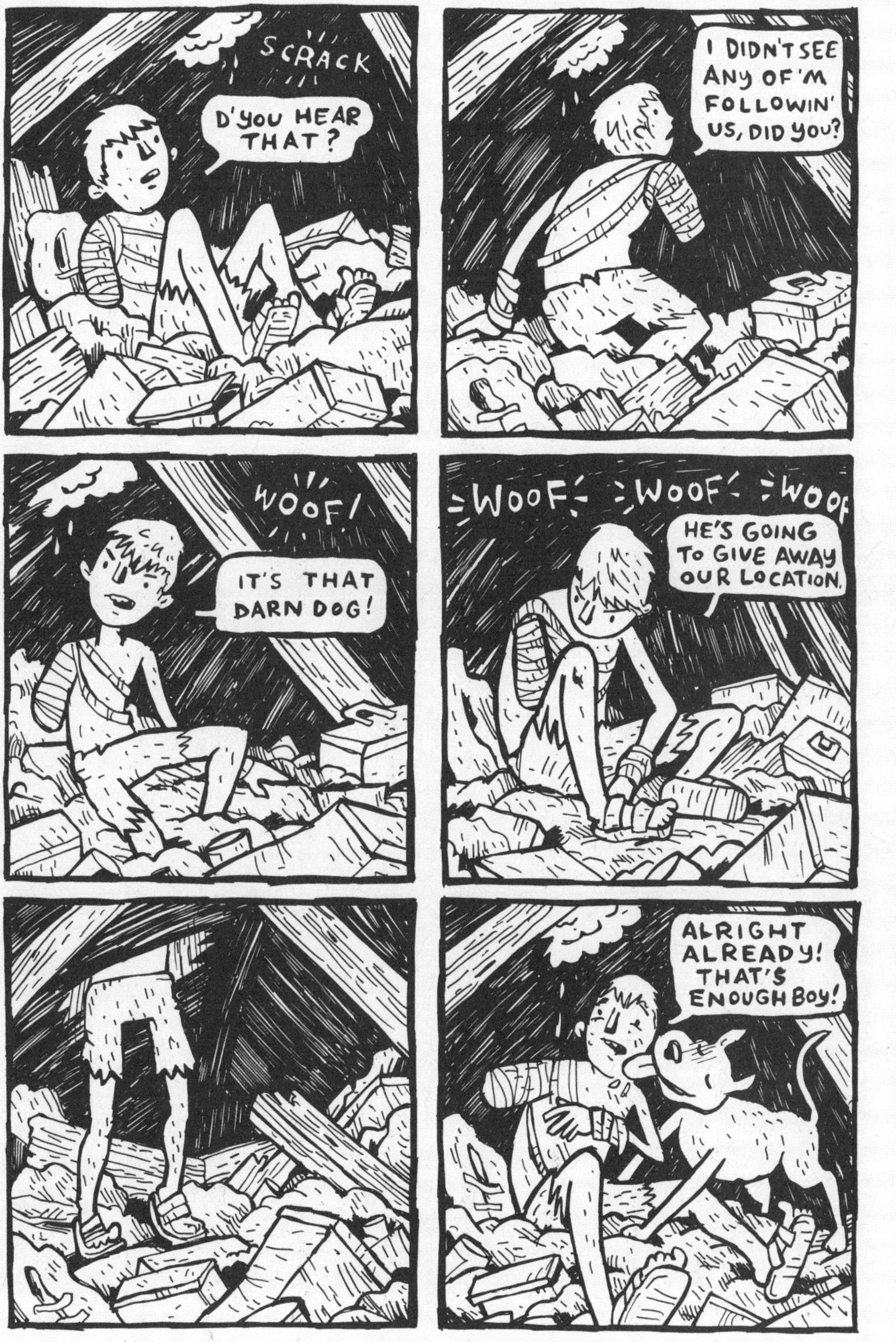
SCRACK
D'YOU HEAR THAT?
I DIDN'T SEE ANY OF 'M FOLLOWIN' US, DID YOU?
WOOF!
IT'S THAT DARN DOG!
WOOF WOOF WOOF
HE'S GOING TO GIVE AWAY OUR LOCATION.
ALRIGHT ALREADY! THAT'S ENOUGH BOY!

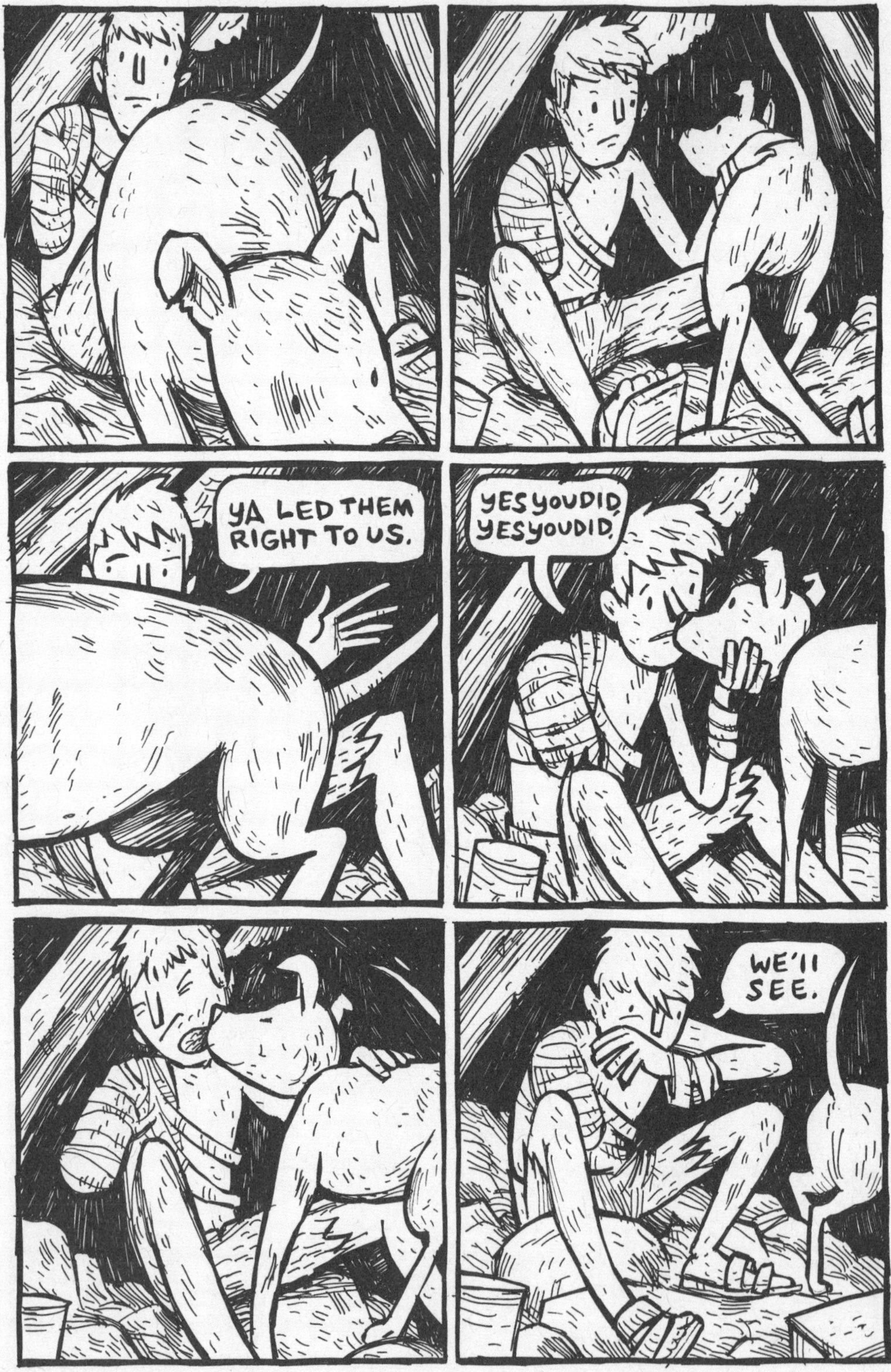
YA LED THEM RIGHT TO US.
YES YOU DID, YES YOU DID.
WE'll SEE.

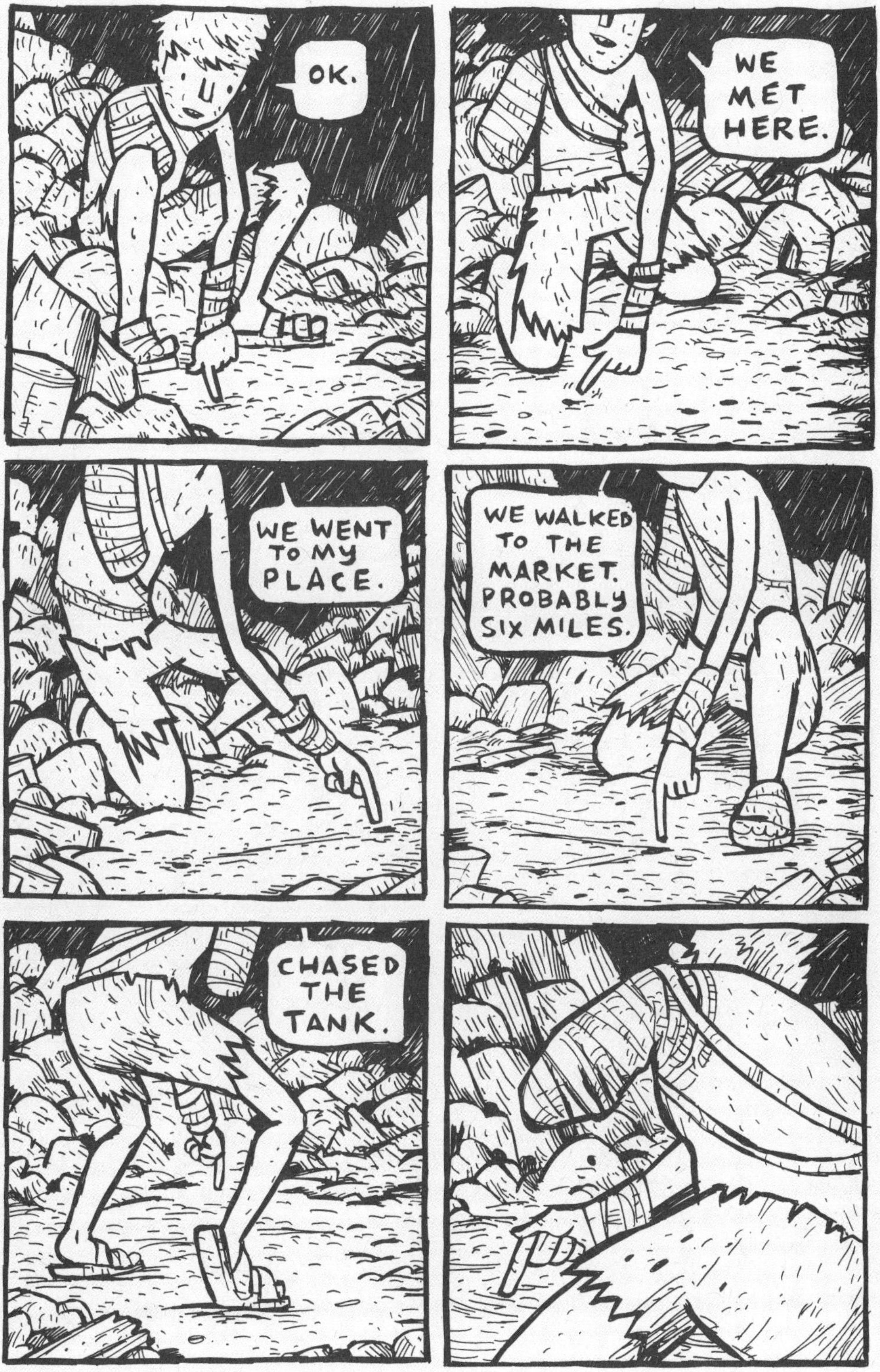
OK.
WE MET HERE.
WE WENT TO MY PLACE.
WE WALKED TO THE MARKET. PROBABLY SIX MILES.
CHASED THE TANK.

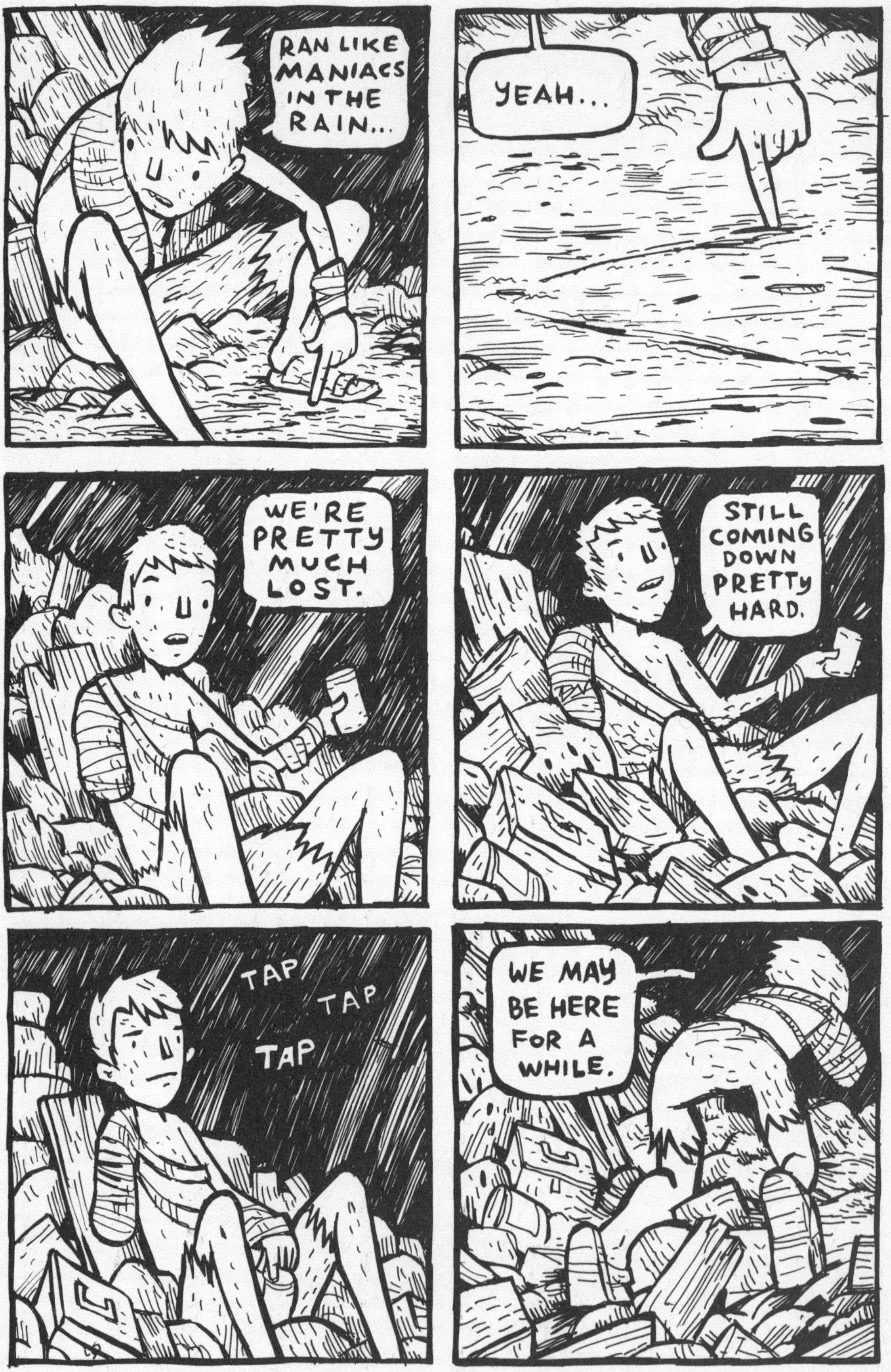
RAN LIKE MANIACS IN THE RAIN...
YEAH...
WE'RE PRETTY MUCH LOST.
STILL COMING DOWN PRETTY HARD.
TAP
TAP
TAP
WE MAY BE HERE FOR A WHILE.

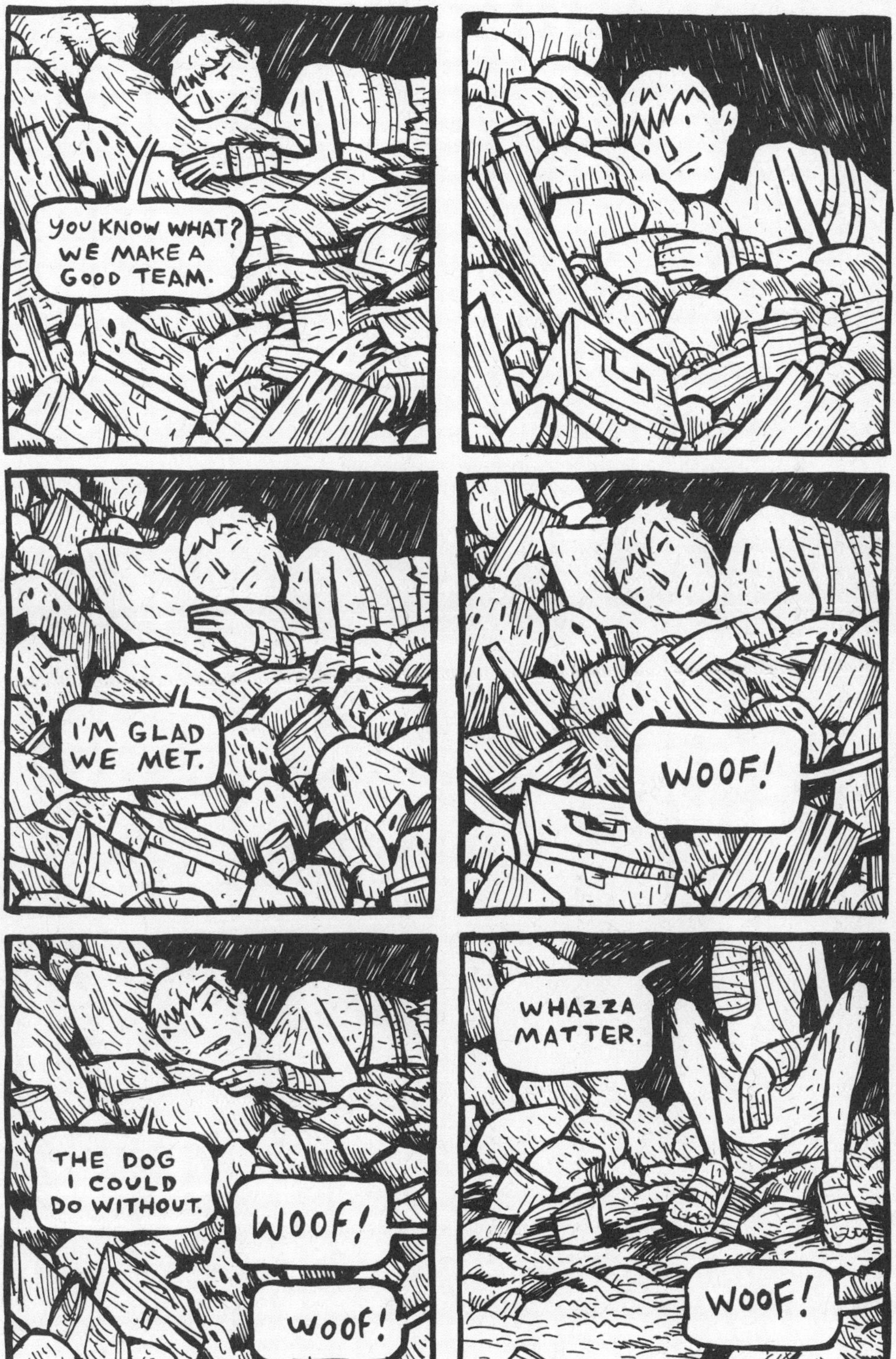
YOU KNOW WHAT? WE MAKE A GOOD TEAM.
I'M GLAD WE MET.
WOOF!
THE DOG I COULD DO WITHOUT.
WOOF!
WOOF!
WHAZZA MATTER.
WOOF!

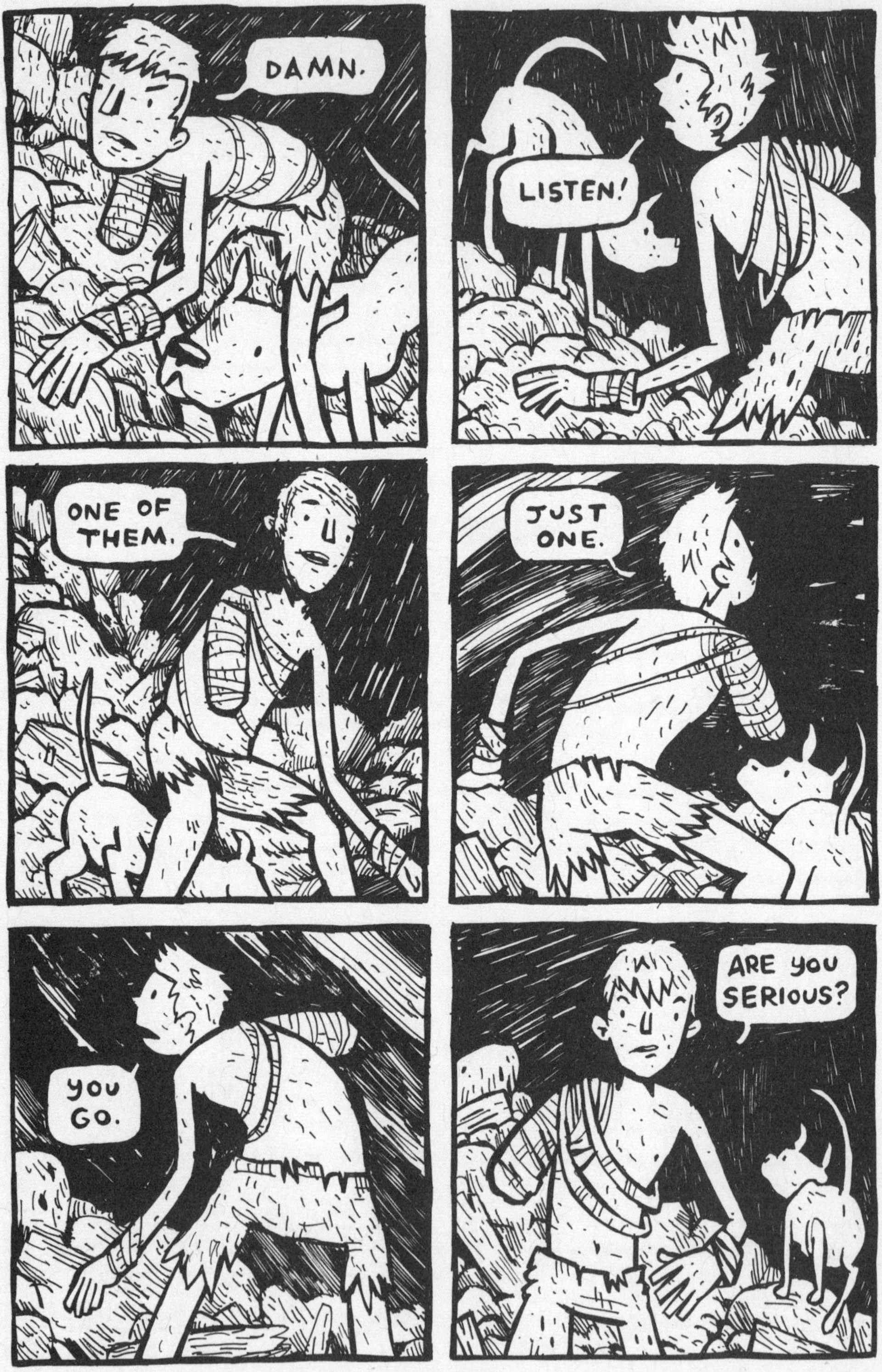
DAMN.
LISTEN!
ONE OF THEM.
JUST ONE.
YOU GO.
ARE YOU SERIOUS?

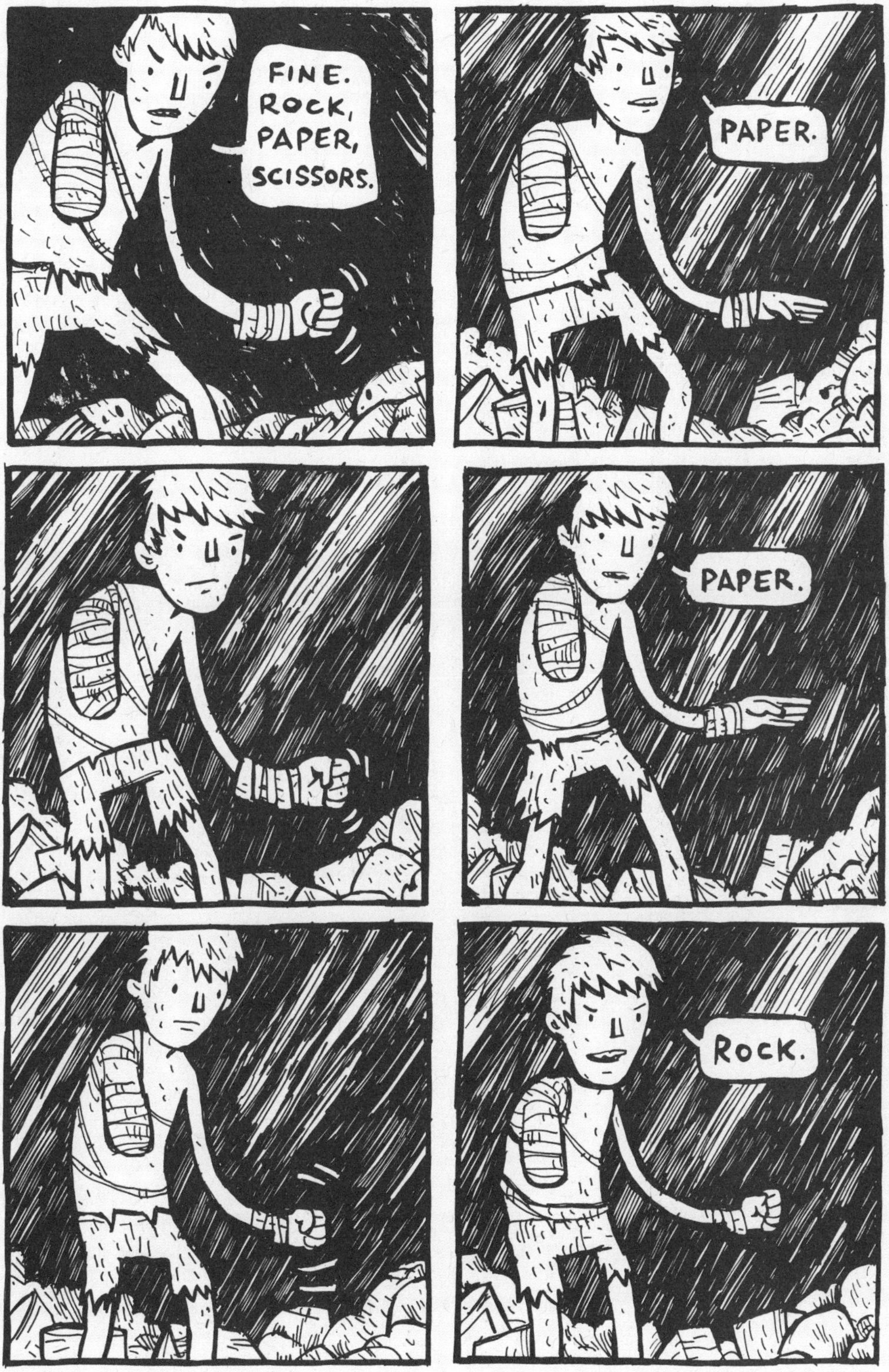
FINE. ROCK, PAPER, SCISSORS.
PAPER.
PAPER.
ROCK.

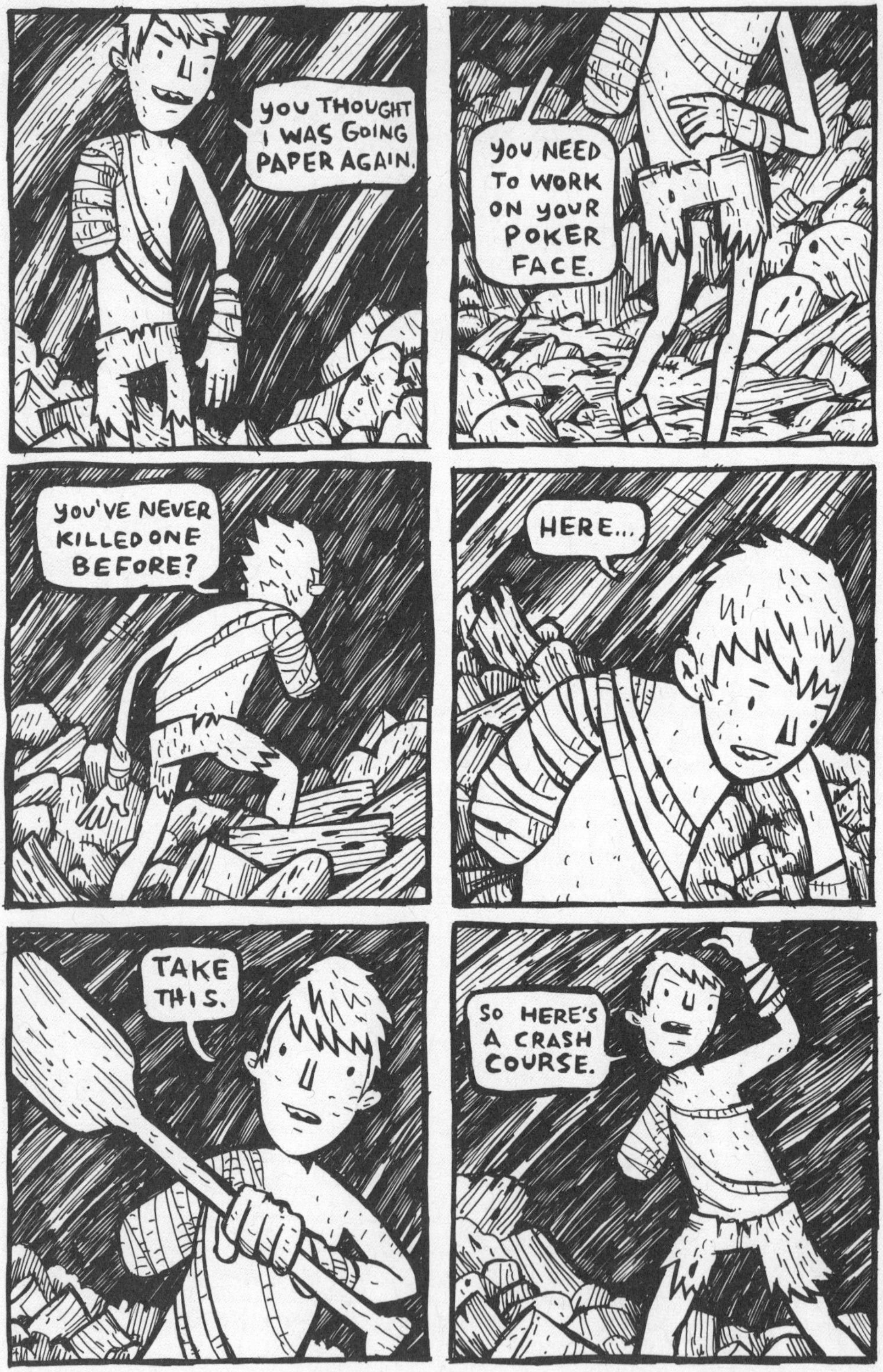
YOU THOUGHT I WAS GOING PAPER AGAIN.
YOU NEED TO WORK ON YOUR POKER FACE.
YOU'VE NEVER KILLED ONE BEFORE?
HERE...
TAKE THIS.
SO HERE'S A CRASH COURSE.

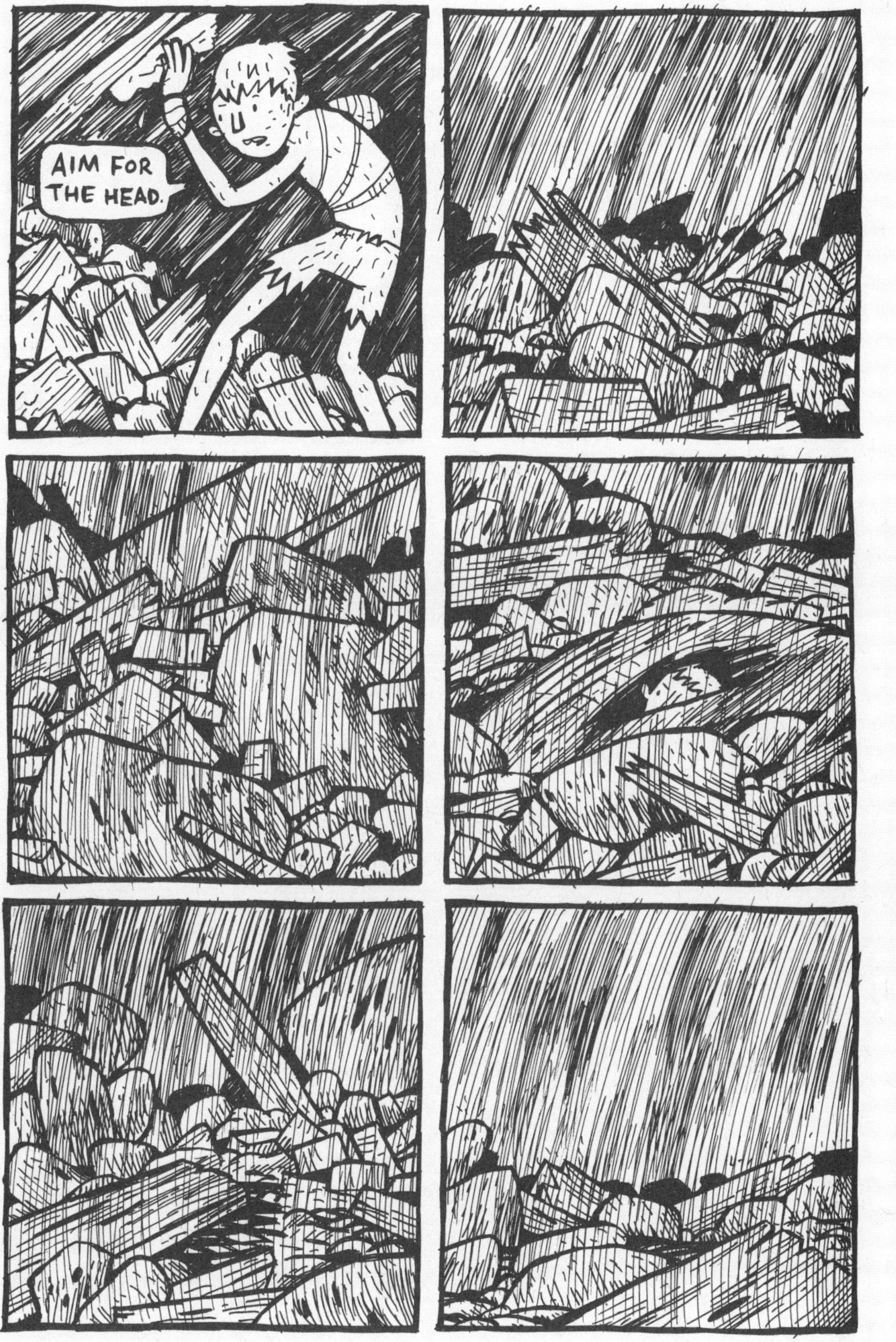
AIM FOR THE HEAD.

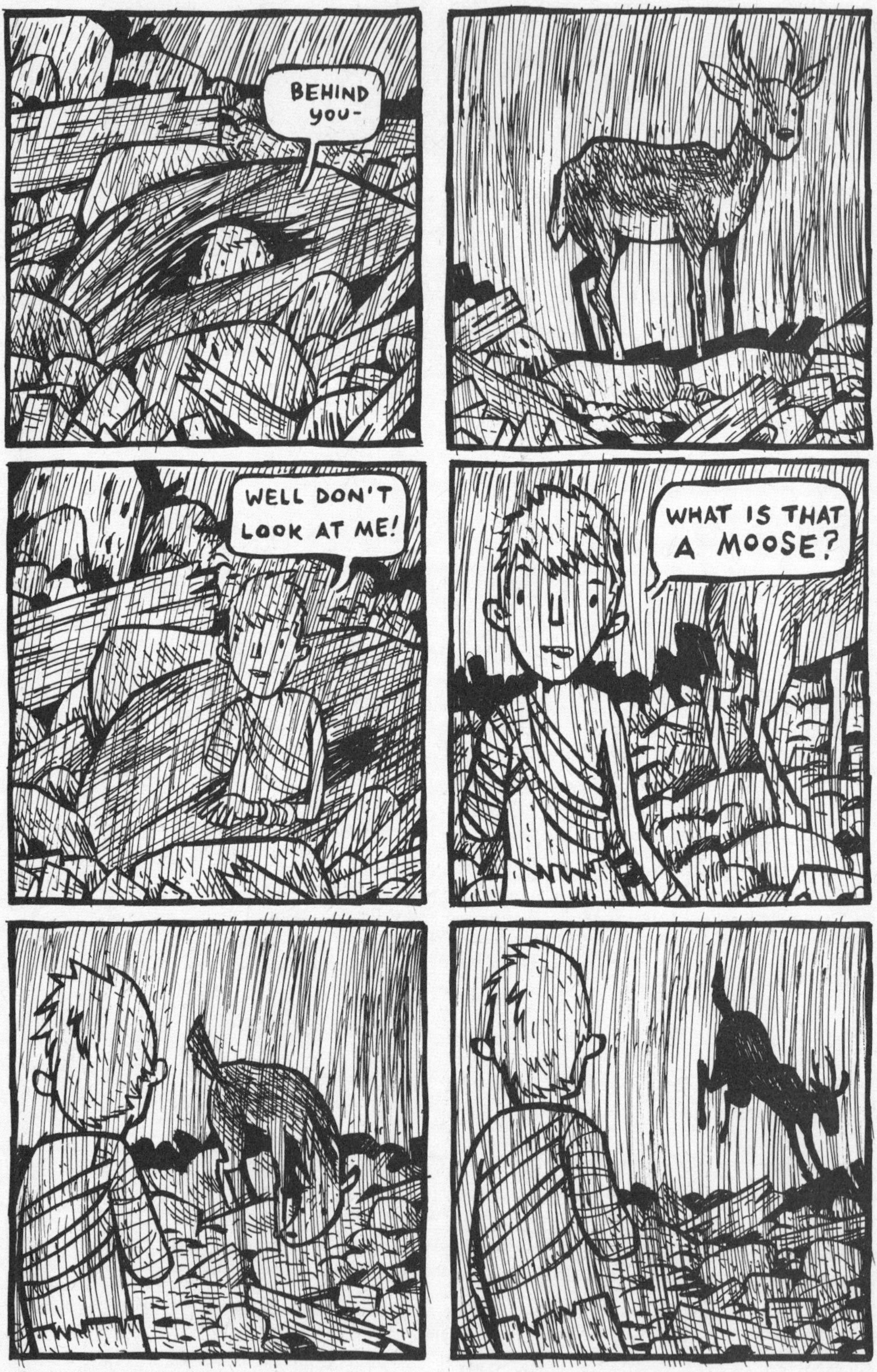
BEHIND you-
WELL DON'T LOOK AT ME!
WHAT IS THAT A MOOSE?

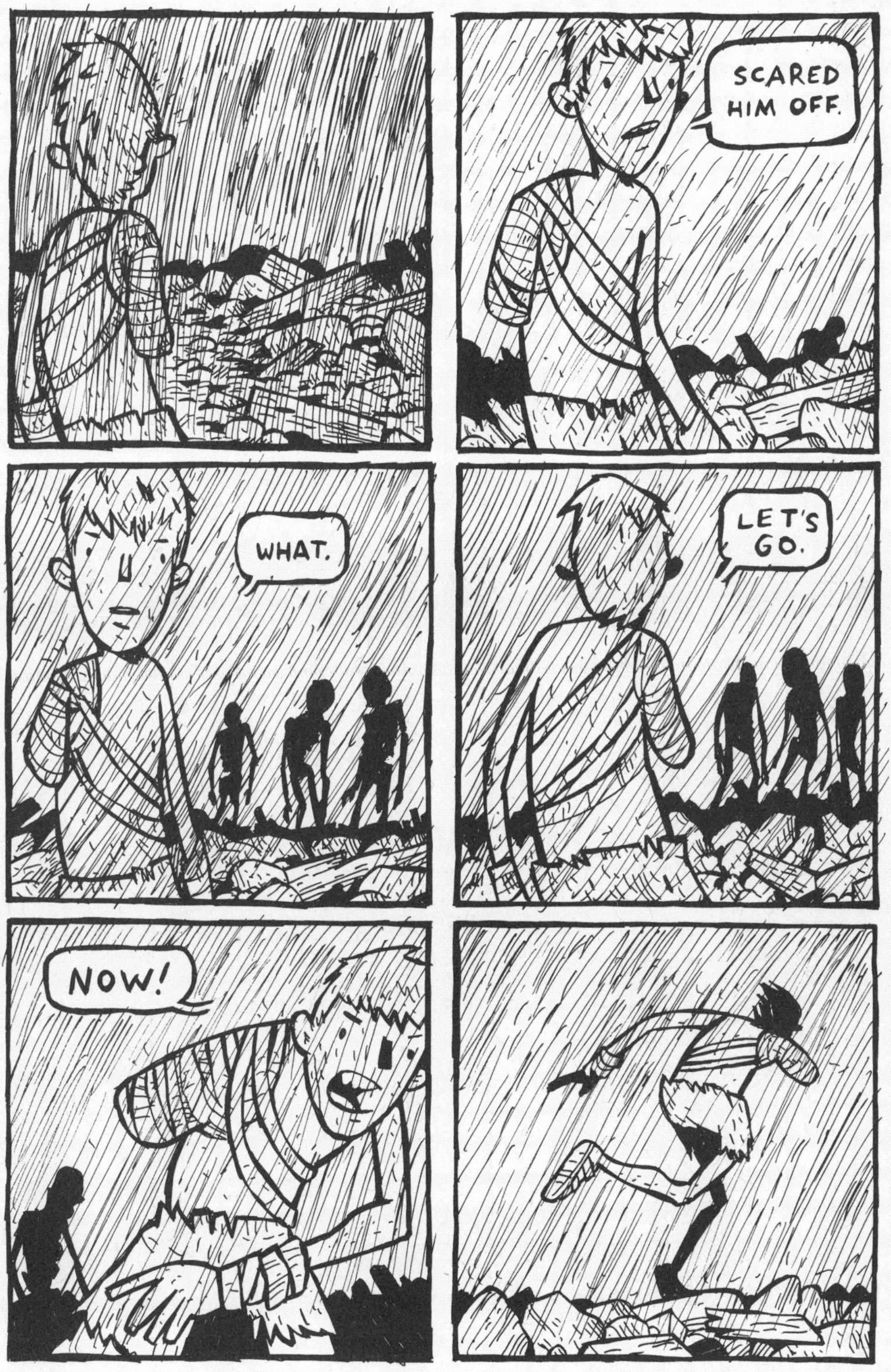
SCARED HIM OFF.
WHAT.
LET'S GO.
NOW!

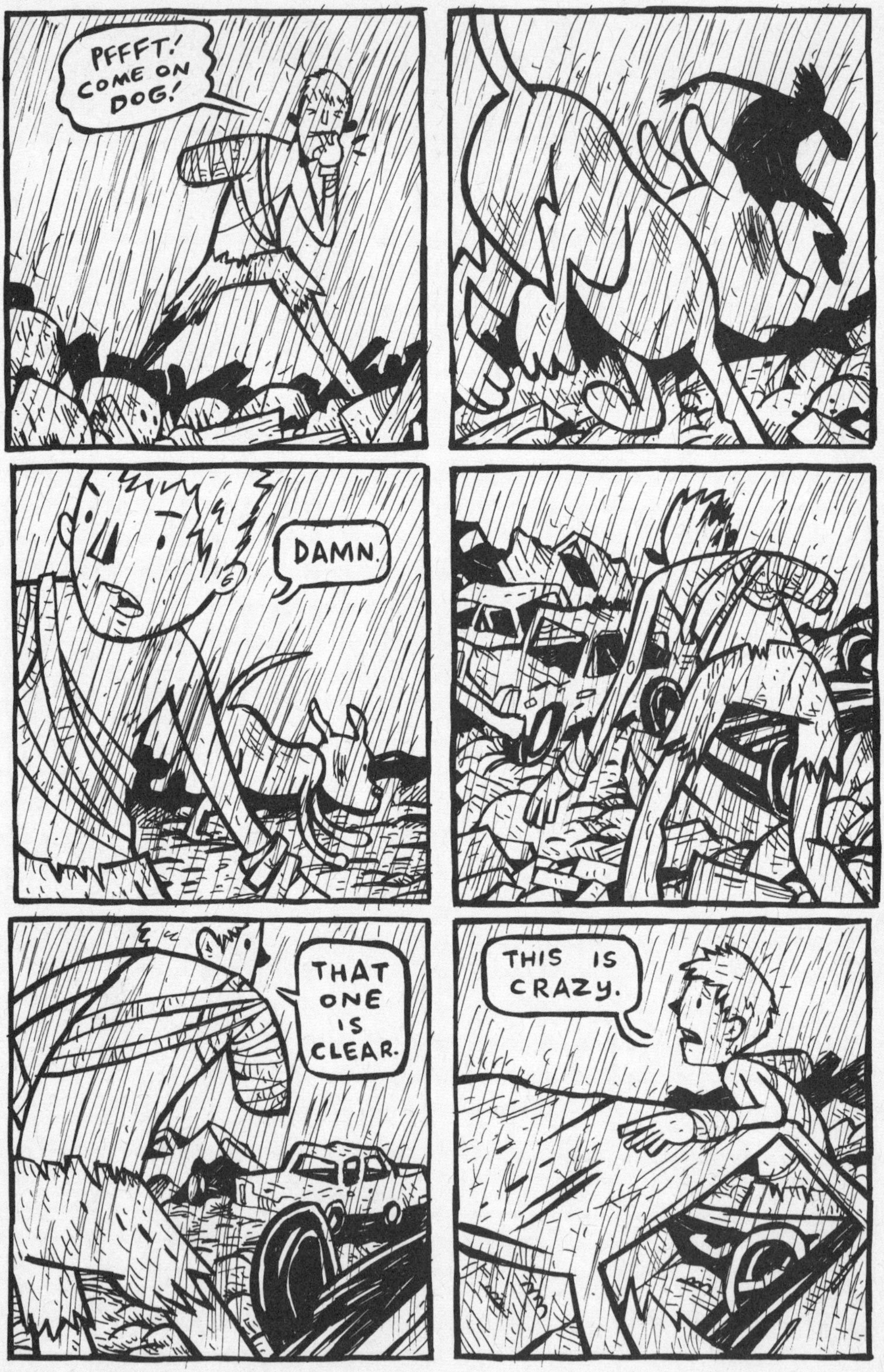
PFFFT! COME ON DOG!
DAMN.
THAT ONE IS CLEAR.
THIS IS CRAZY.

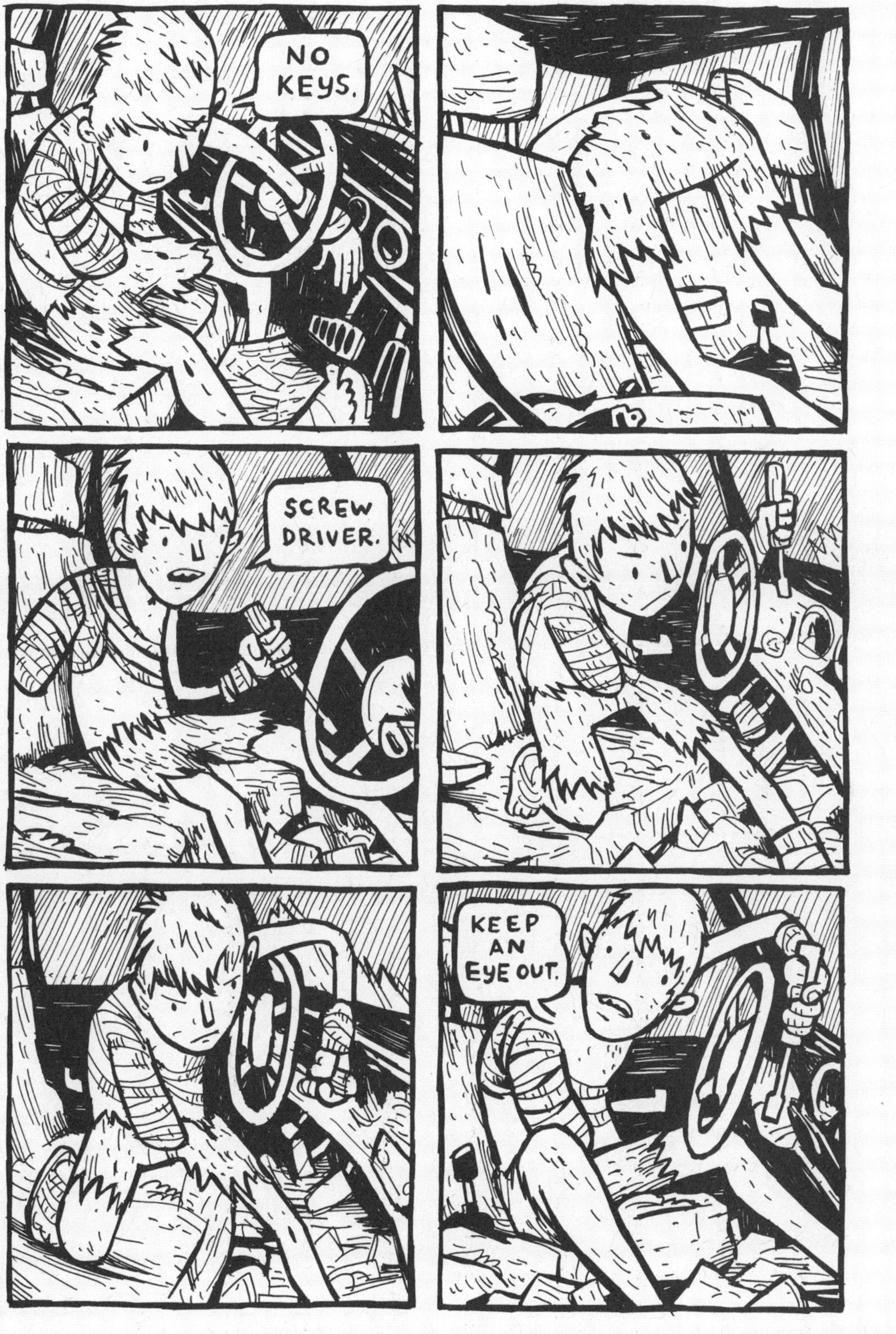
NO KEYS.
SCREW DRIVER.
KEEP AN EYE OUT.

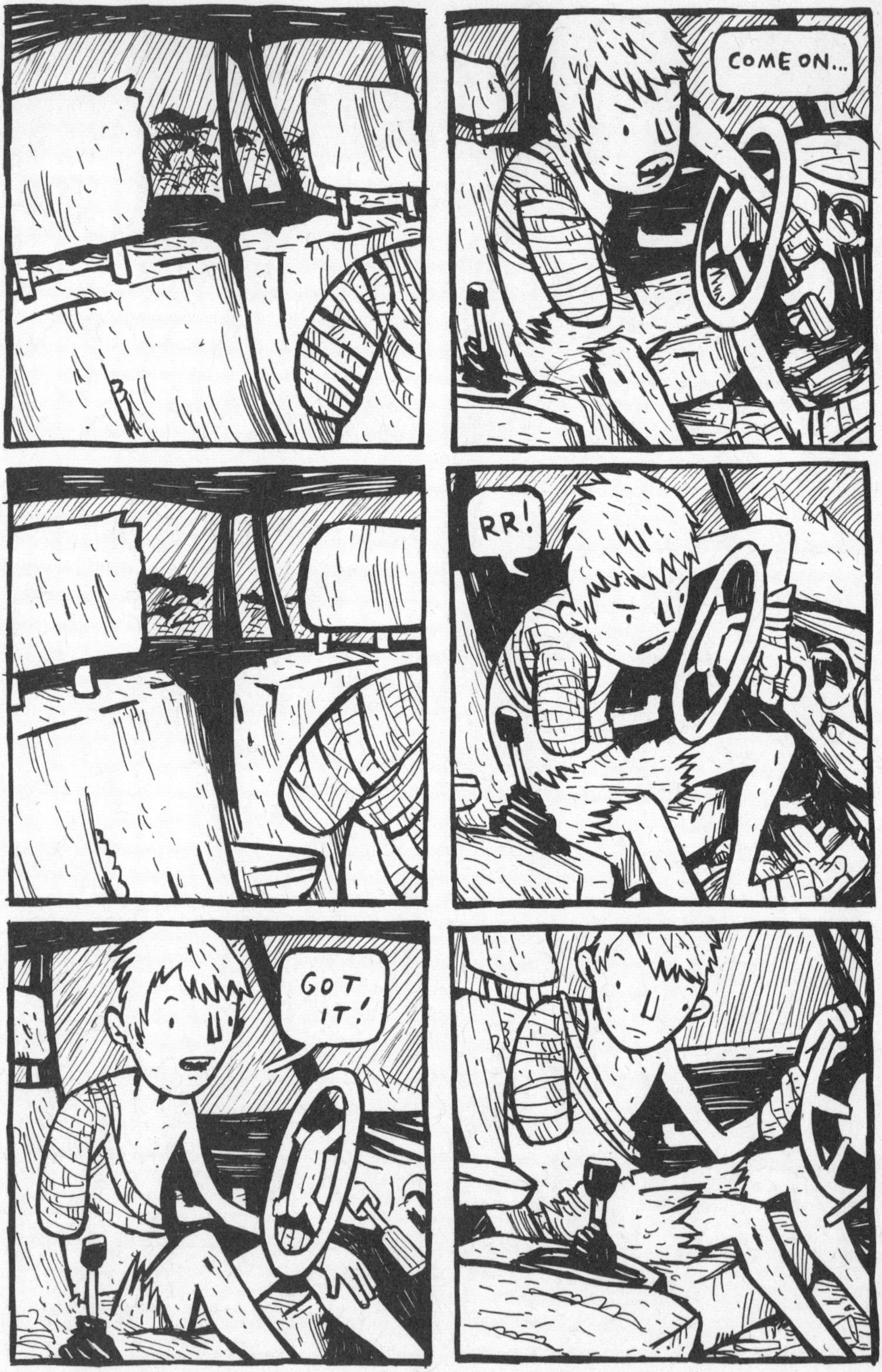
COME ON...
RR!
GOT IT!

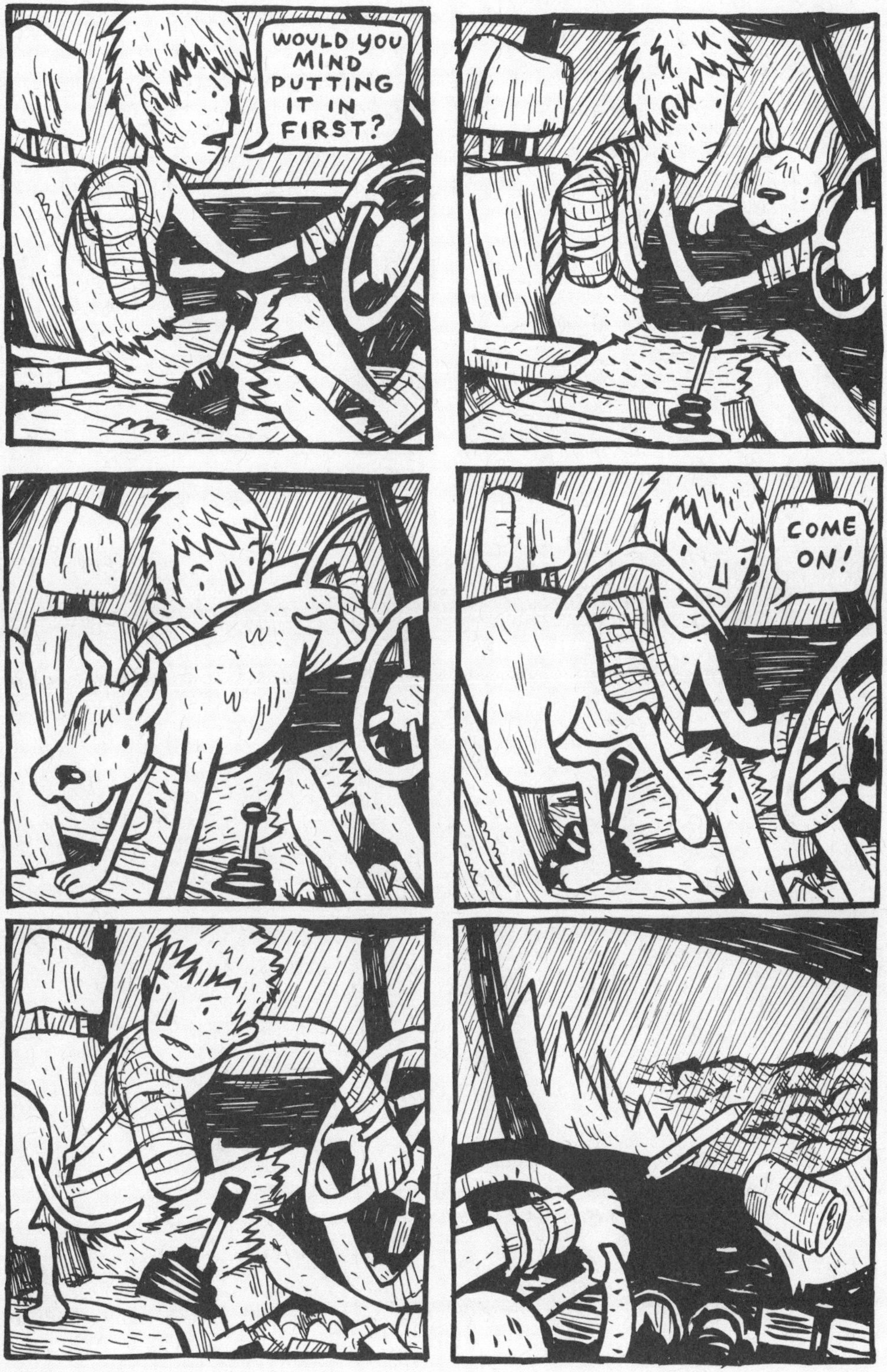
WOULD YOU MIND PUTTING IT IN FIRST?
COME ON!

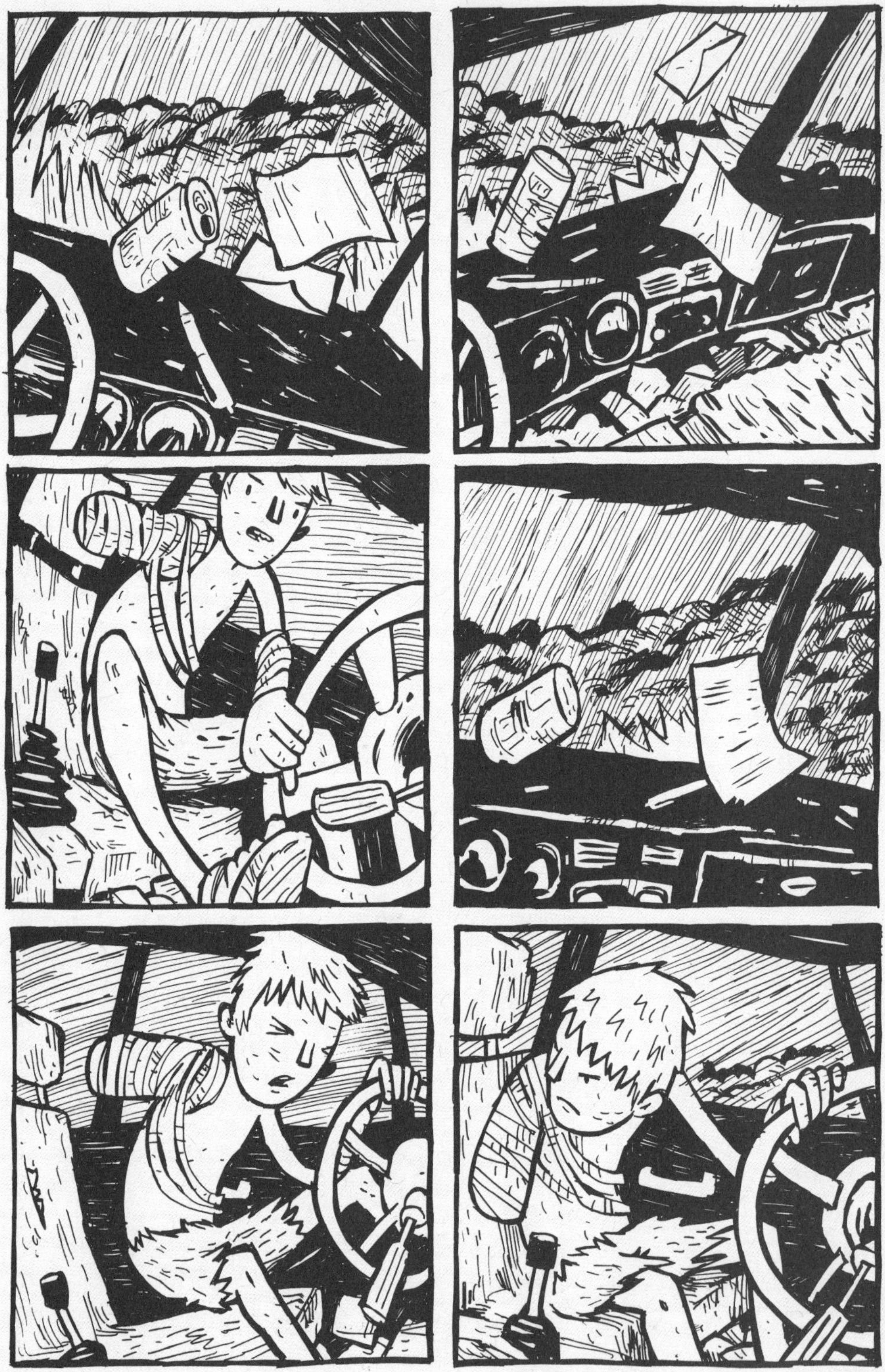

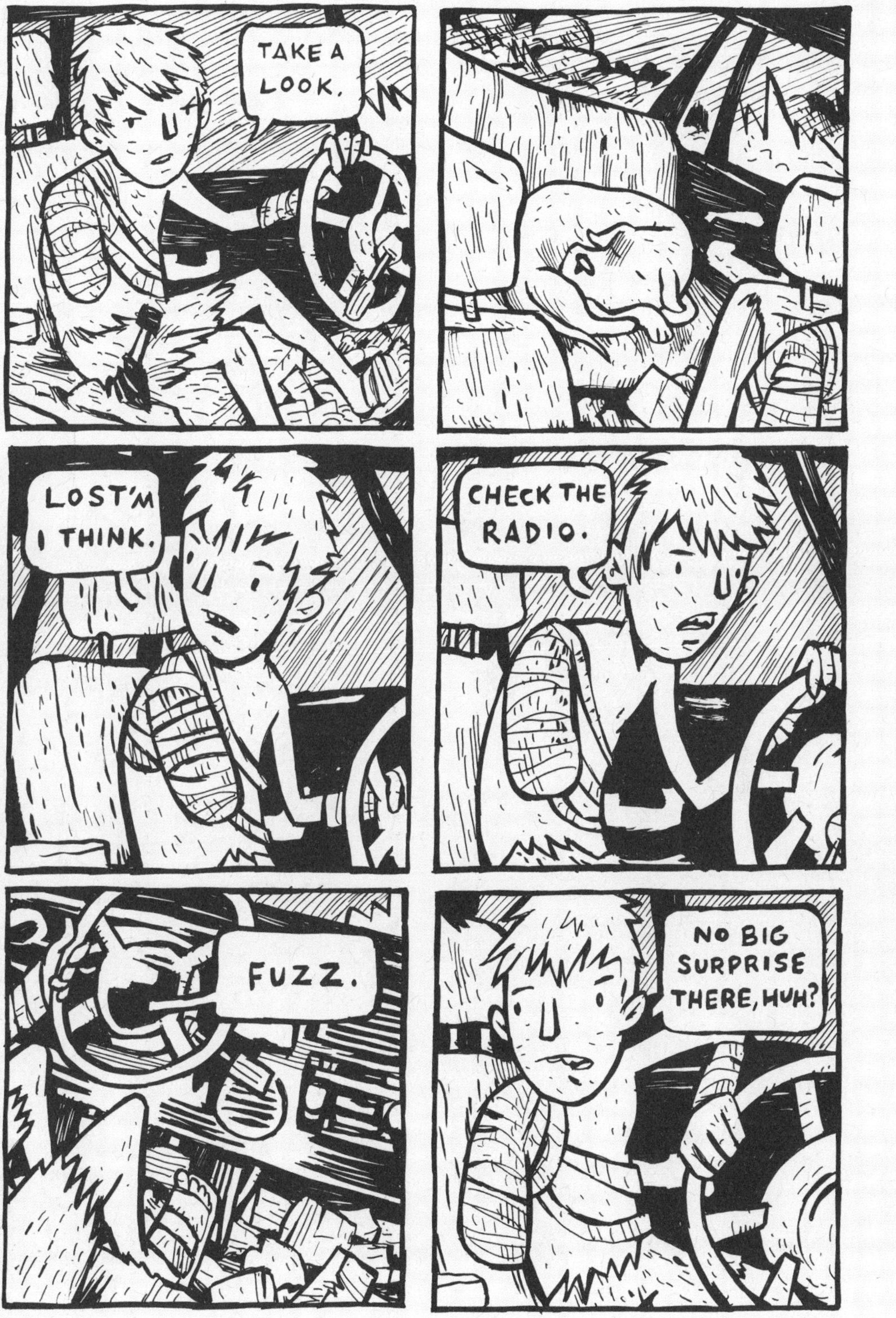
TAKE A LOOK.
LOST'M I THINK.
CHECK THE RADIO.
FUZZ.
NO BIG SURPRISE THERE, HUH?

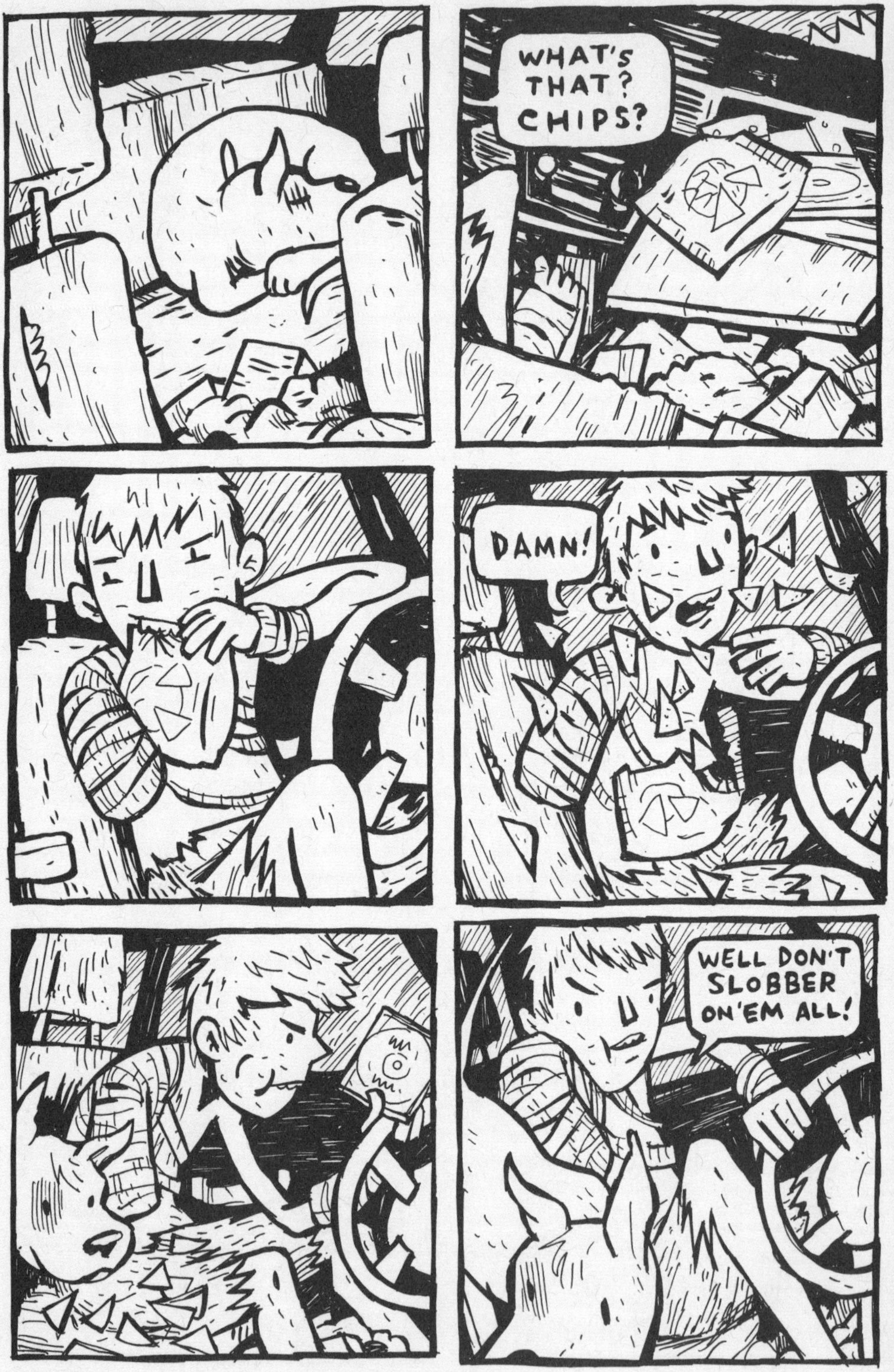
WHAT'S THAT? CHIPS?
DAMN!
WELL DON'T SLOBBER ON'EM ALL!

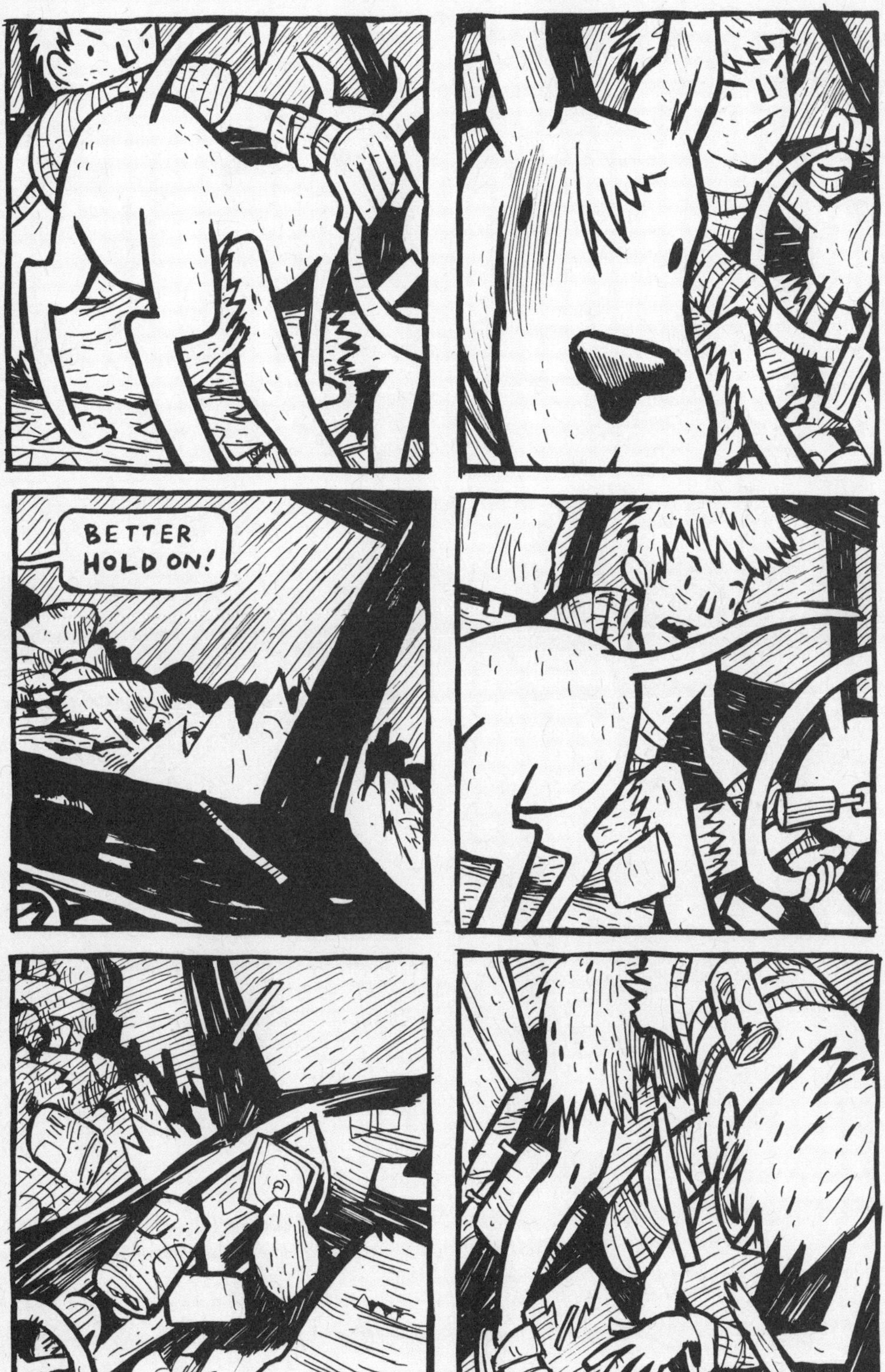
BETTER HOLD ON!

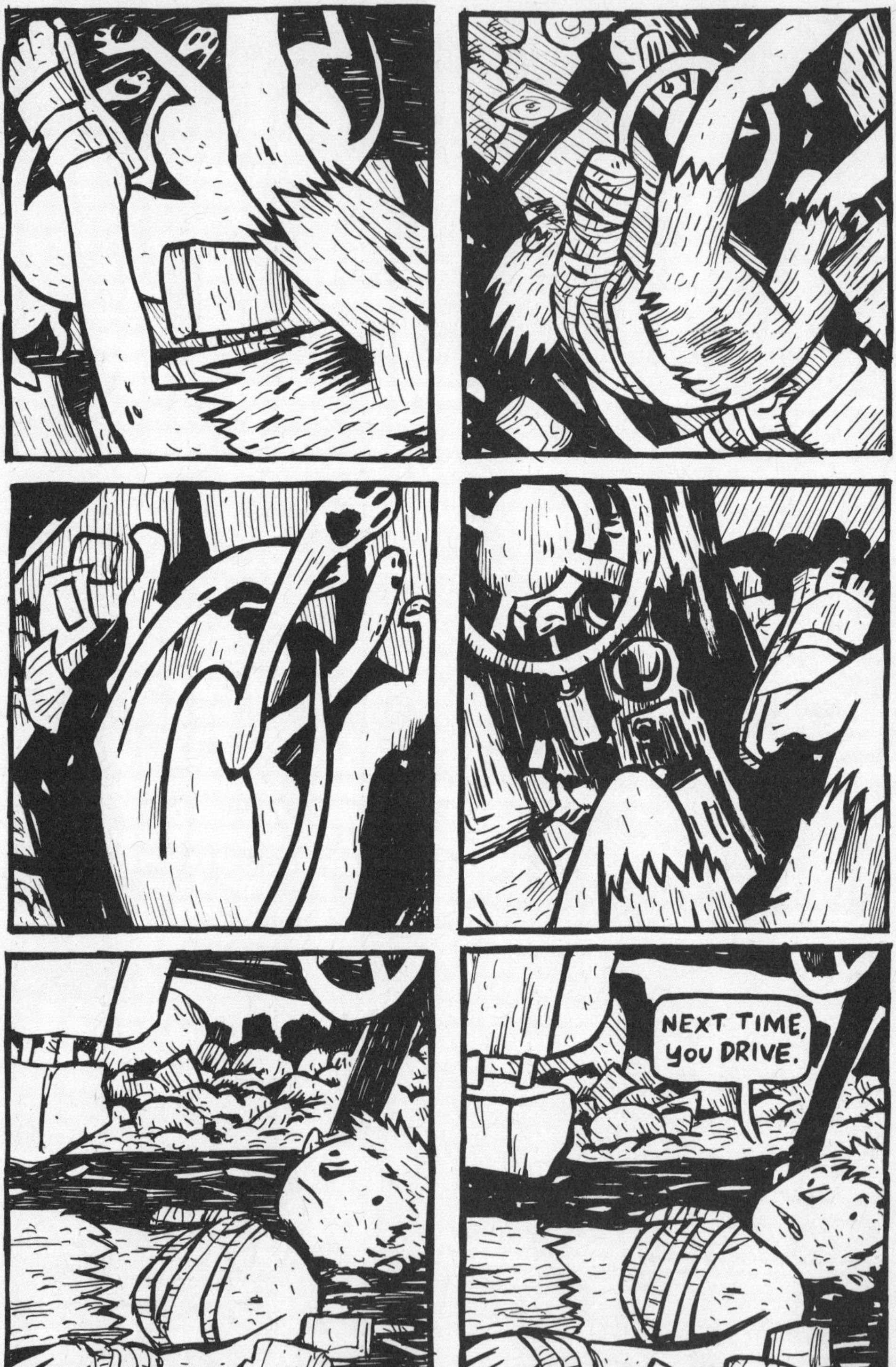
NEXT TIME, YOU DRIVE.

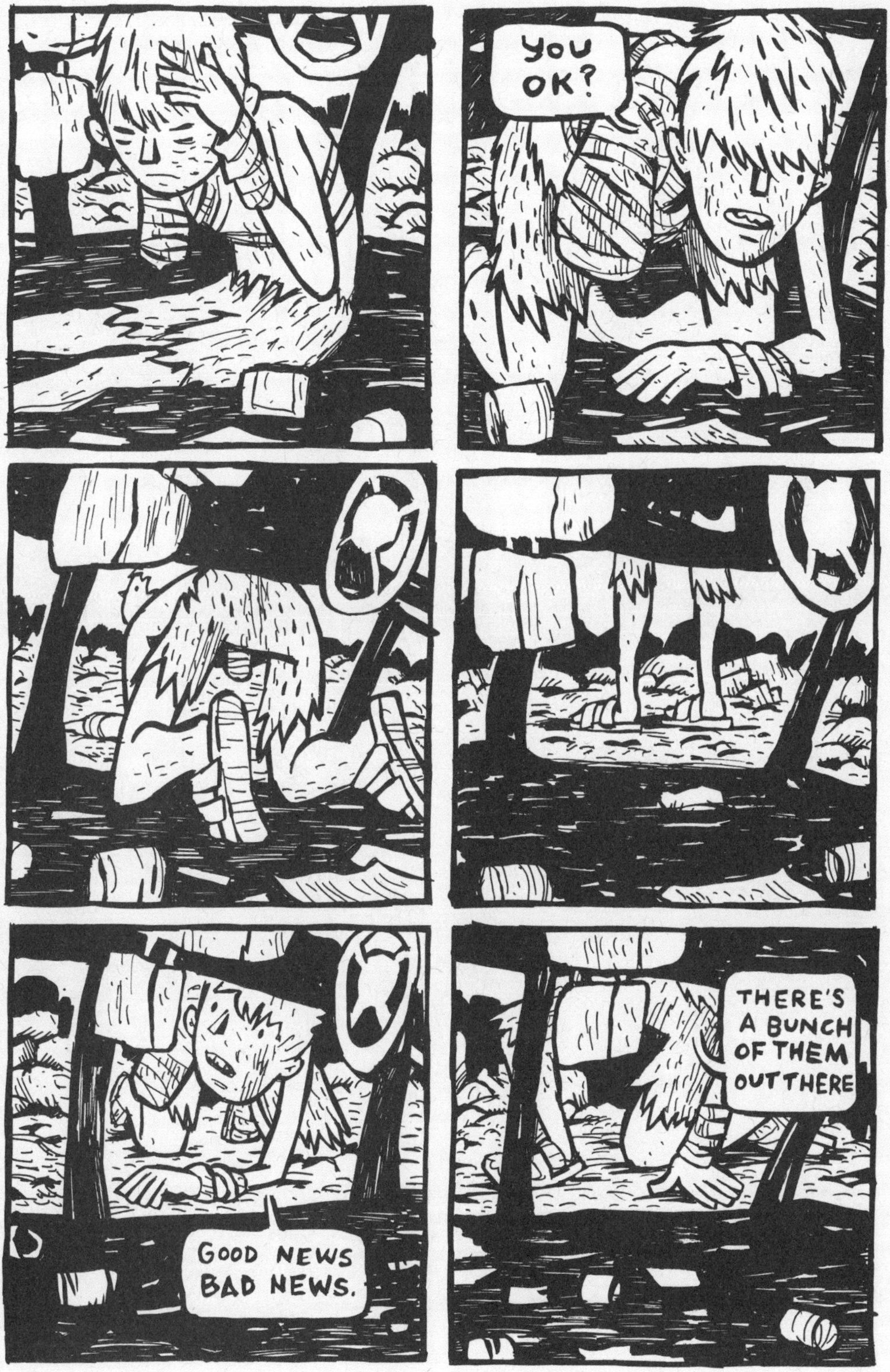
YOU OK?
GOOD NEWS BAD NEWS.
THERE'S A BUNCH OF THEM OUT THERE

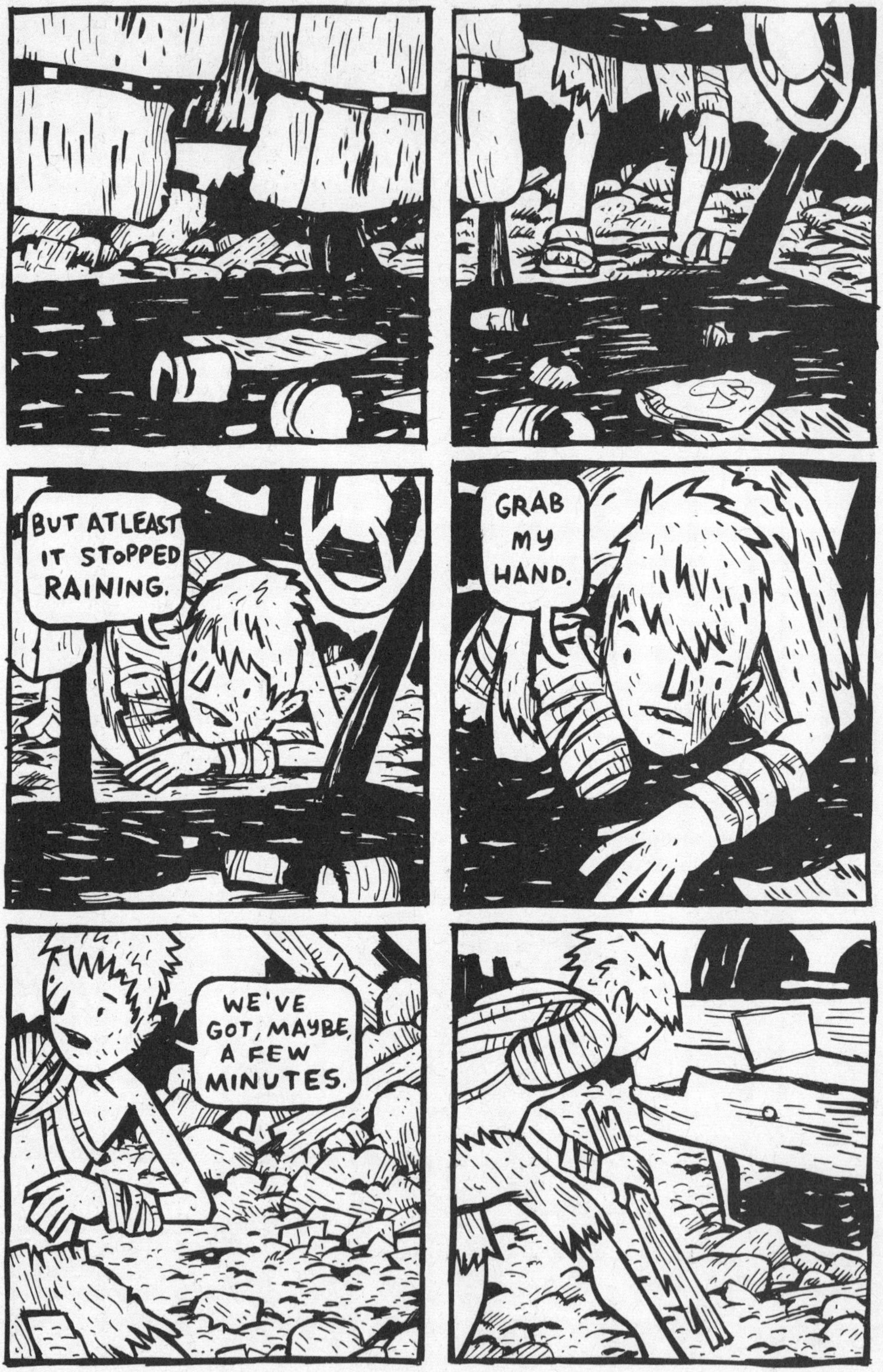
BUT ATLEAST IT STOPPED RAINING.
GRAB MY HAND.
WE'VE GOT, MAYBE, A FEW MINUTES.

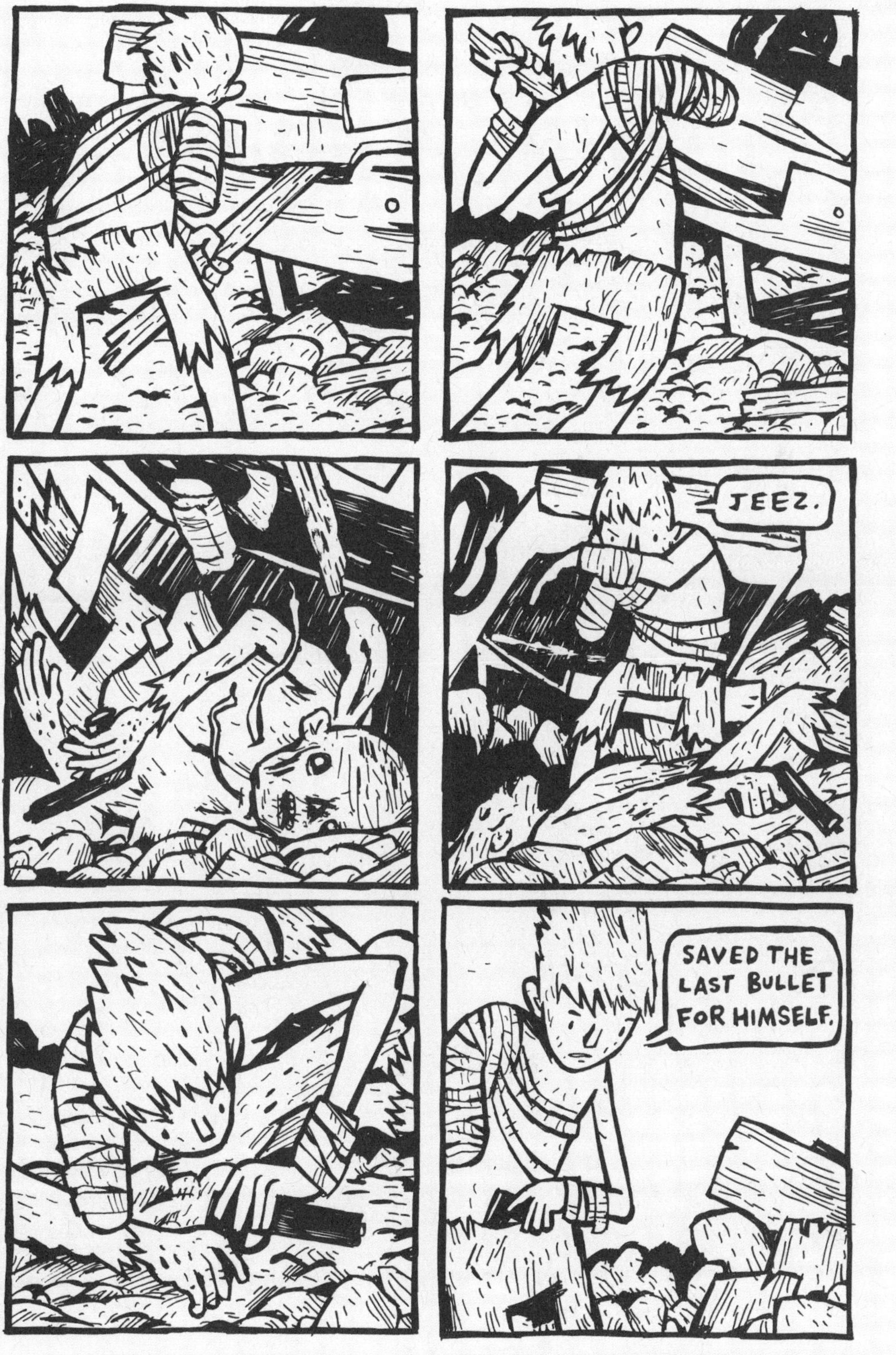
JEEZ.
SAVED THE LAST BULLET FOR HIMSELF.

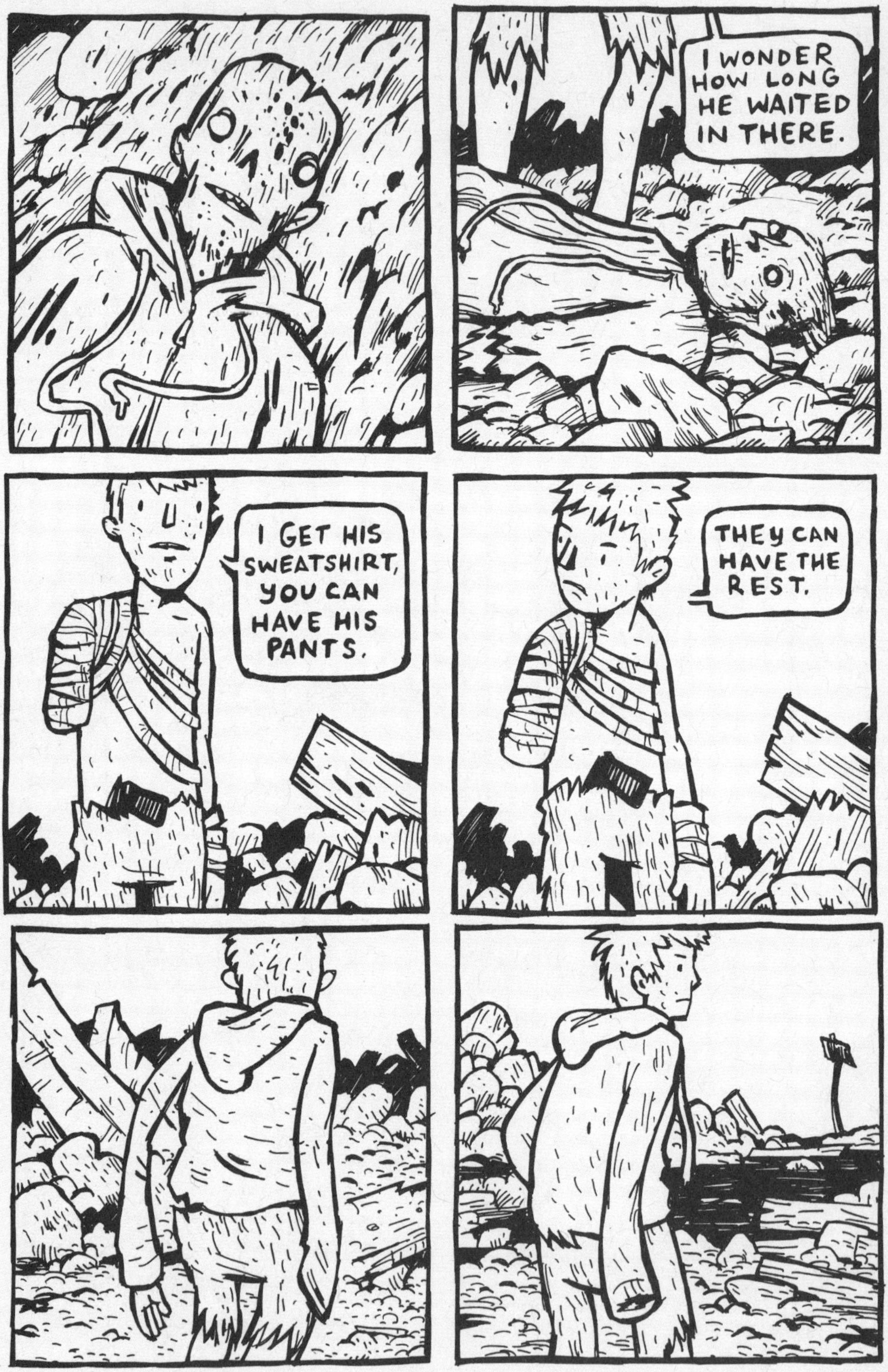
I WONDER HOW LONG HE WAITED IN THERE.
I GET HIS SWEATSHIRT, YOU CAN HAVE HIS PANTS.
THEY CAN HAVE THE REST.

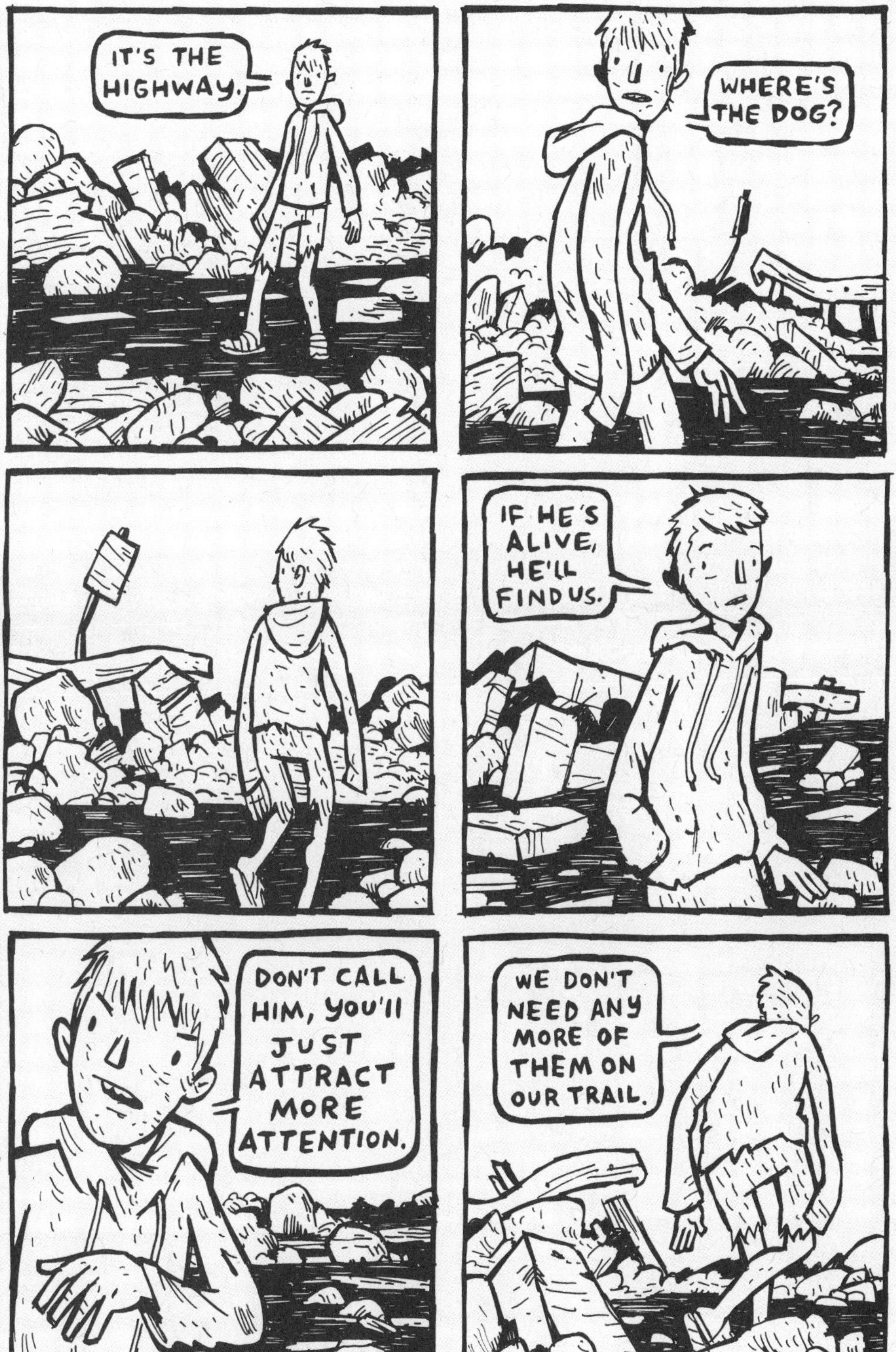
IT'S THE HIGHWAY.
WHERE'S THE DOG?
IF HE'S ALIVE, HE'LL FIND US.
DON'T CALL HIM, YOU'LL JUST ATTRACT MORE ATTENTION.
WE DON'T NEED ANY MORE OF THEM ON OUR TRAIL.

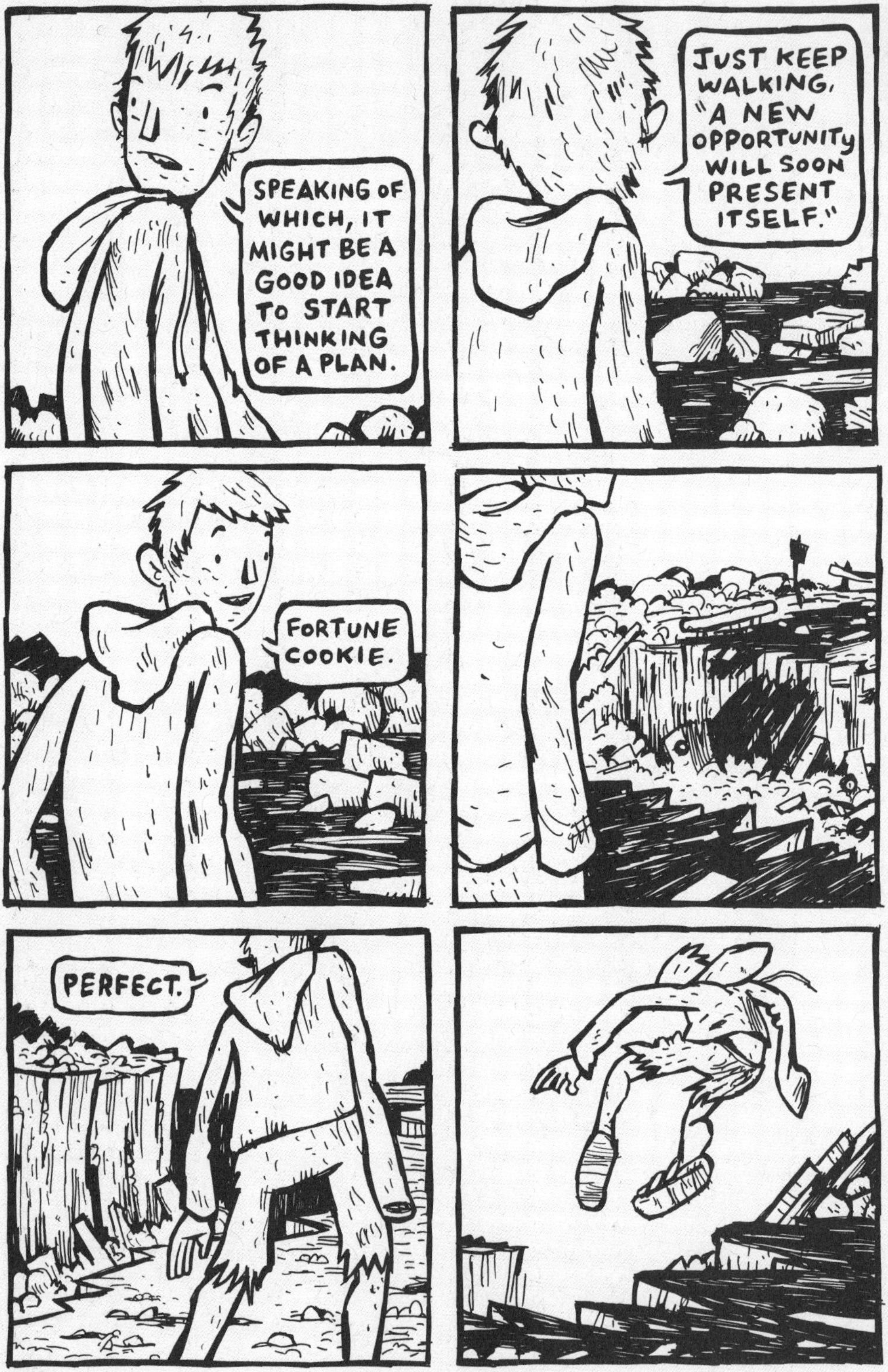
SPEAKING OF WHICH, IT MIGHT BE A GOOD IDEA TO START THINKING OF A PLAN.
JUST KEEP WALKING. "A NEW OPPORTUNITY WILL SOON PRESENT ITSELF."
FORTUNE COOKIE.
PERFECT.

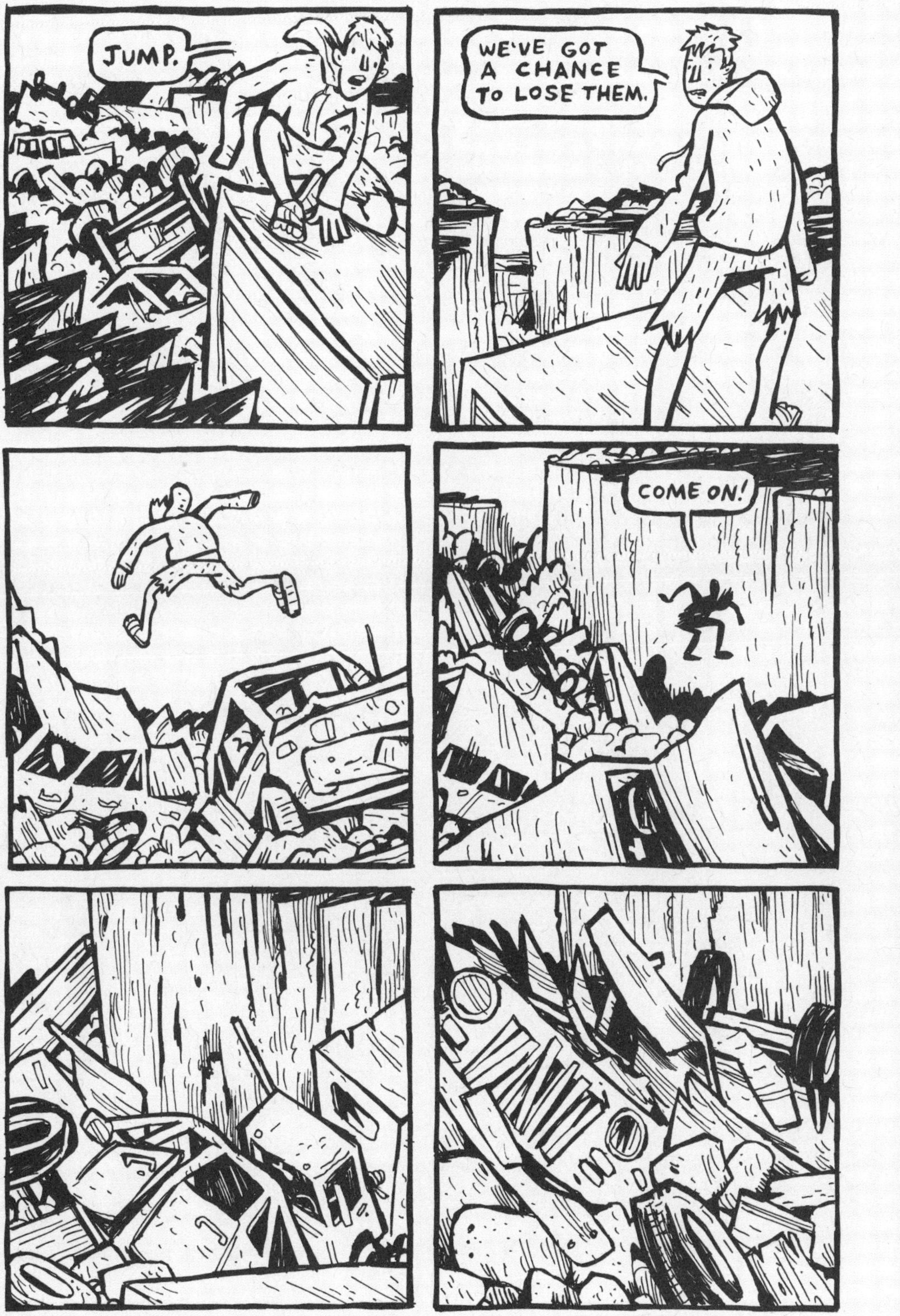
JUMP.
WE'VE GOT A CHANCE TO LOSE THEM.
COME ON!

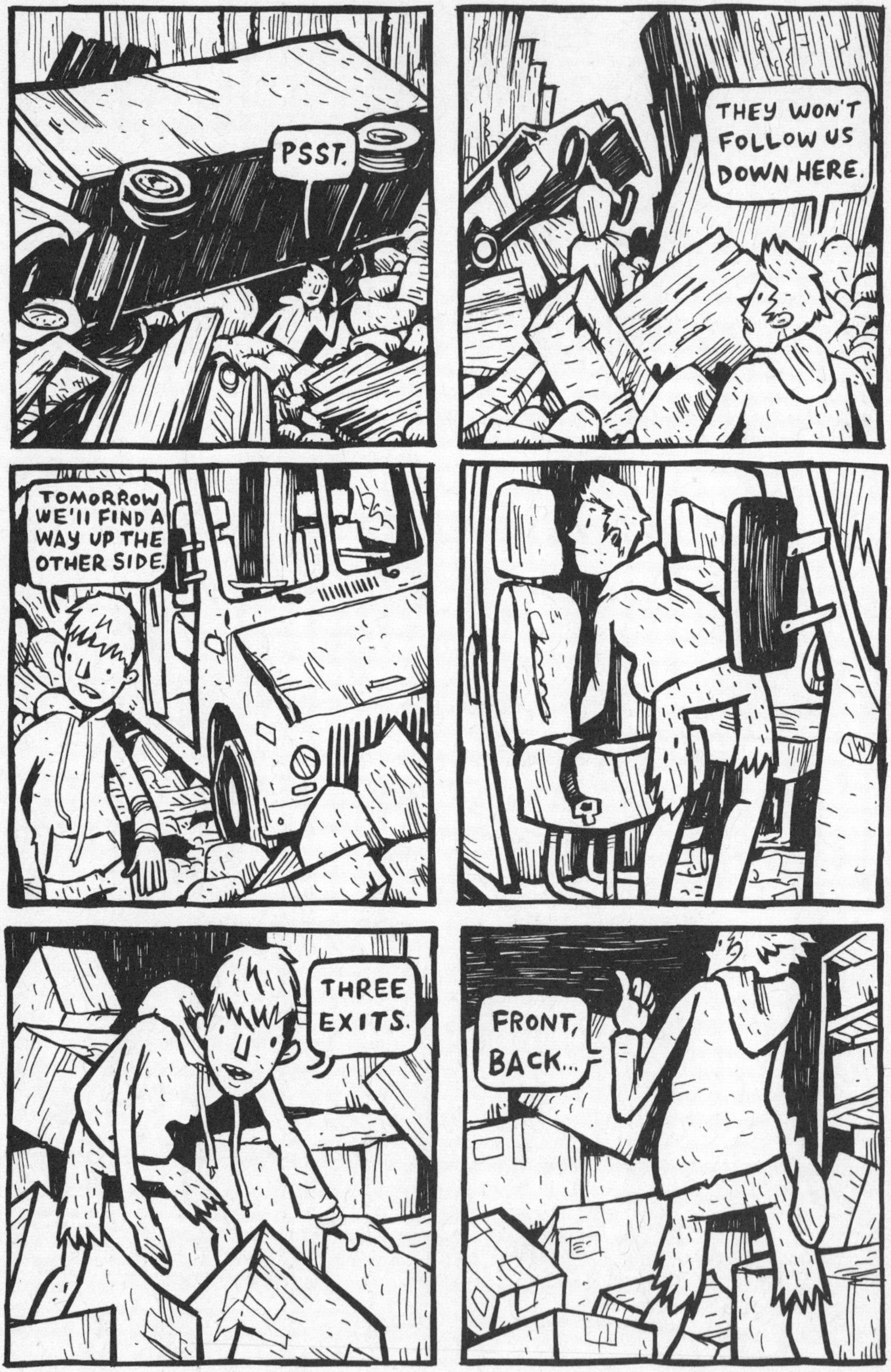
PSST.
THEY WON'T FOLLOW US DOWN HERE.
TOMORROW WE'll FIND A WAY UP THE OTHER SIDE.
THREE EXITS.
FRONT, BACK...

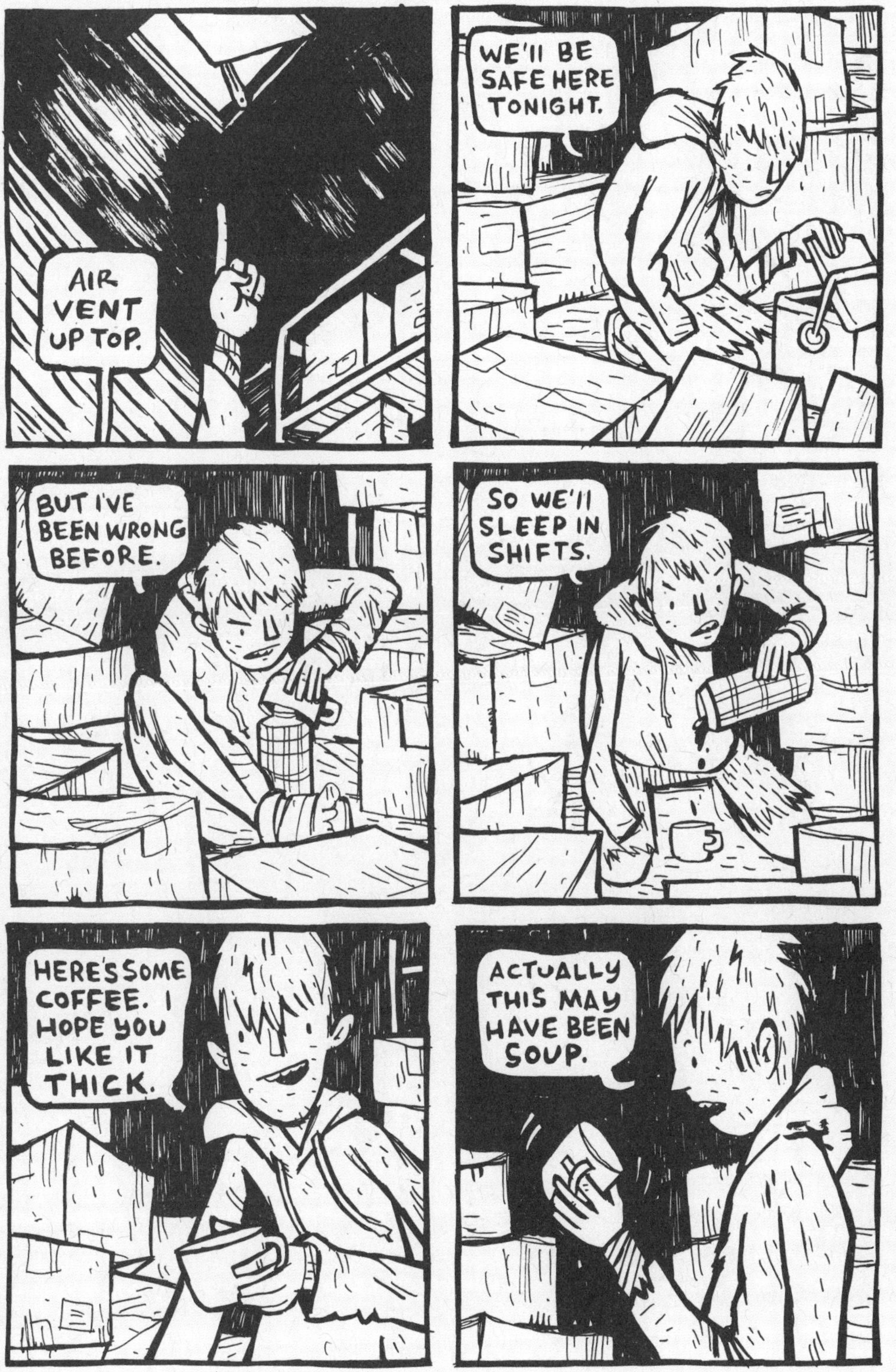
AIR VENT UP TOP.
WE'll BE SAFE HERE TONIGHT.
BUT I'VE BEEN WRONG BEFORE.
SO WE'll SLEEP IN SHIFTS.
HERE'S SOME COFFEE. I HOPE YOU LIKE IT THICK.
ACTUALLY THIS MAY HAVE BEEN SOUP.

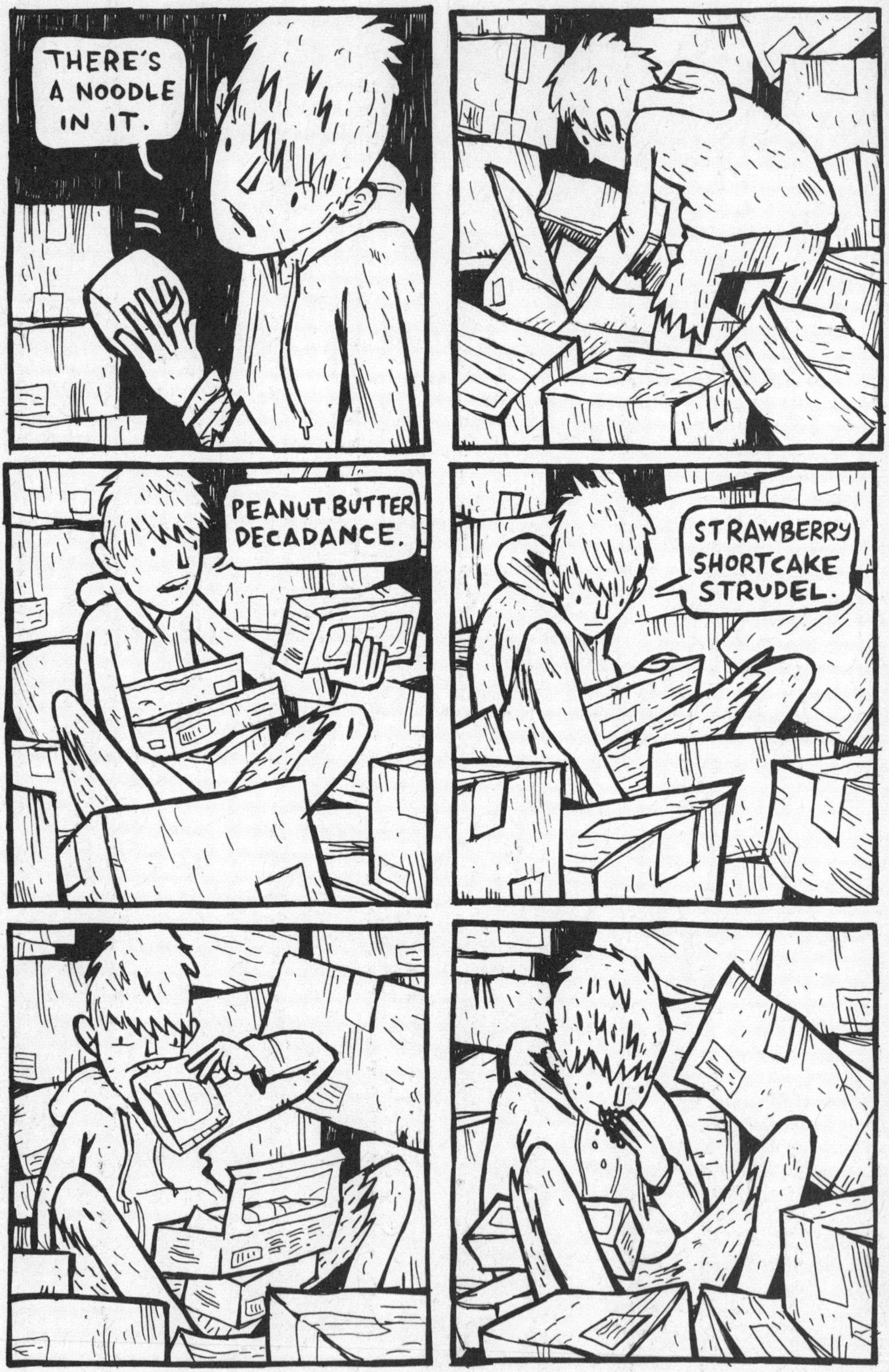
THERE'S A NOODLE IN IT.
PEANUT BUTTER DECADANCE.
STRAWBERRY SHORTCAKE STRUDEL.

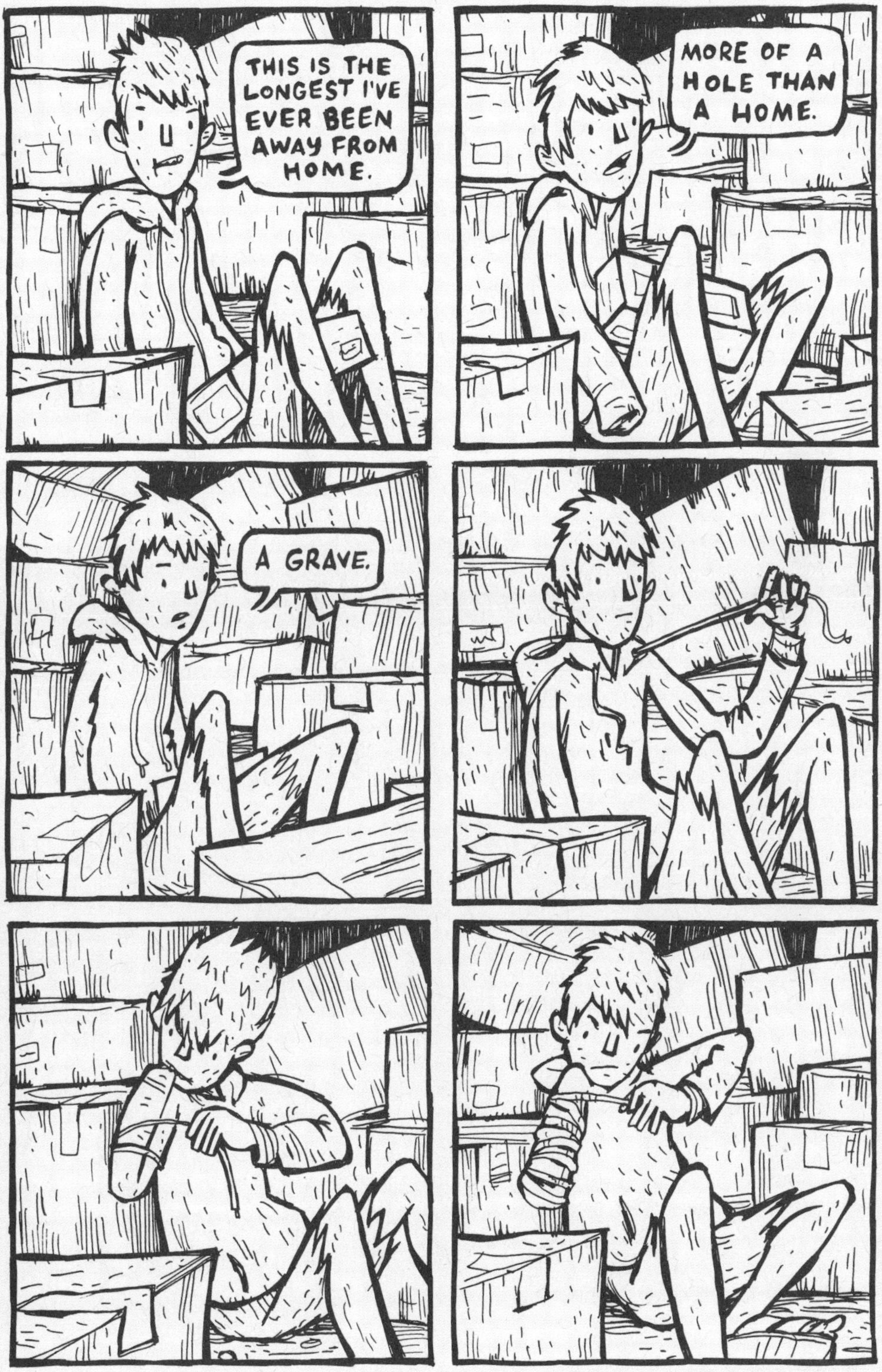
THIS IS THE LONGEST I'VE EVER BEEN AWAY FROM HOME.
MORE OF A HOLE THAN A HOME.
A GRAVE.

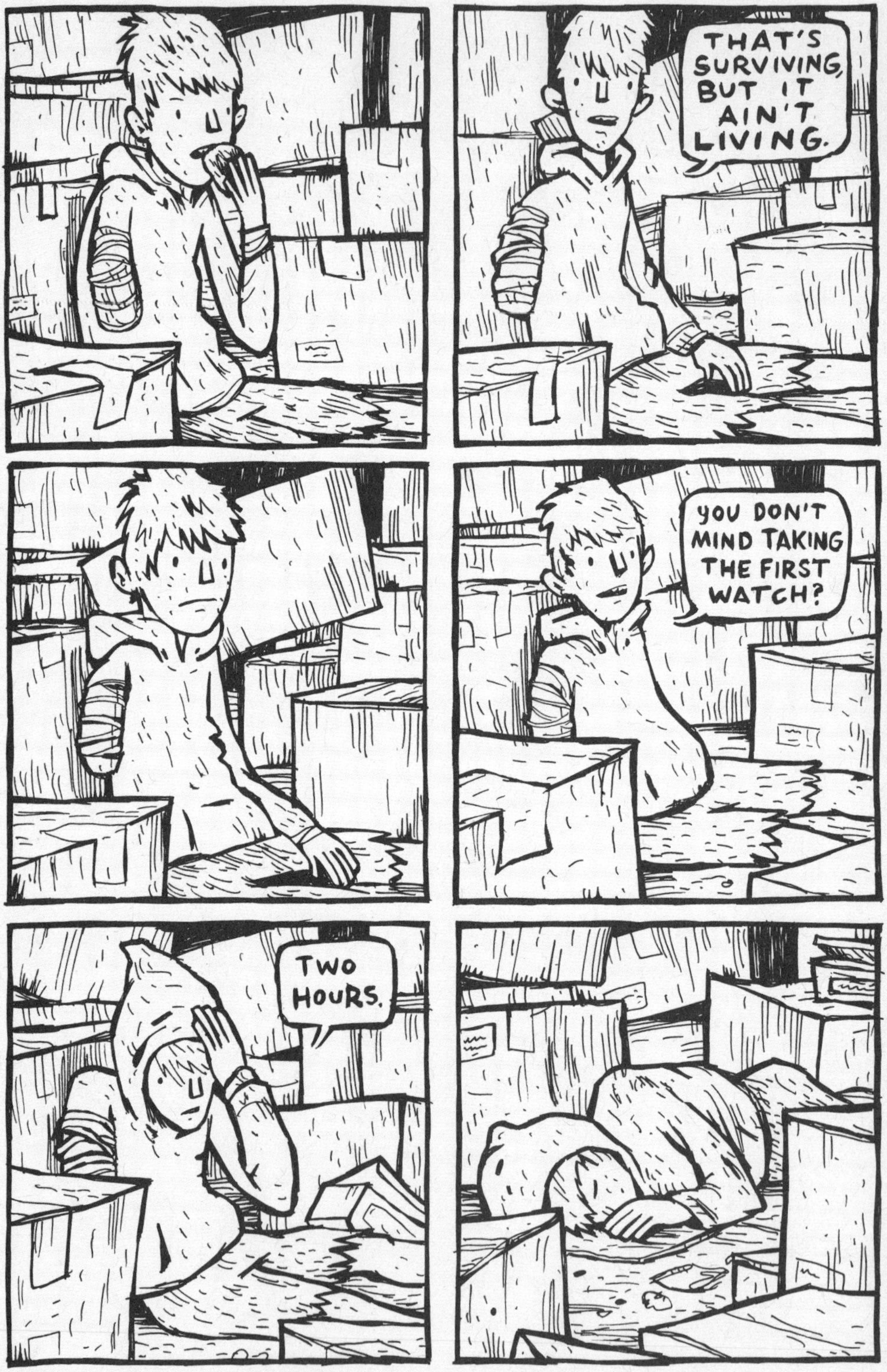
THAT'S SURVIVING, BUT IT AIN'T LIVING.
YOU DON'T MIND TAKING THE FIRST WATCH?
TWO HOURS.

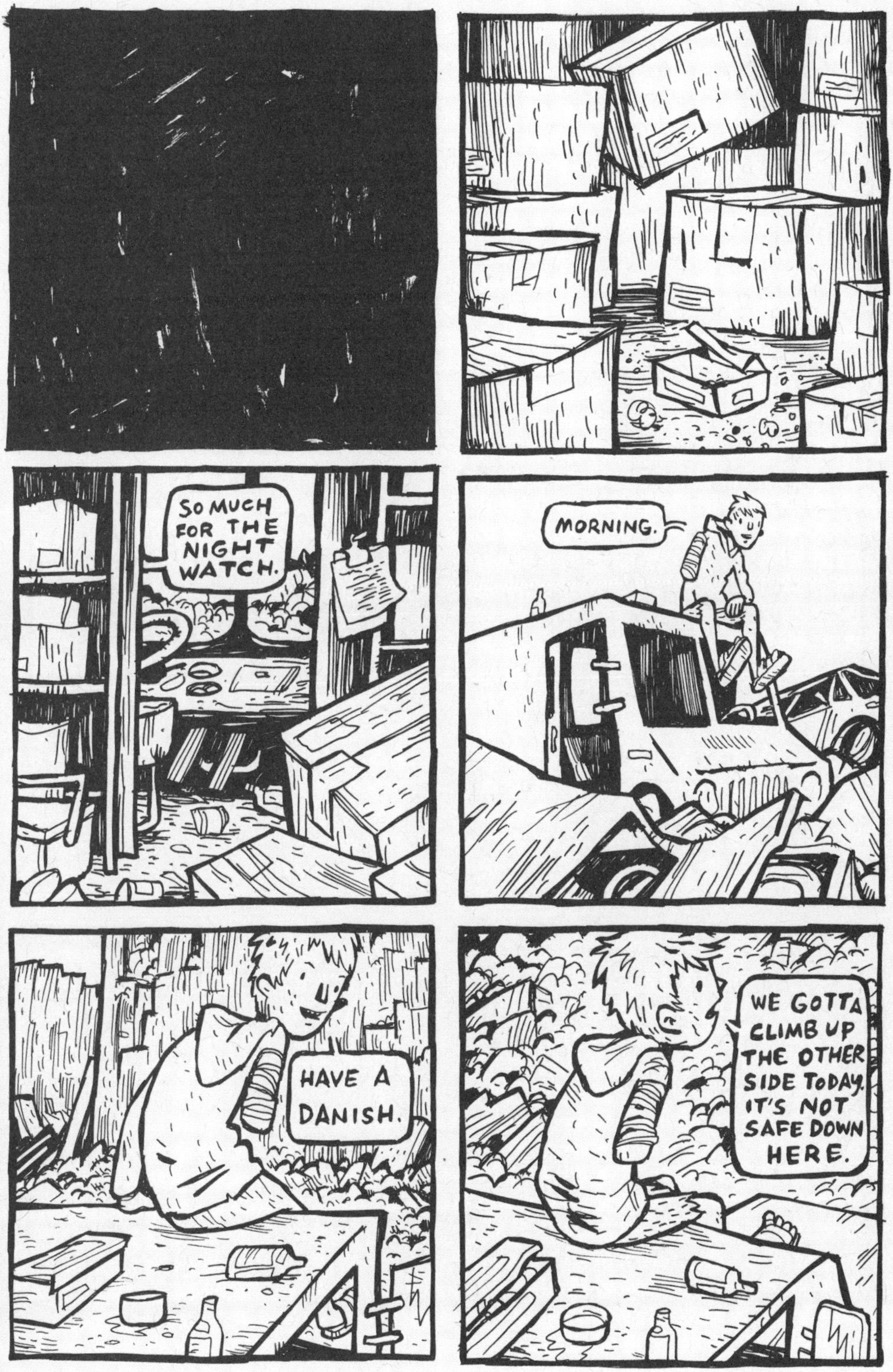
SO MUCH FOR THE NIGHT WATCH.
MORNING.
HAVE A DANISH.
WE GOTTA CLIMB UP THE OTHER SIDE TODAY. IT'S NOT SAFE DOWN HERE.

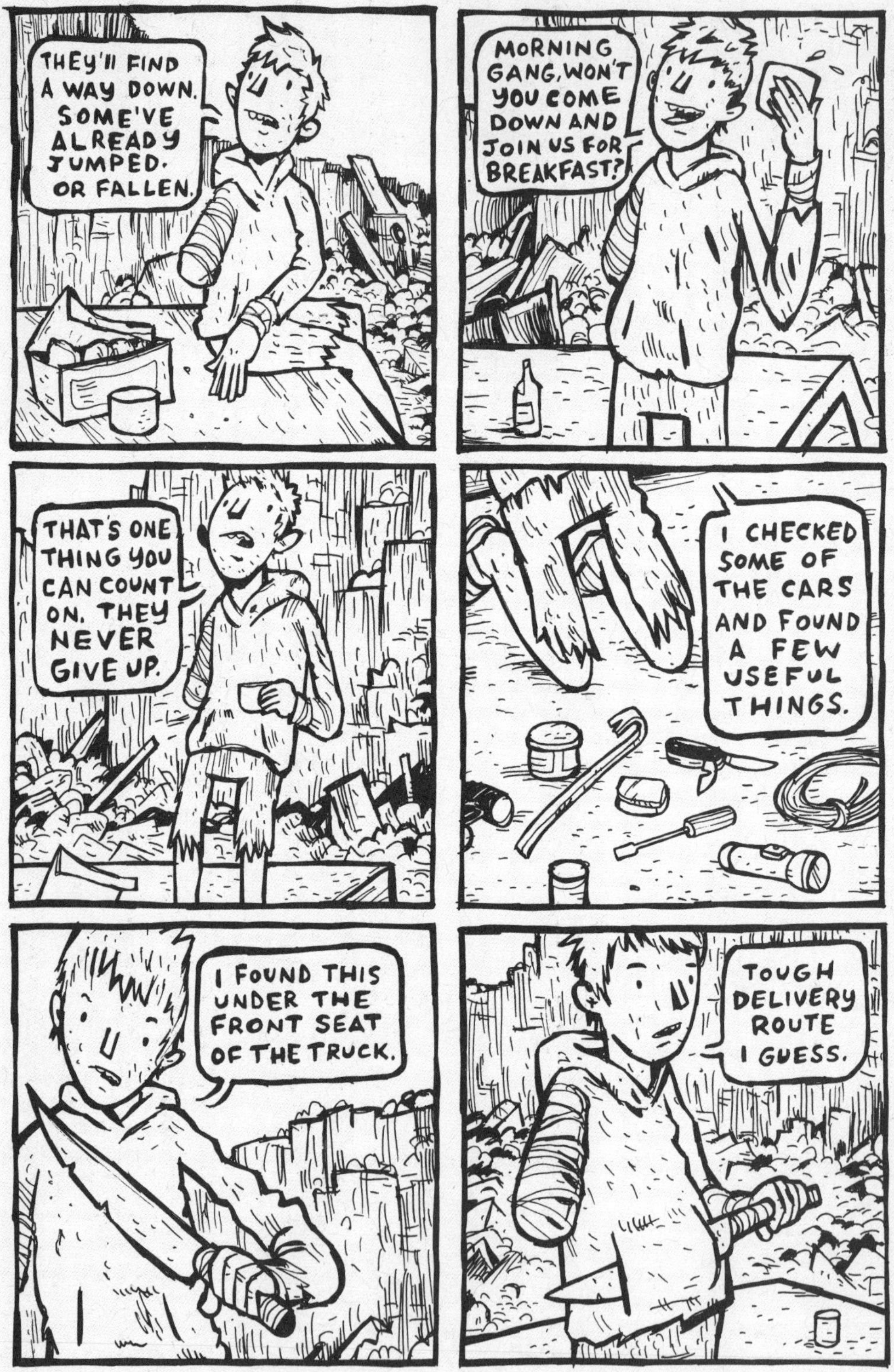
THEY'LL FIND A WAY DOWN. SOME'VE ALREADY JUMPED. OR FALLEN.
MORNING GANG, WON'T YOU COME DOWN AND JOIN US FOR BREAKFAST?
THAT'S ONE THING YOU CAN COUNT ON. THEY NEVER GIVE UP.
I CHECKED SOME OF THE CARS AND FOUND A FEW USEFUL THINGS.
I FOUND THIS UNDER THE FRONT SEAT OF THE TRUCK.
TOUGH DELIVERY ROUTE I GUESS.

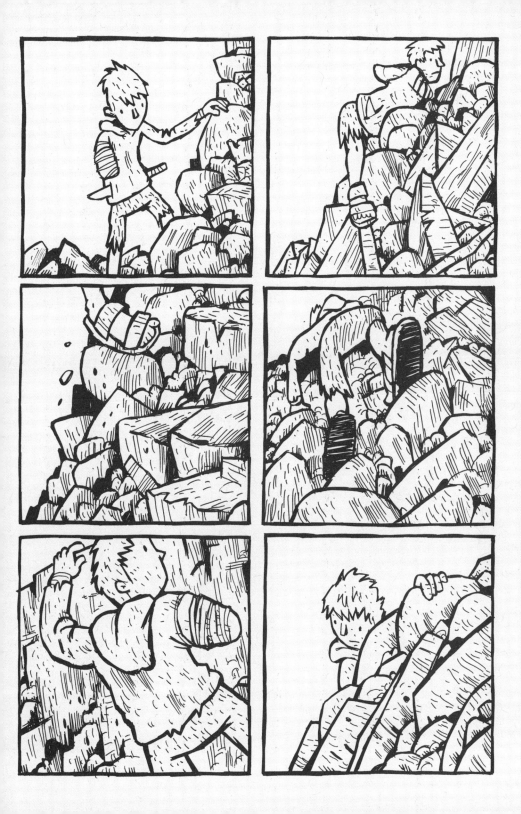

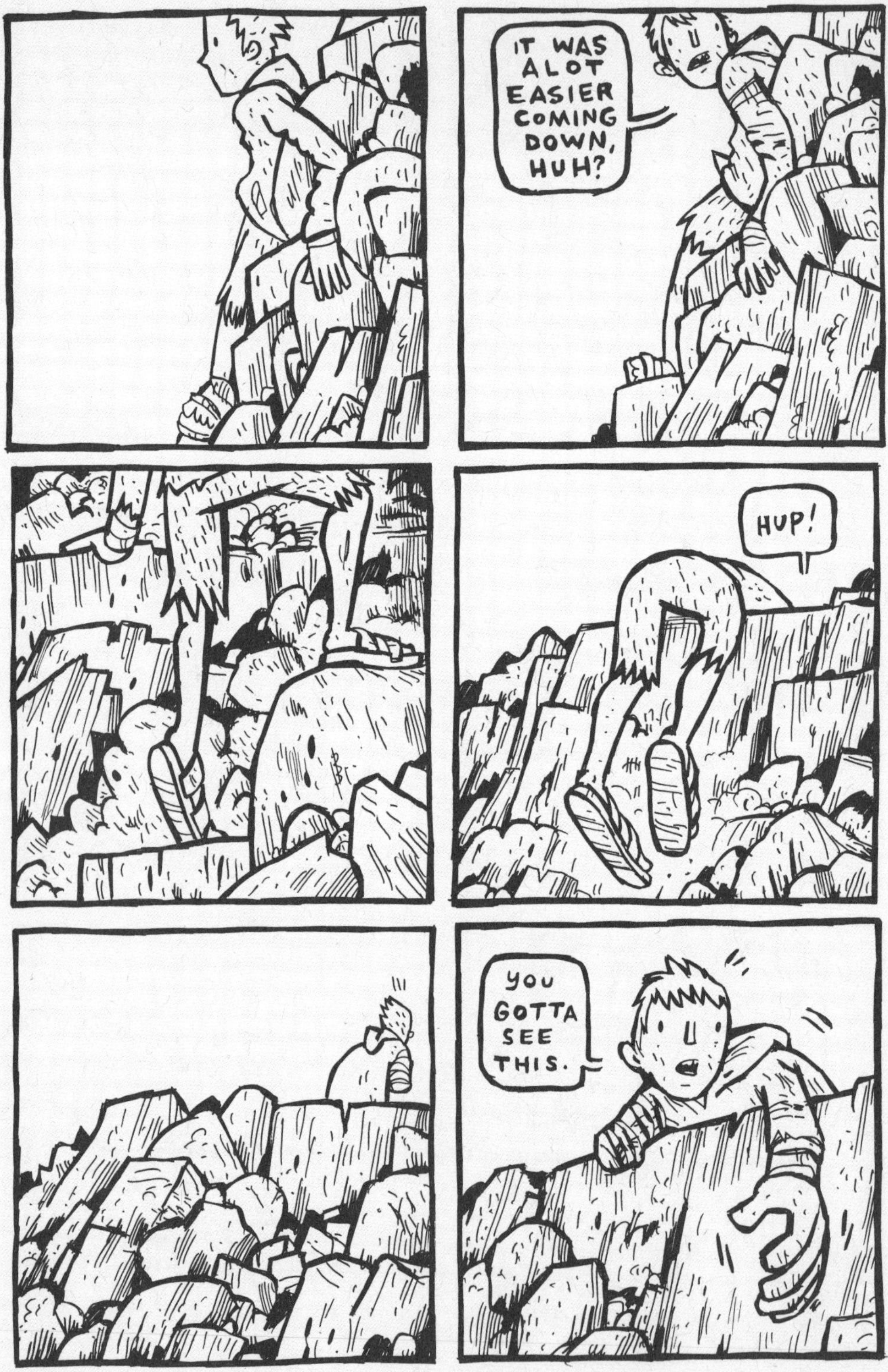
IT WAS ALOT EASIER COMING DOWN, HUH?
HUP!
YOU GOTTA SEE THIS.

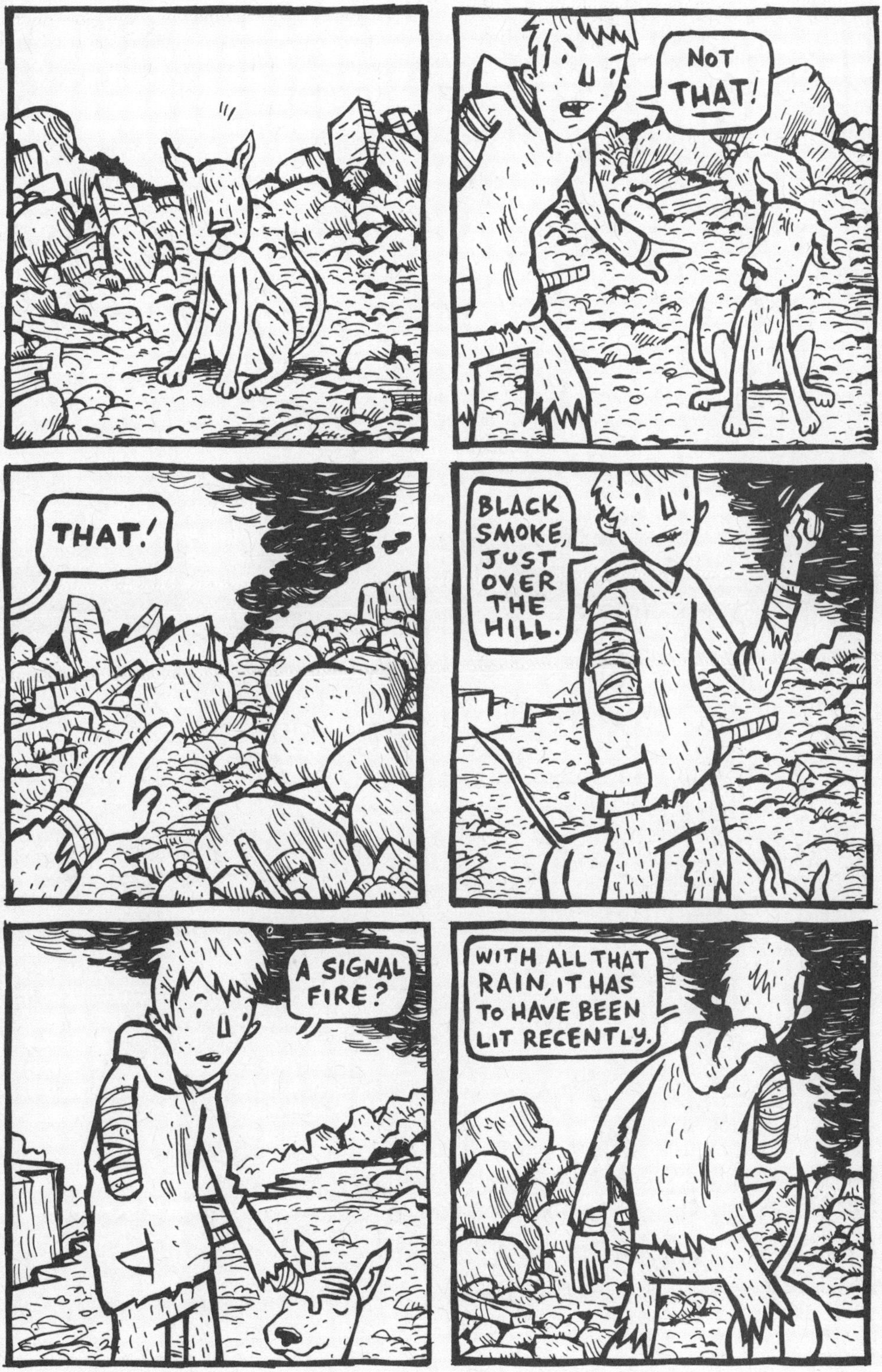
NOT THAT!
THAT!
BLACK SMOKE, JUST OVER THE HILL.
A SIGNAL FIRE?
WITH ALL THAT RAIN, IT HAS TO HAVE BEEN LIT RECENTLY.

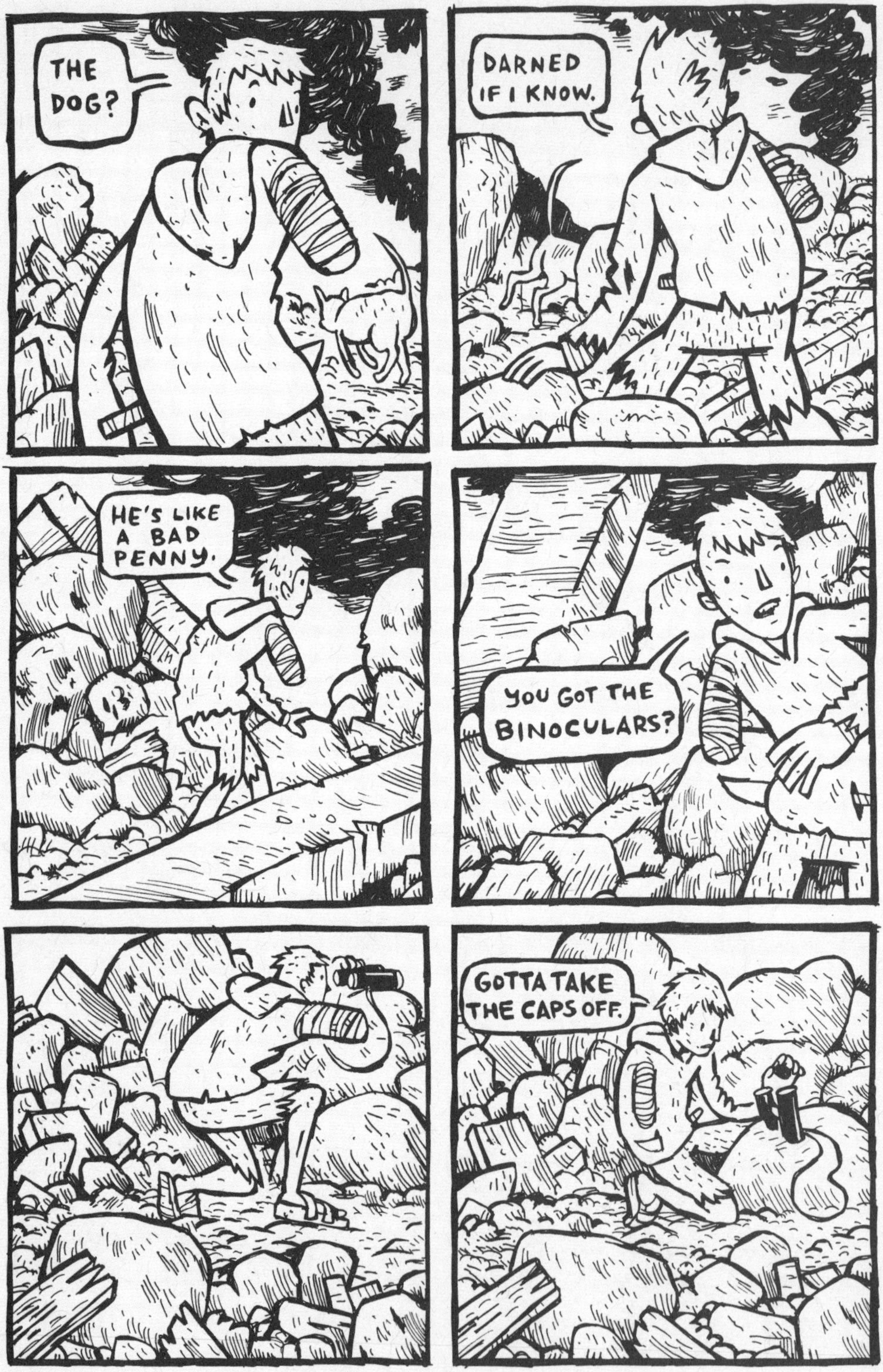
THE DOG?
DARNED IF I KNOW.
HE'S LIKE A BAD PENNY.
YOU GOT THE BINOCULARS?
GOTTA TAKE THE CAPS OFF.

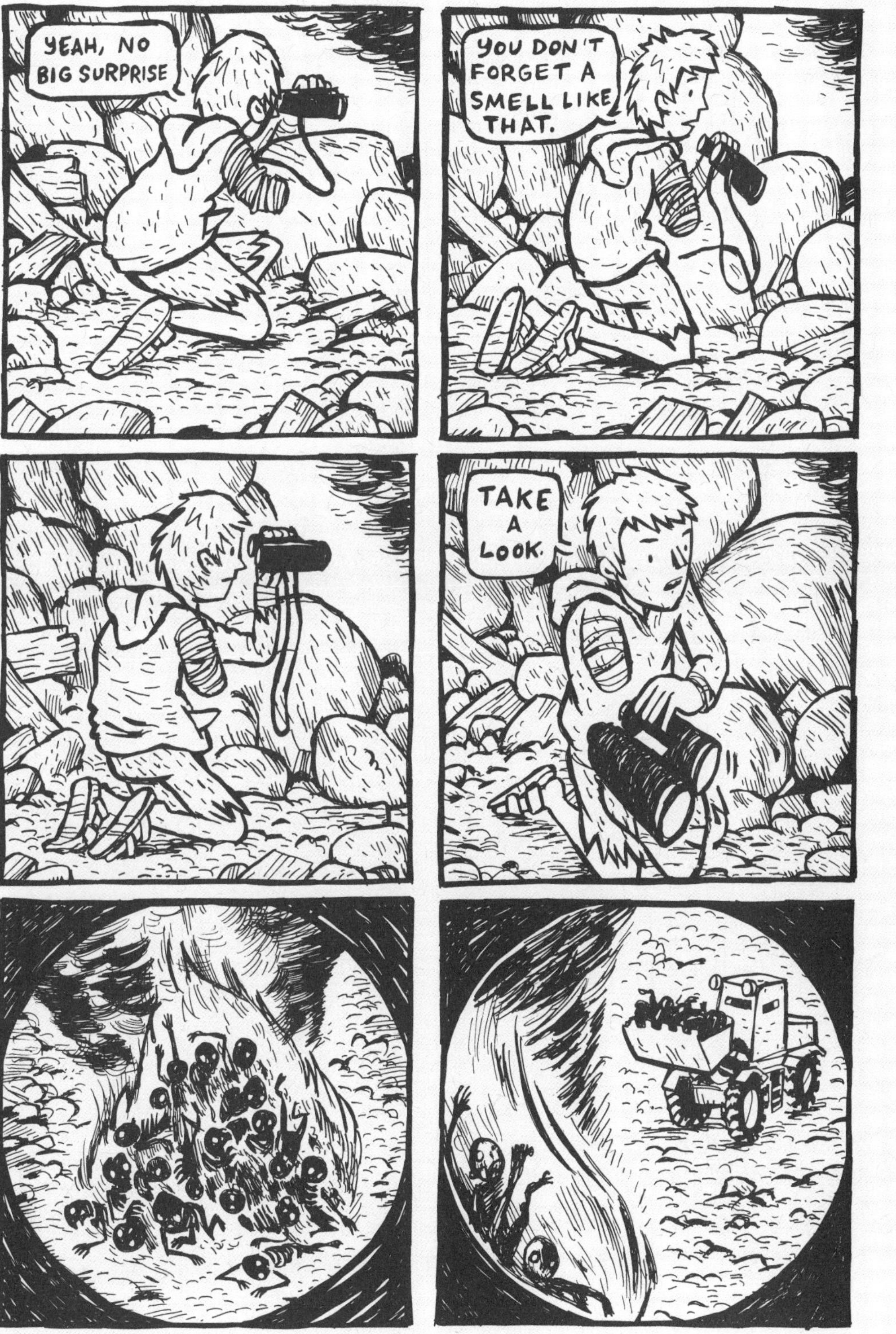
YEAH, NO BIG SURPRISE
YOU DON'T FORGET A SMELL LIKE THAT.
TAKE A LOOK.

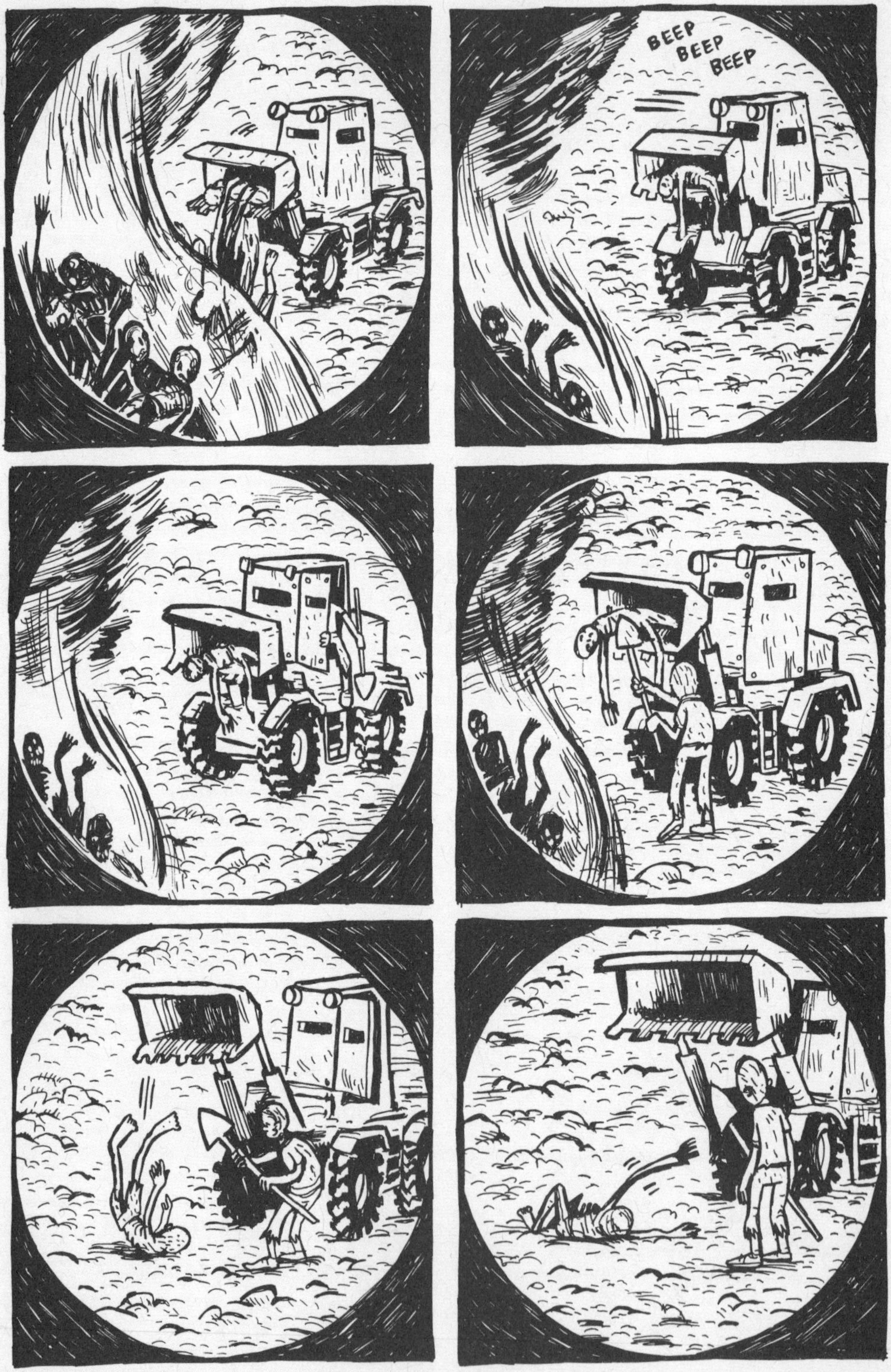
BEEP
BEEP
BEEP

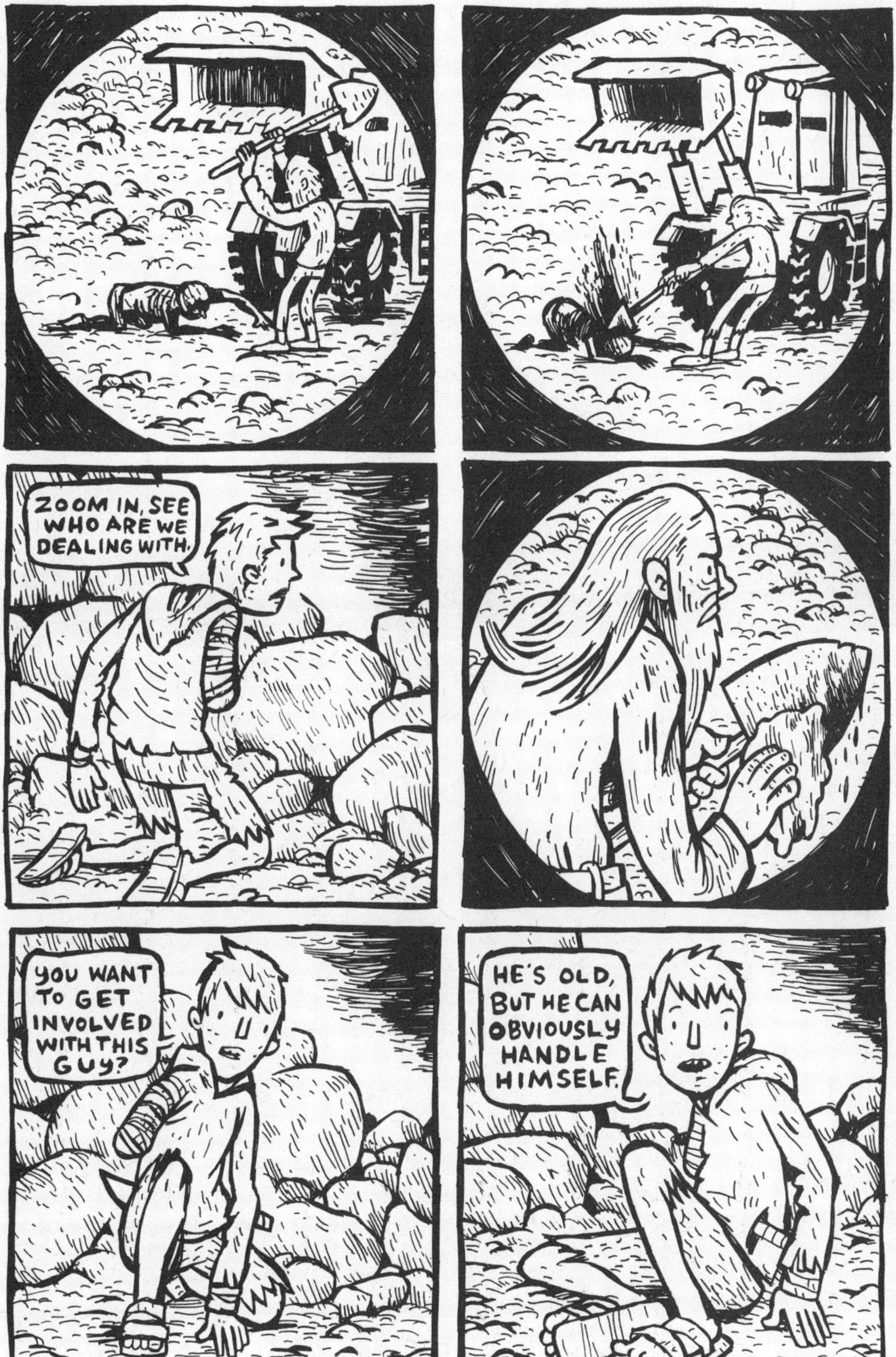
ZOOM IN, SEE WHO ARE WE DEALING WITH.
YOU WANT TO GET INVOLVED WITH THIS GUY?
HE'S OLD, BUT HE CAN OBVIOUSLY HANDLE HIMSELF.

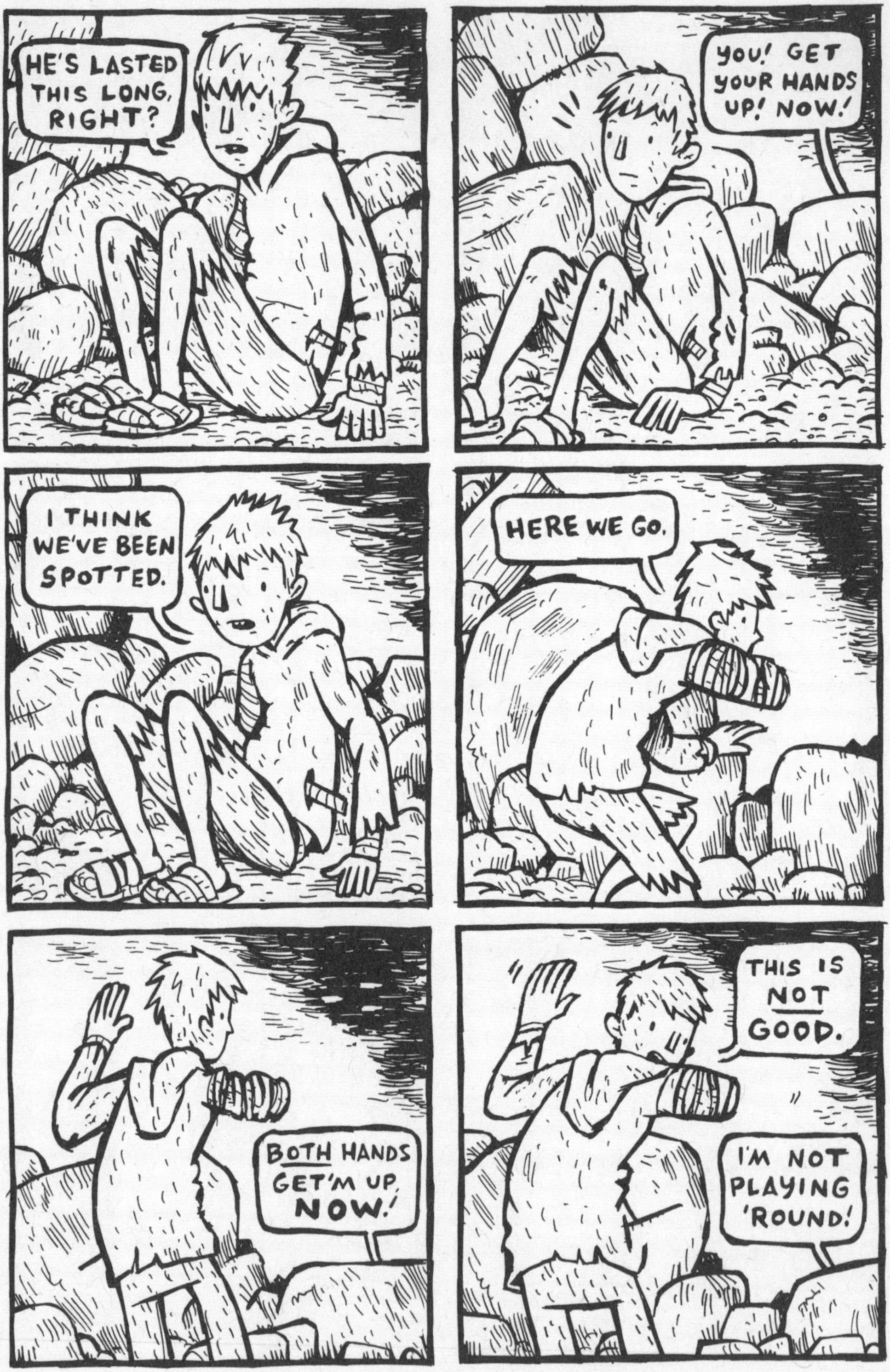
HE'S LASTED THIS LONG, RIGHT?
YOU! GET YOUR HANDS UP! NOW!
I THINK WE'VE BEEN SPOTTED.
HERE WE GO.
BOTH HANDS GET'M UP, NOW!
THIS IS NOT GOOD.
I'M NOT PLAYING 'ROUND!

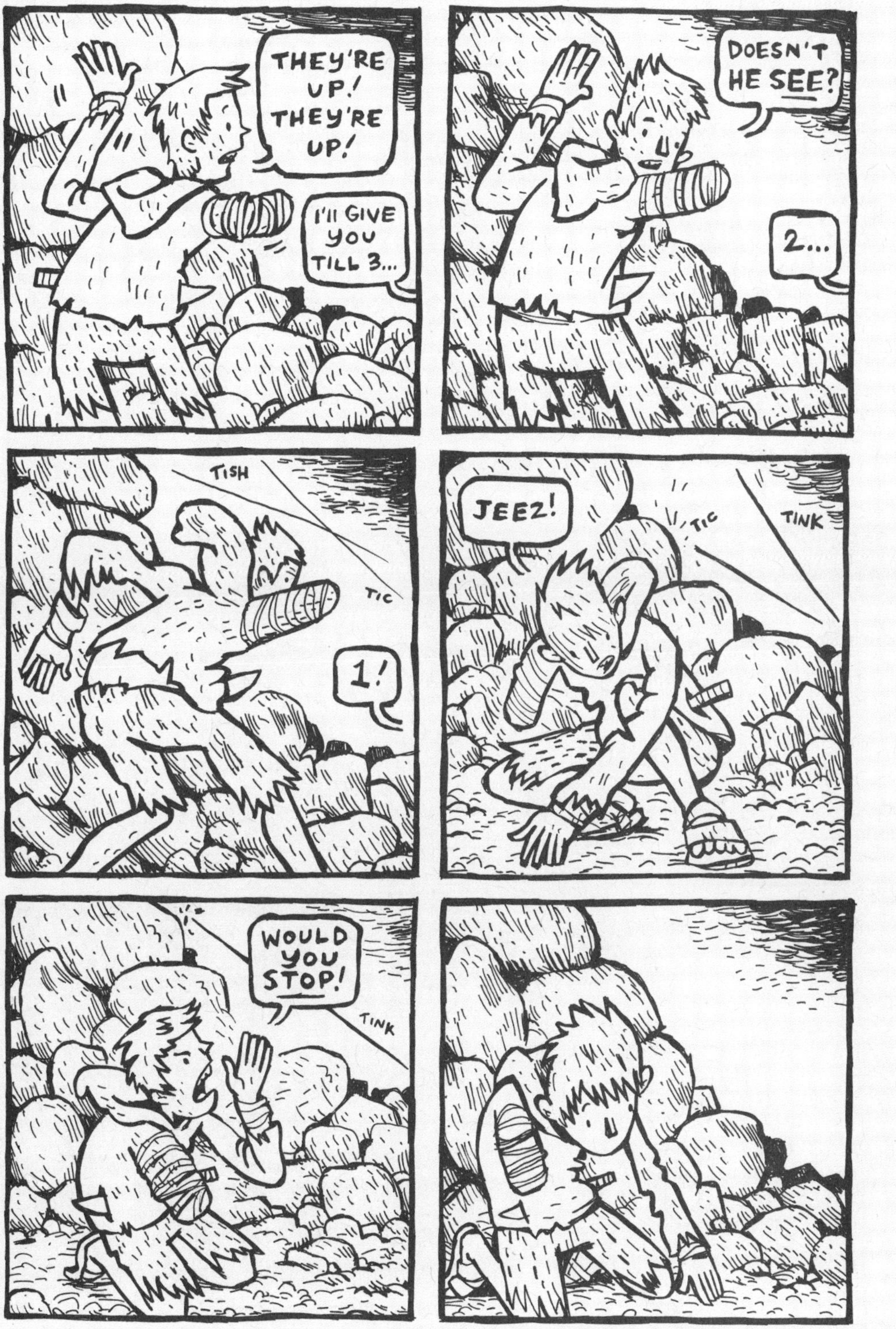
THEY'RE UP! THEY'RE UP!
I'll GIVE YOU TILL 3...
DOESN'T HE SEE?
2...
TISH
TIC
1!
JEEZ!
TIC
TINK
WOULD YOU STOP!
TINK

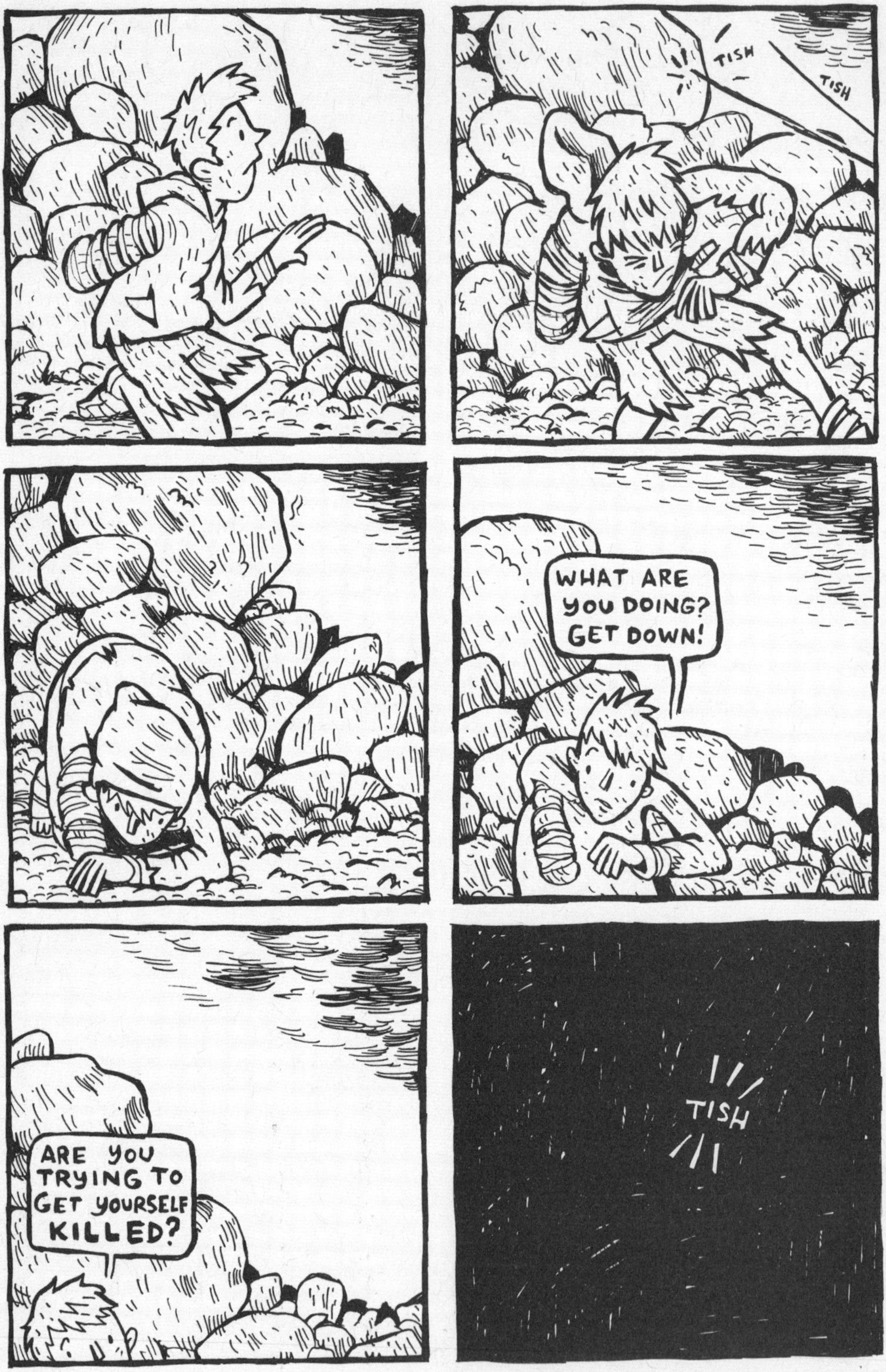
TISH
TISH
WHAT ARE YOU DOING? GET DOWN!
ARE YOU TRYING TO GET YOURSELF KILLED?
TISH

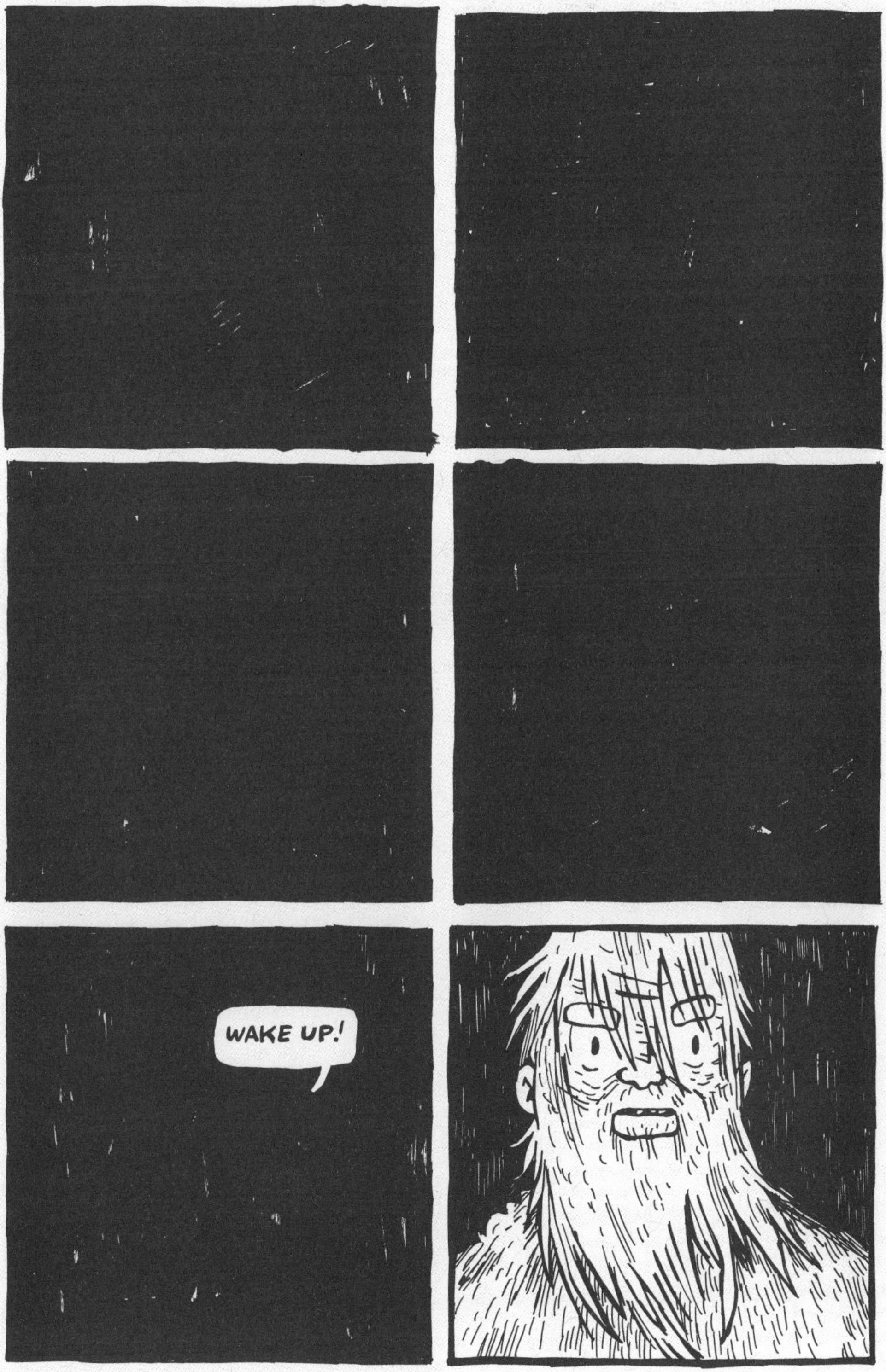
WAKE UP!

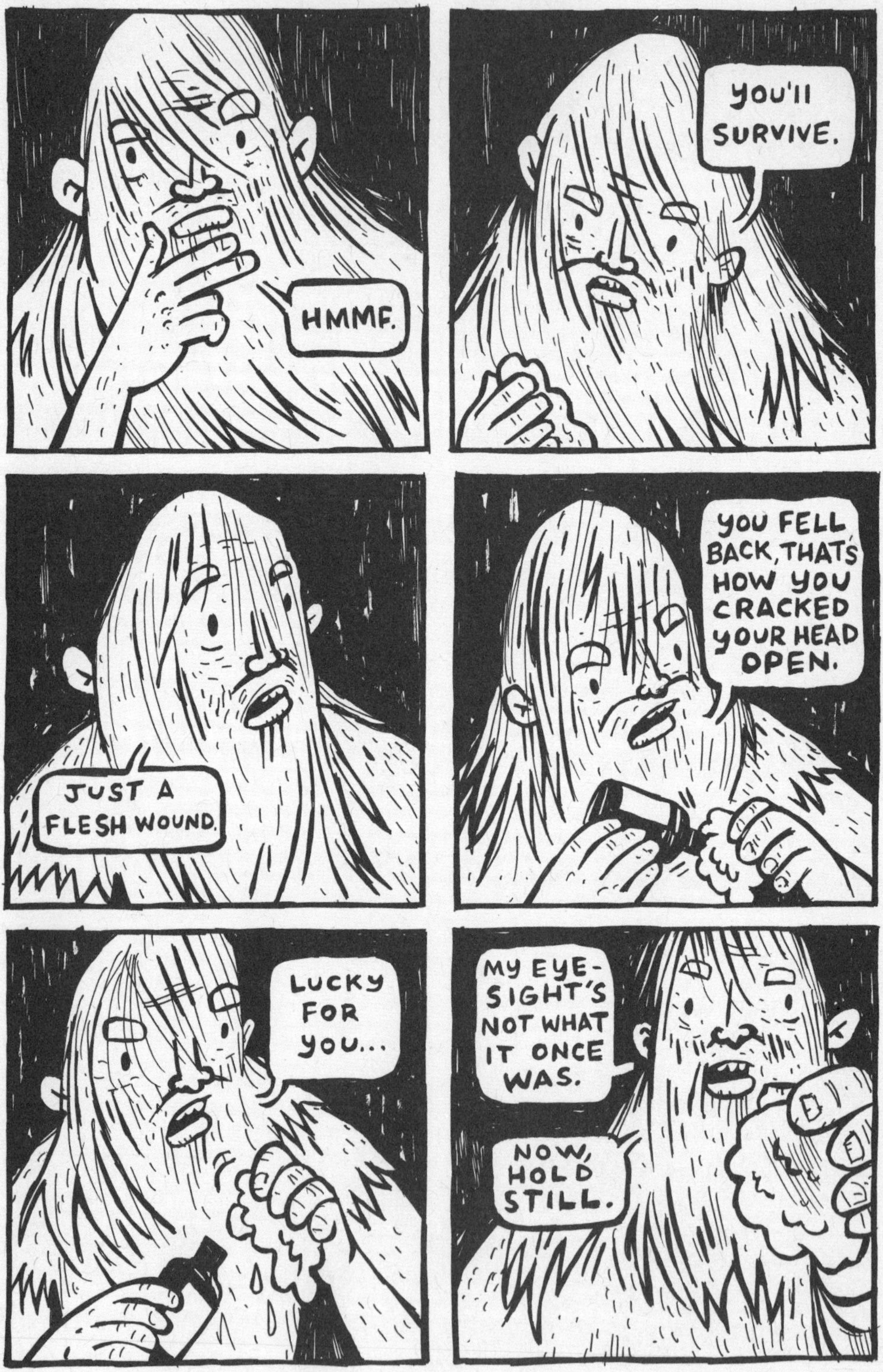
HMMF.
YOU'LL SURVIVE.
JUST A FLESH WOUND.
YOU FELL BACK, THAT'S HOW YOU CRACKED YOUR HEAD OPEN.
LUCKY FOR YOU...
MY EYE-SIGHT'S NOT WHAT IT ONCE WAS.
NOW, HOLD STILL.

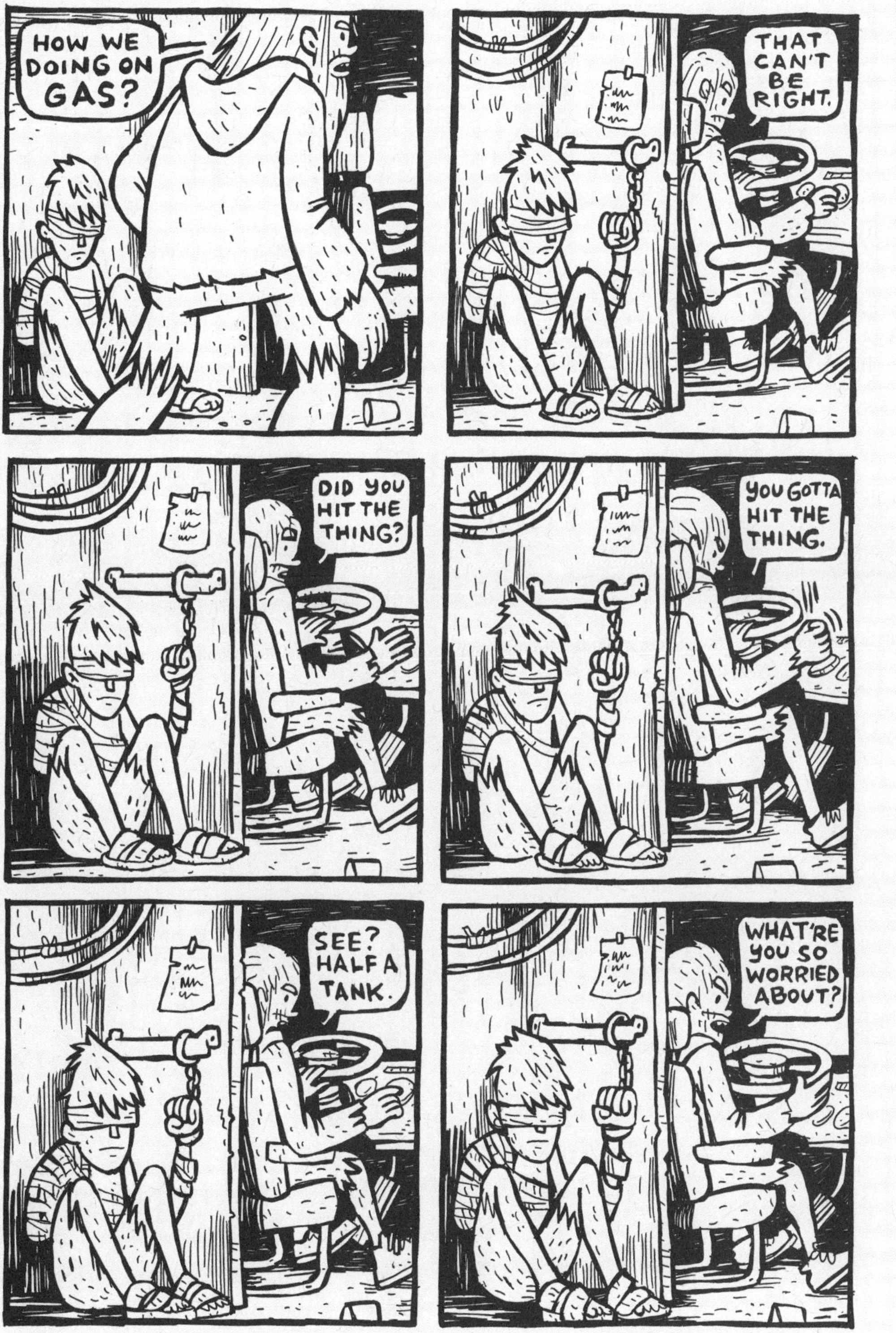
HOW WE DOING ON GAS?
THAT CAN'T BE RIGHT.
DID YOU HIT THE THING?
YOU GOTTA HIT THE THING.
SEE? HALF A TANK.
WHAT'RE YOU SO WORRIED ABOUT?

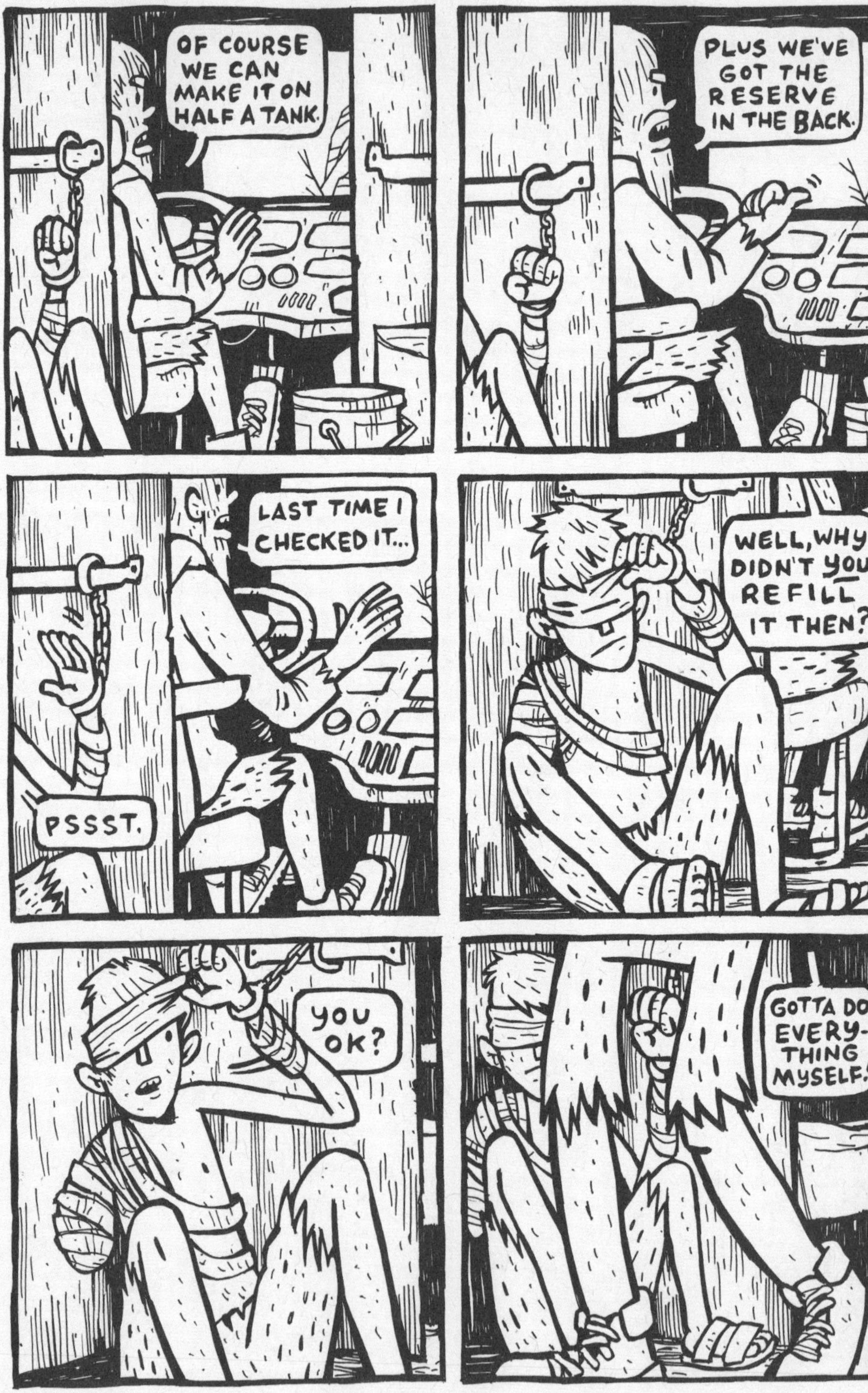
OF COURSE WE CAN MAKE IT ON HALF A TANK.
PLUS WE'VE GOT THE RESERVE IN THE BACK.
LAST TIME I CHECKED IT...
PSSST.
WELL, WHY DIDN'T YOU REFILL IT THEN?
YOU OK?
GOTTA DO EVERY-THING MYSELF!

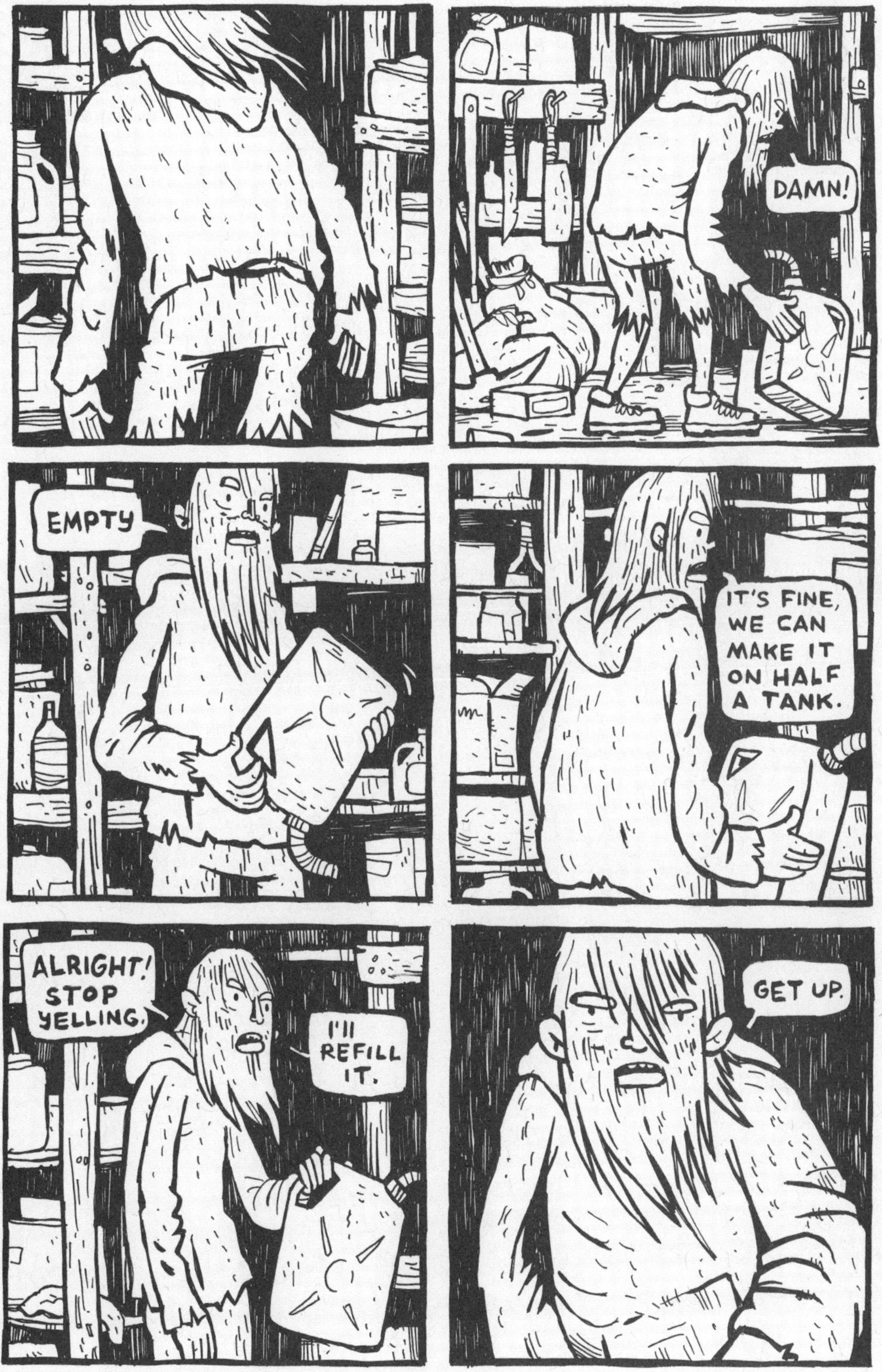
DAMN!
EMPTY
IT'S FINE, WE CAN MAKE IT ON HALF A TANK.
ALRIGHT! STOP YELLING.
I'll REFILL IT.
GET UP.

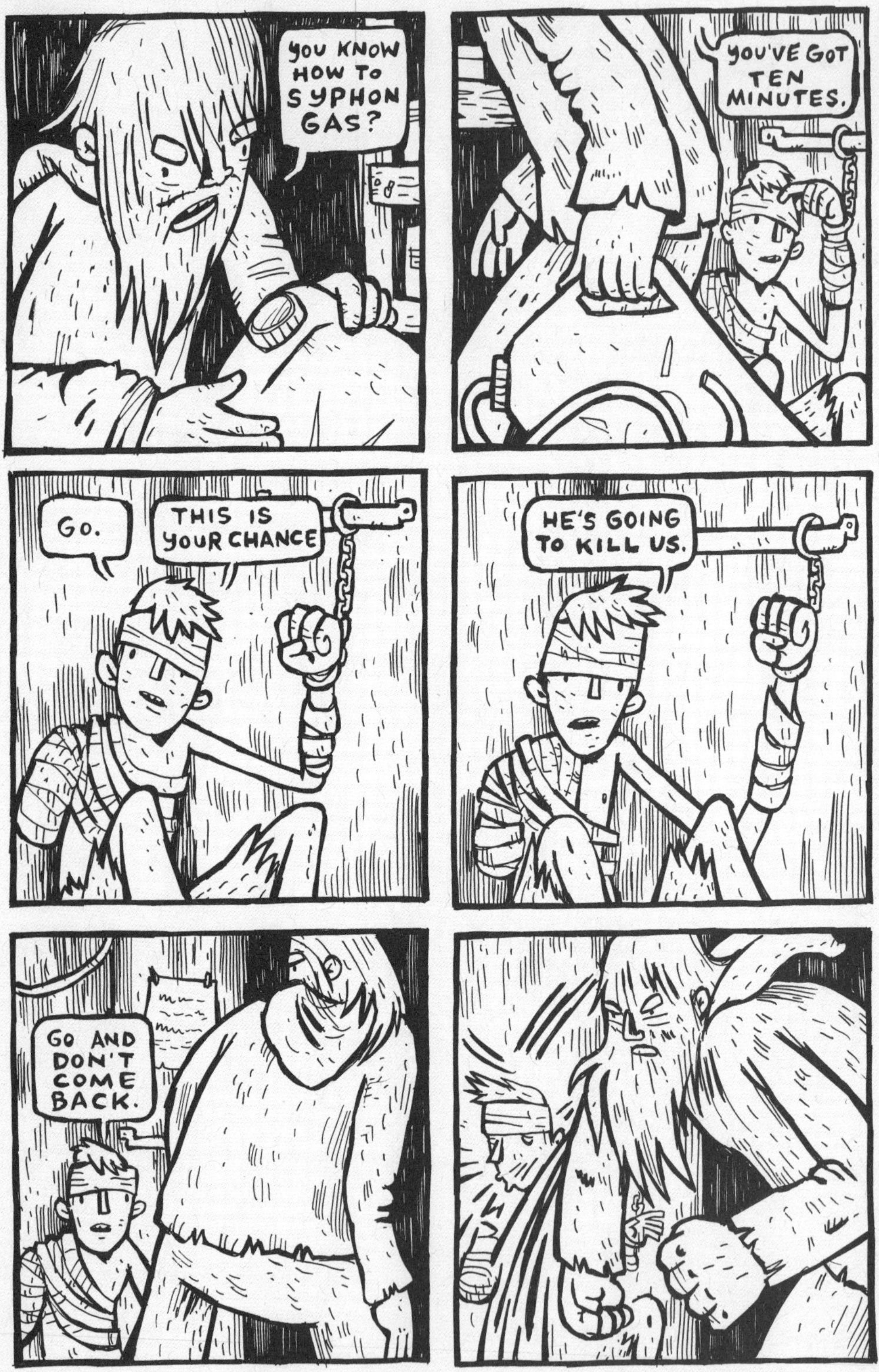
YOU KNOW HOW TO SYPHON GAS?
YOU'VE GOT TEN MINUTES.
GO.
THIS IS YOUR CHANCE
HE'S GOING TO KILL US.
GO AND DON'T COME BACK.

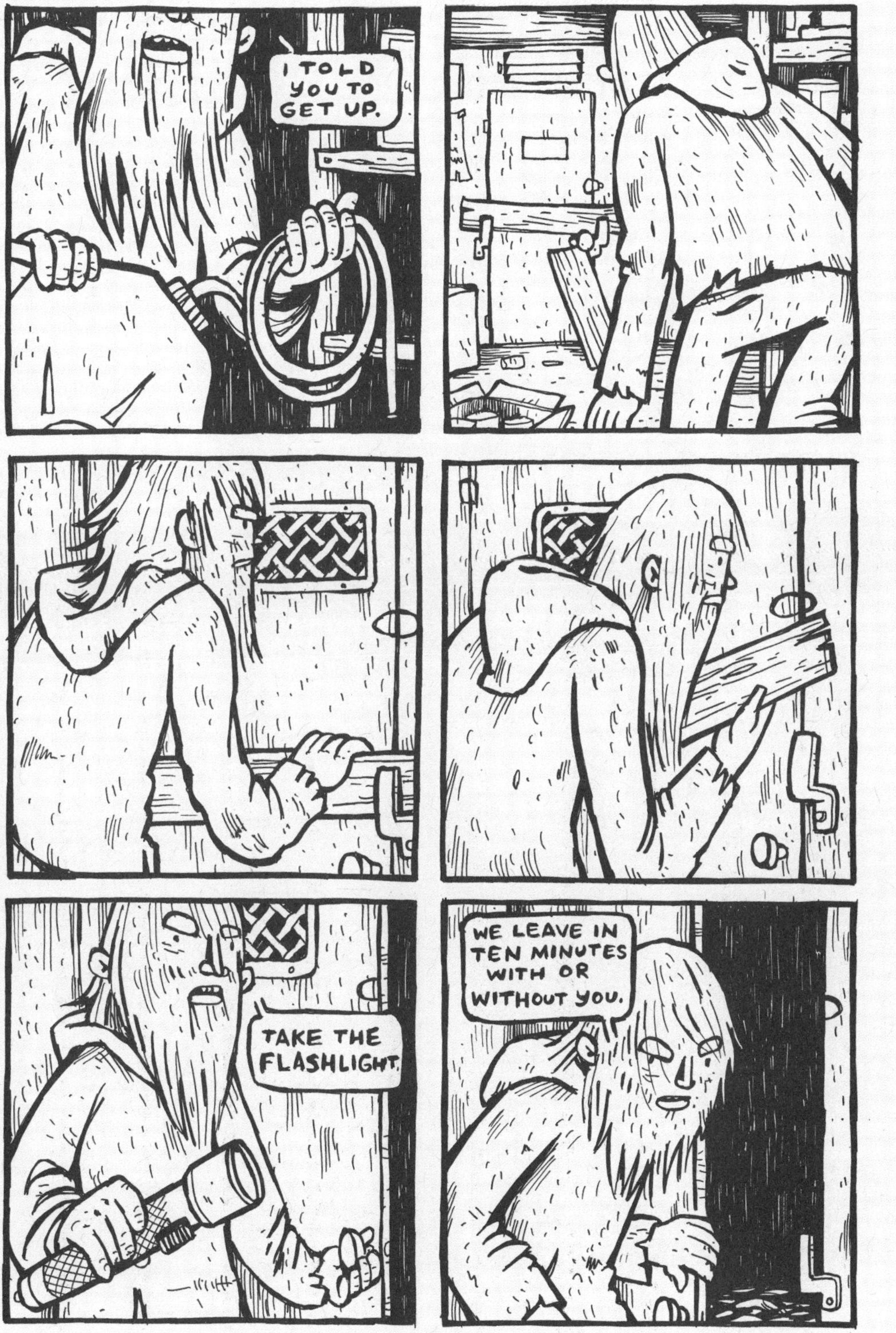
I TOLD YOU TO GET UP.
TAKE THE FLASHLIGHT.
WE LEAVE IN TEN MINUTES WITH OR WITHOUT YOU.

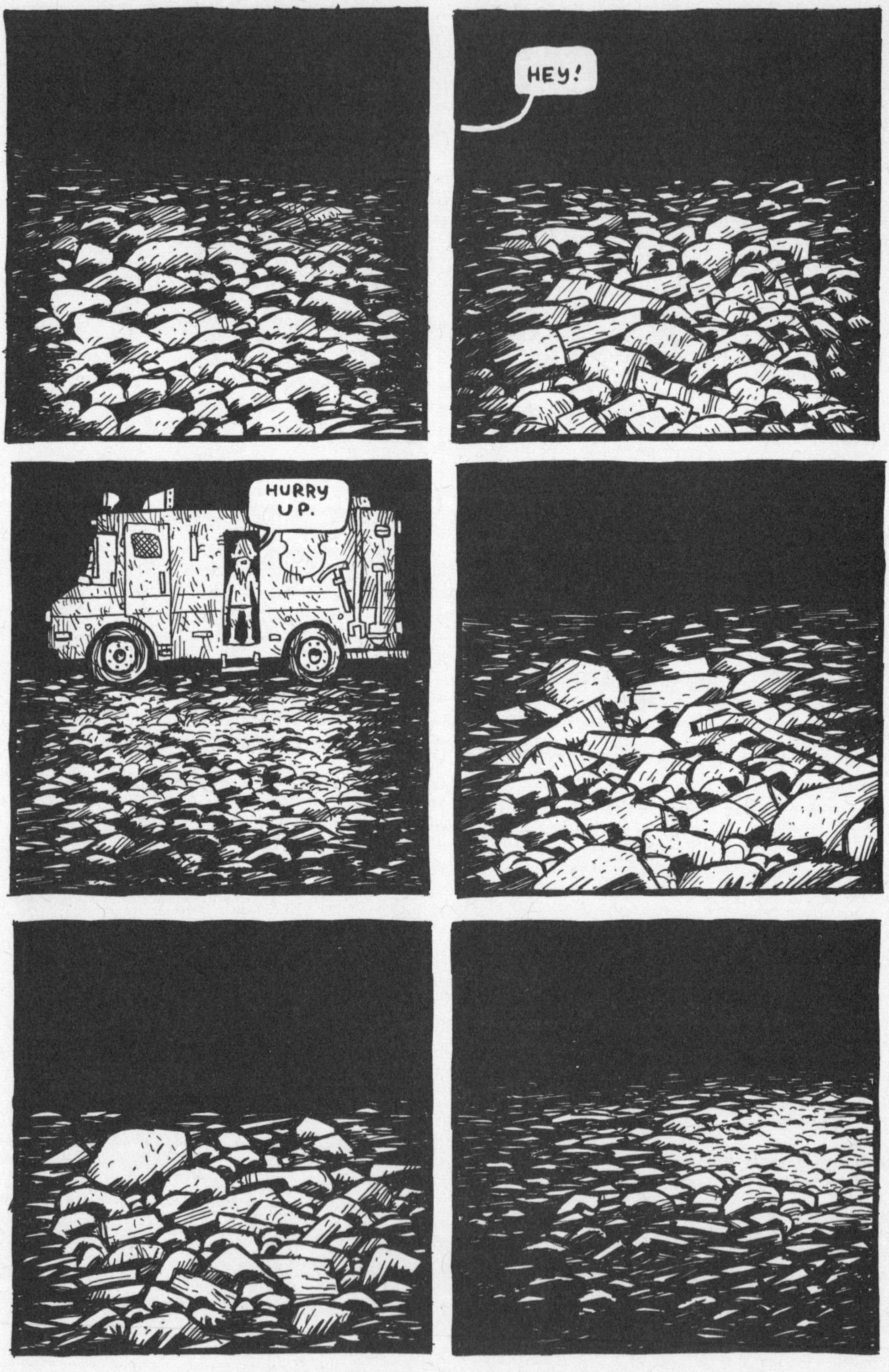
HEY!
HURRY UP.

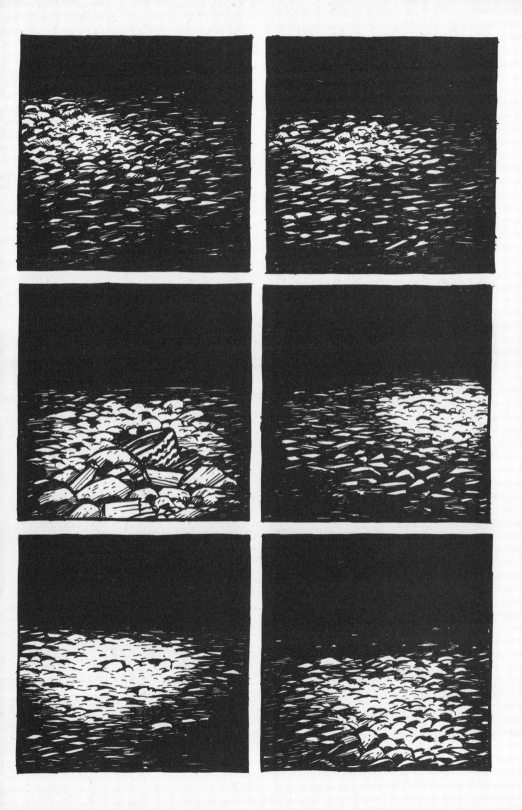

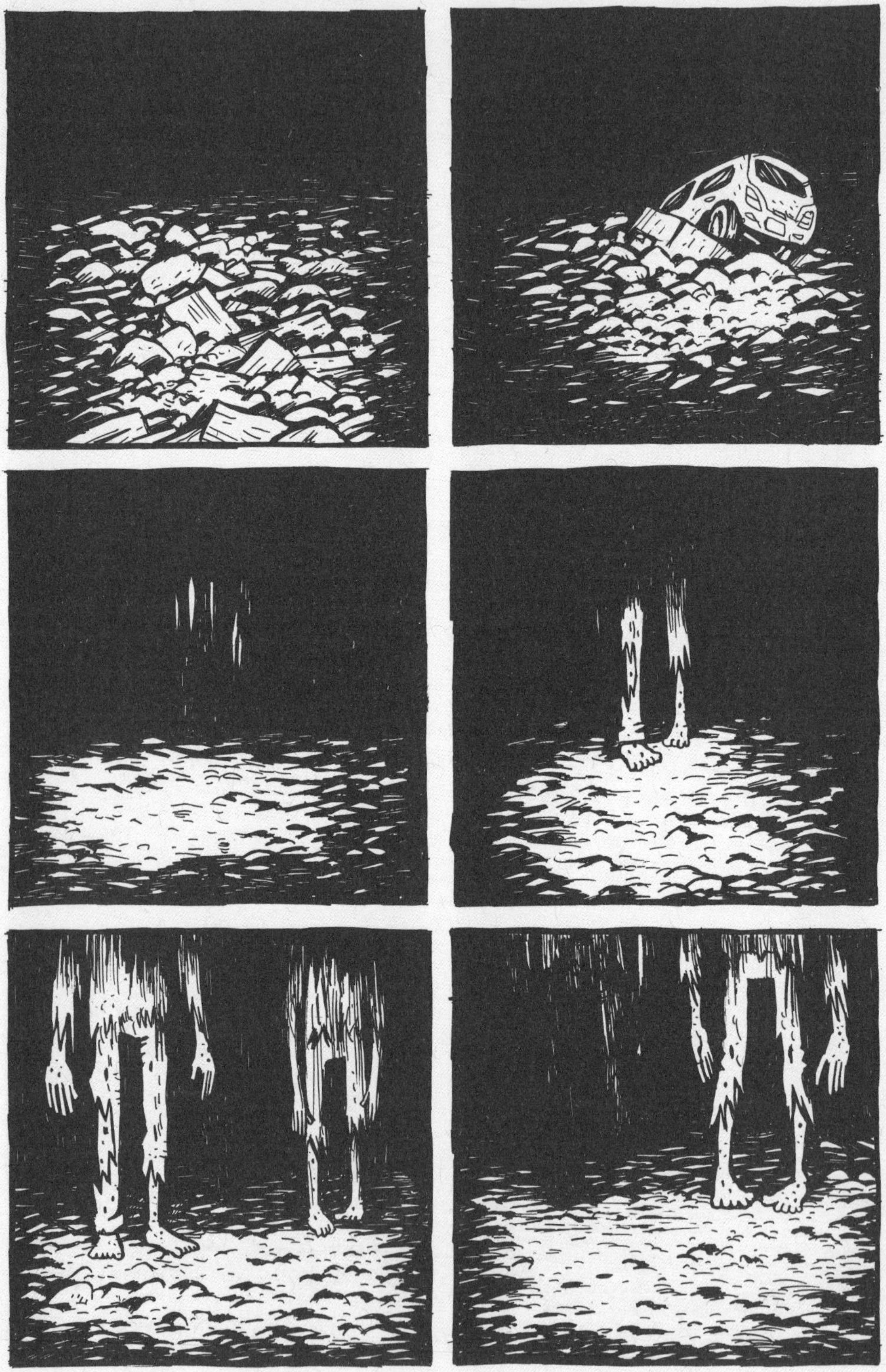

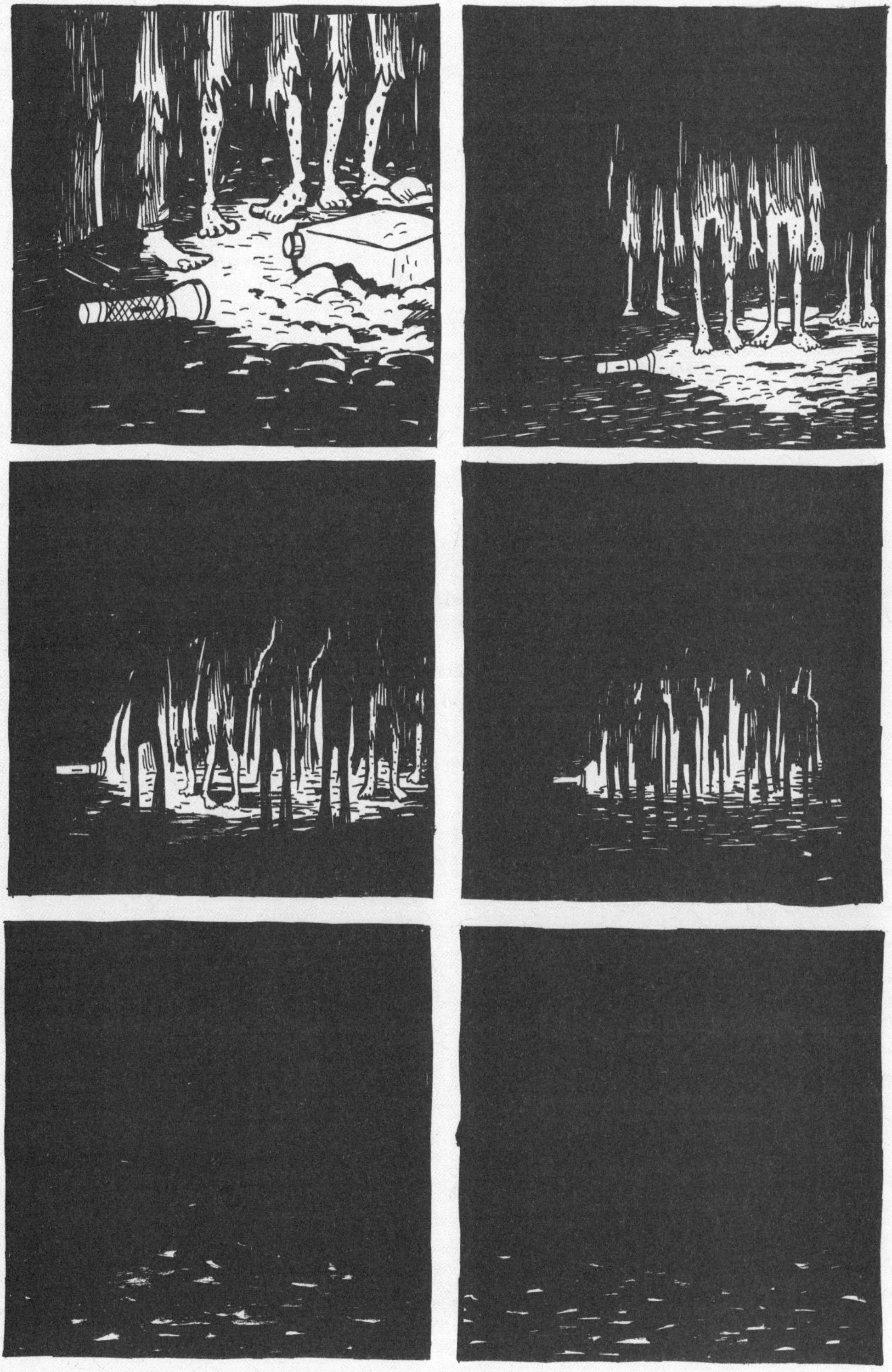

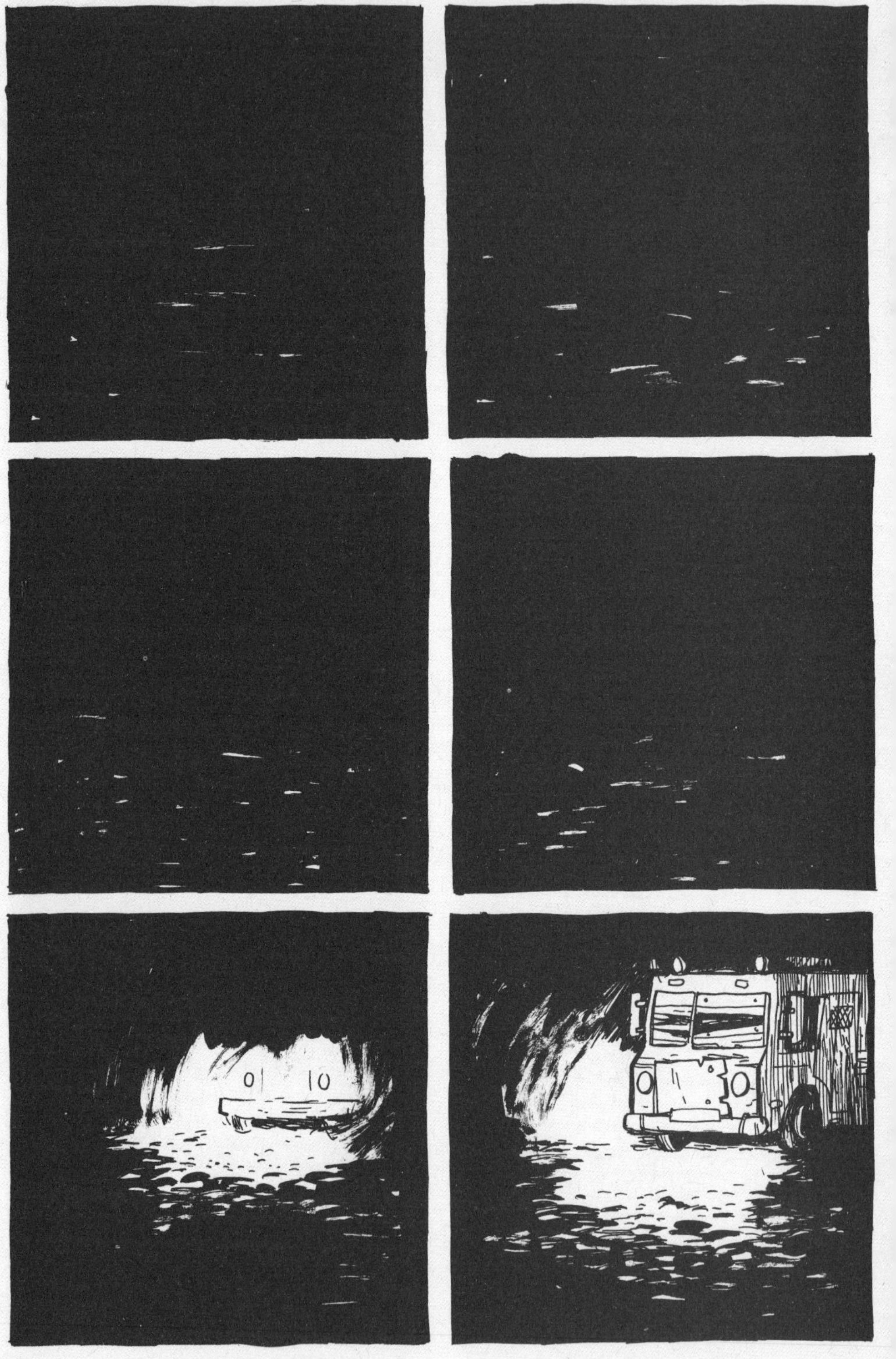

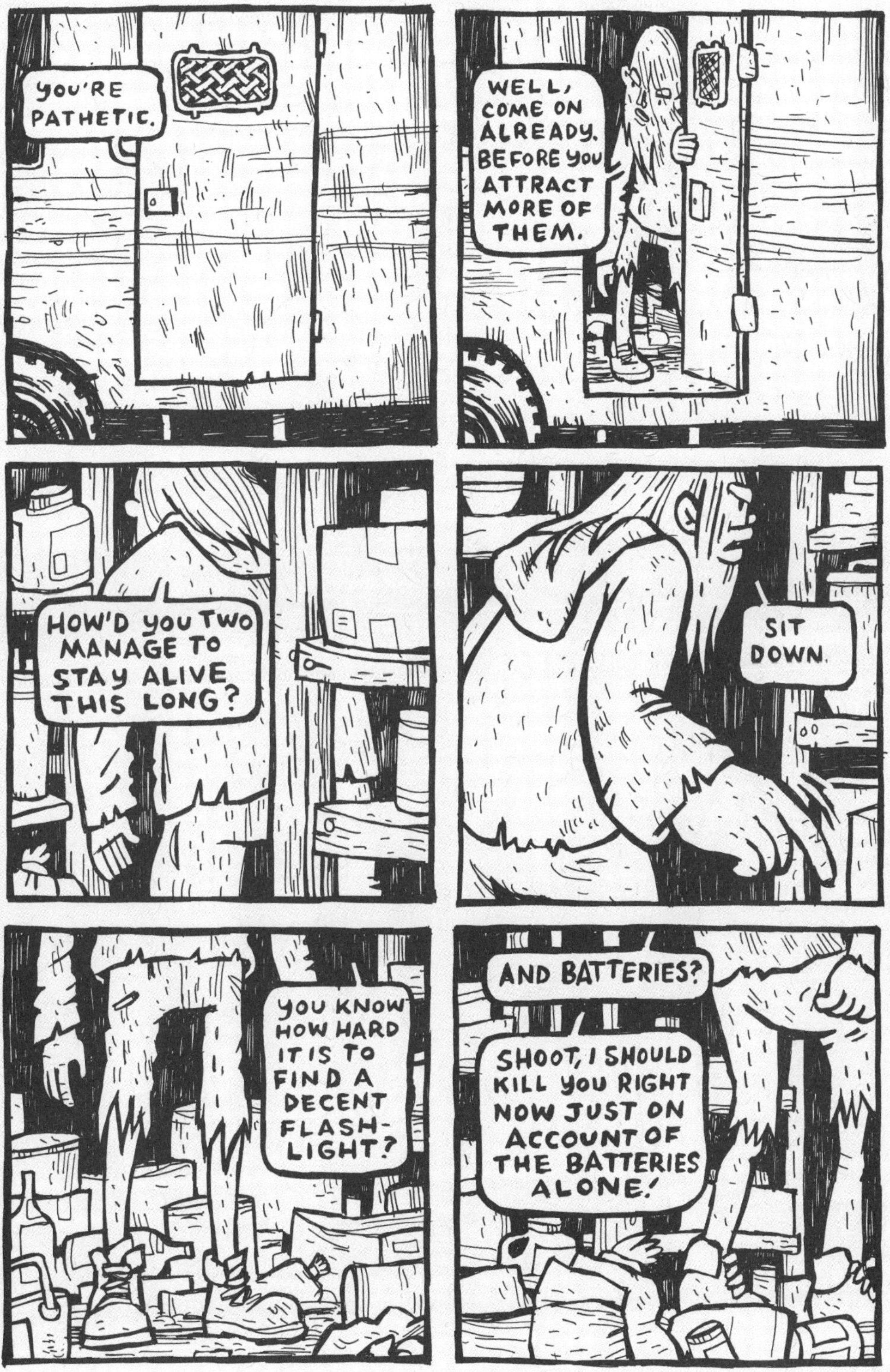
YOU'RE PATHETIC.
WELL, COME ON ALREADY. BEFORE YOU ATTRACT MORE OF THEM.
HOW'D YOU TWO MANAGE TO STAY ALIVE THIS LONG?
SIT DOWN.
YOU KNOW HOW HARD IT IS TO FIND A DECENT FLASH-LIGHT?
AND BATTERIES?
SHOOT, I SHOULD KILL YOU RIGHT NOW JUST ON ACCOUNT OF THE BATTERIES ALONE!

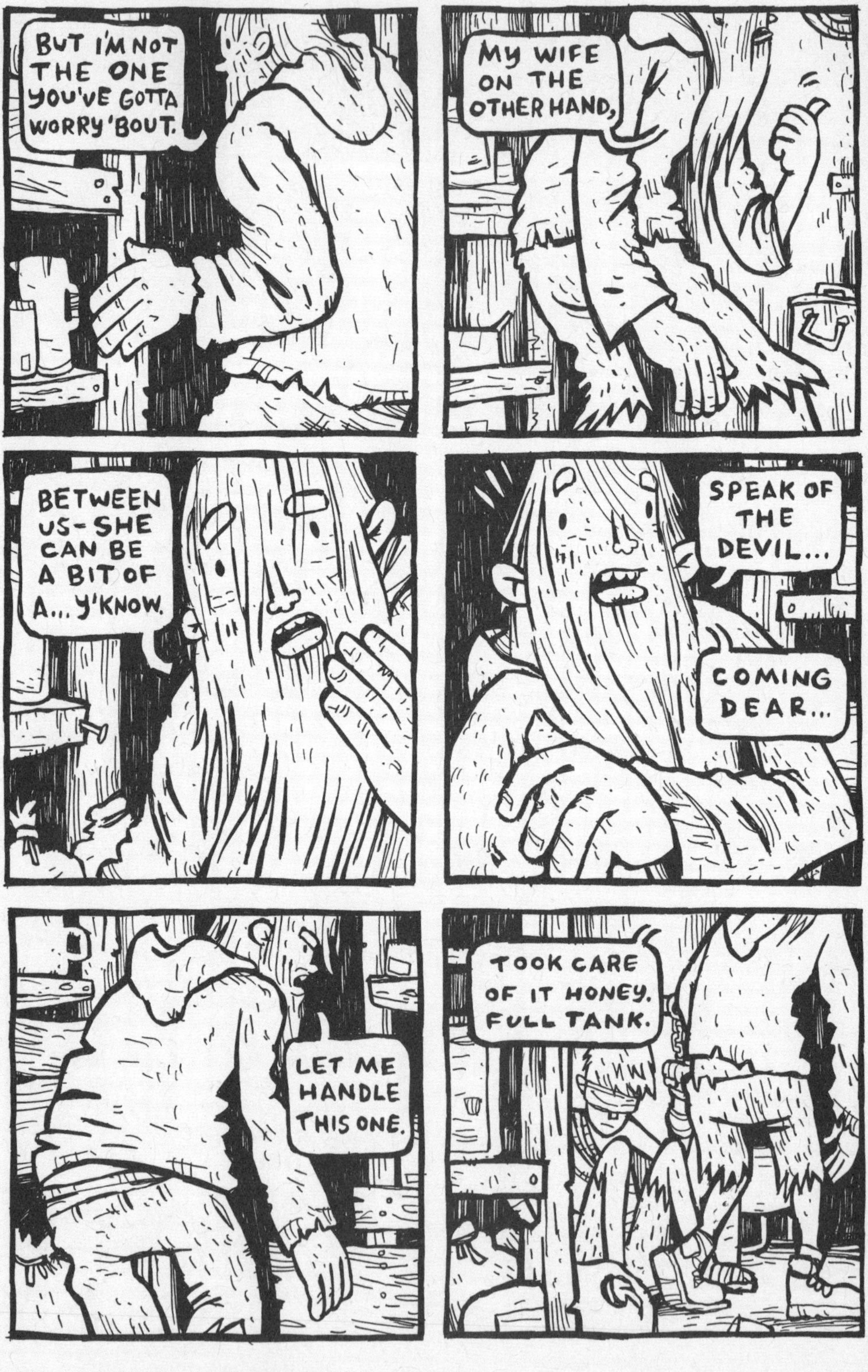

BUT I'M NOT THE ONE YOU'VE GOTTA WORRY 'BOUT.
MY WIFE ON THE OTHER HAND,
BETWEEN US- SHE CAN BE A BIT OF A... Y'KNOW.
SPEAK OF THE DEVIL...
COMING DEAR...
LET ME HANDLE THIS ONE.
TOOK CARE OF IT HONEY. FULL TANK.

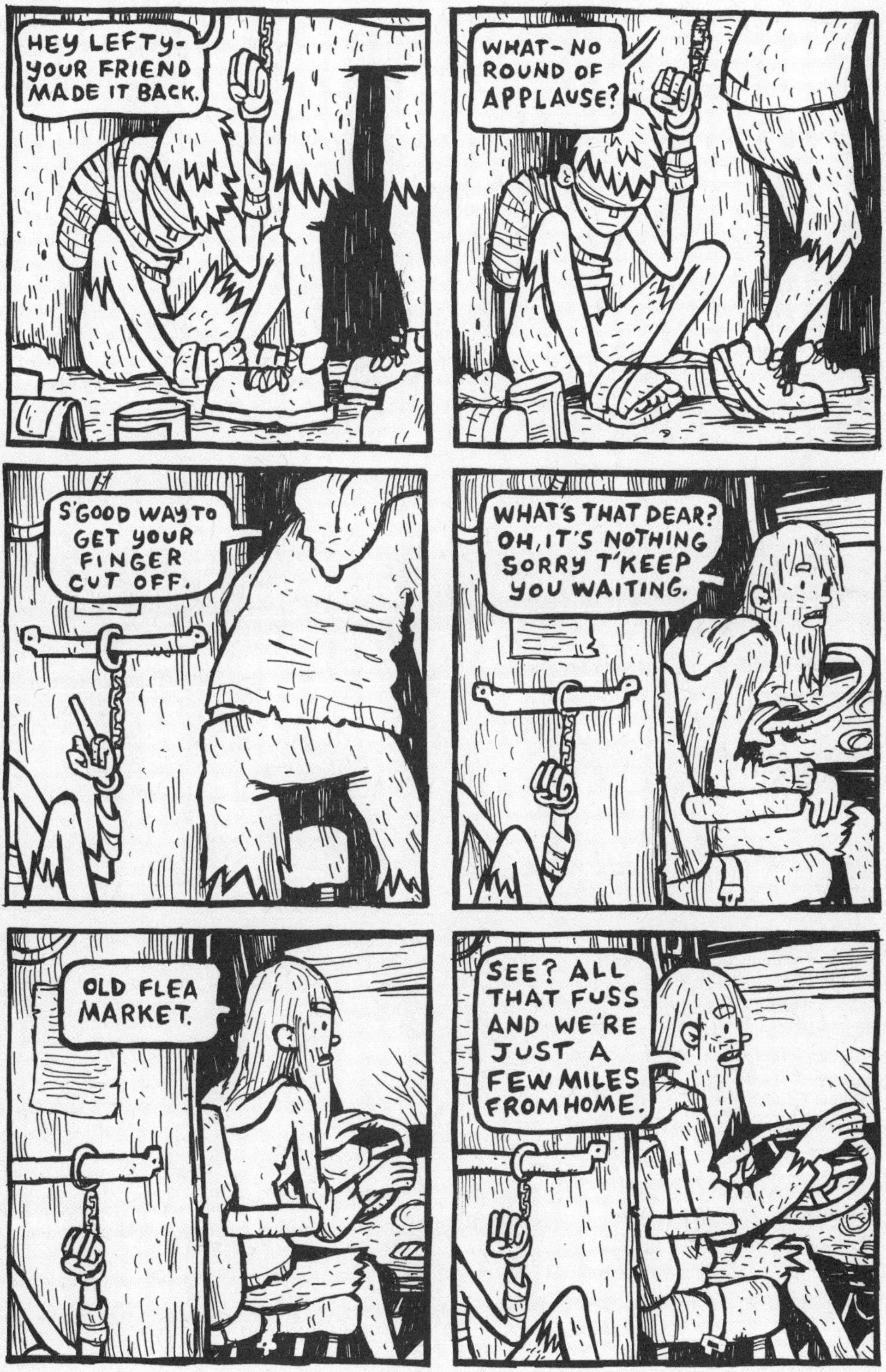
HEY LEFTY-
YOUR FRIEND
MADE IT BACK.
WHAT- NO
ROUND OF
APPLAUSE?
S'GOOD WAY TO
GET YOUR
FINGER
CUT OFF.
WHAT'S THAT DEAR?
OH, IT'S NOTHING
SORRY T'KEEP
YOU WAITING.
OLD FLEA
MARKET.
SEE? ALL
THAT FUSS
AND WE'RE
JUST A
FEW MILES
FROM HOME.

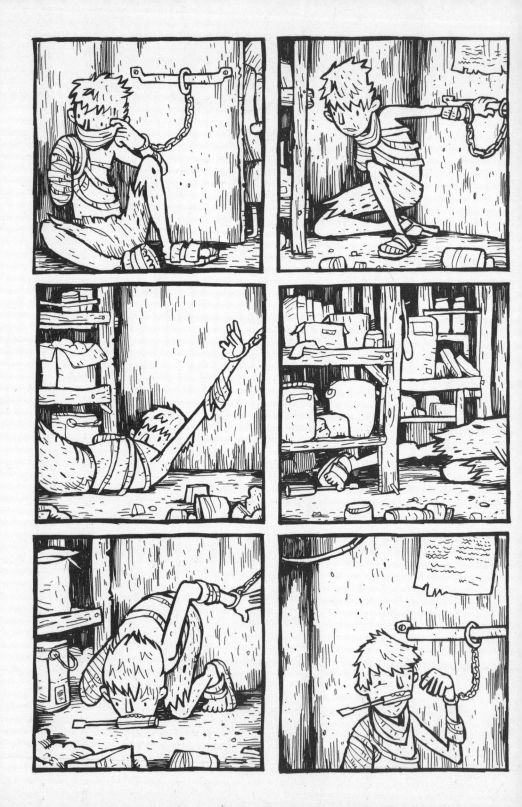

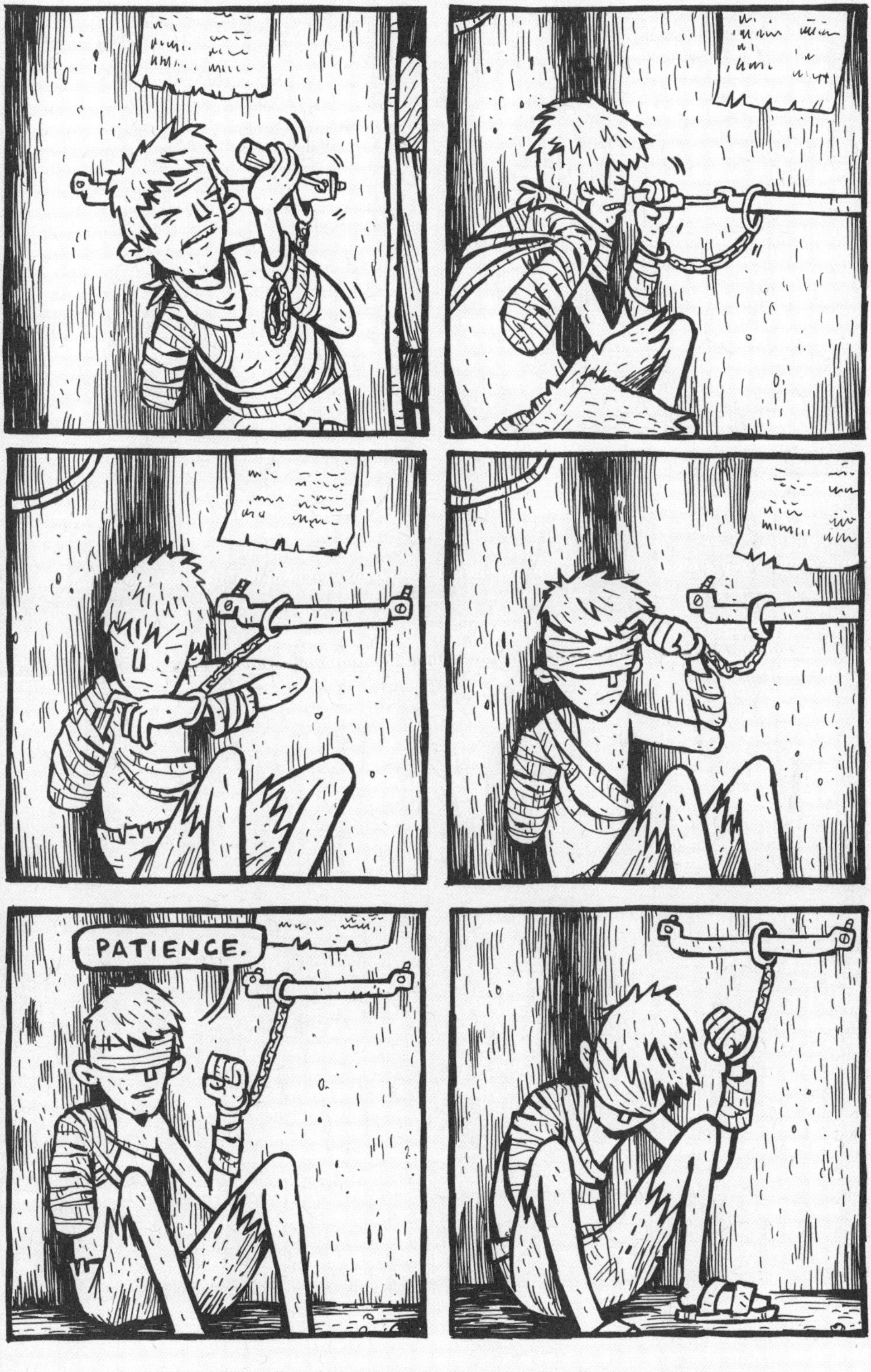
PATIENCE.

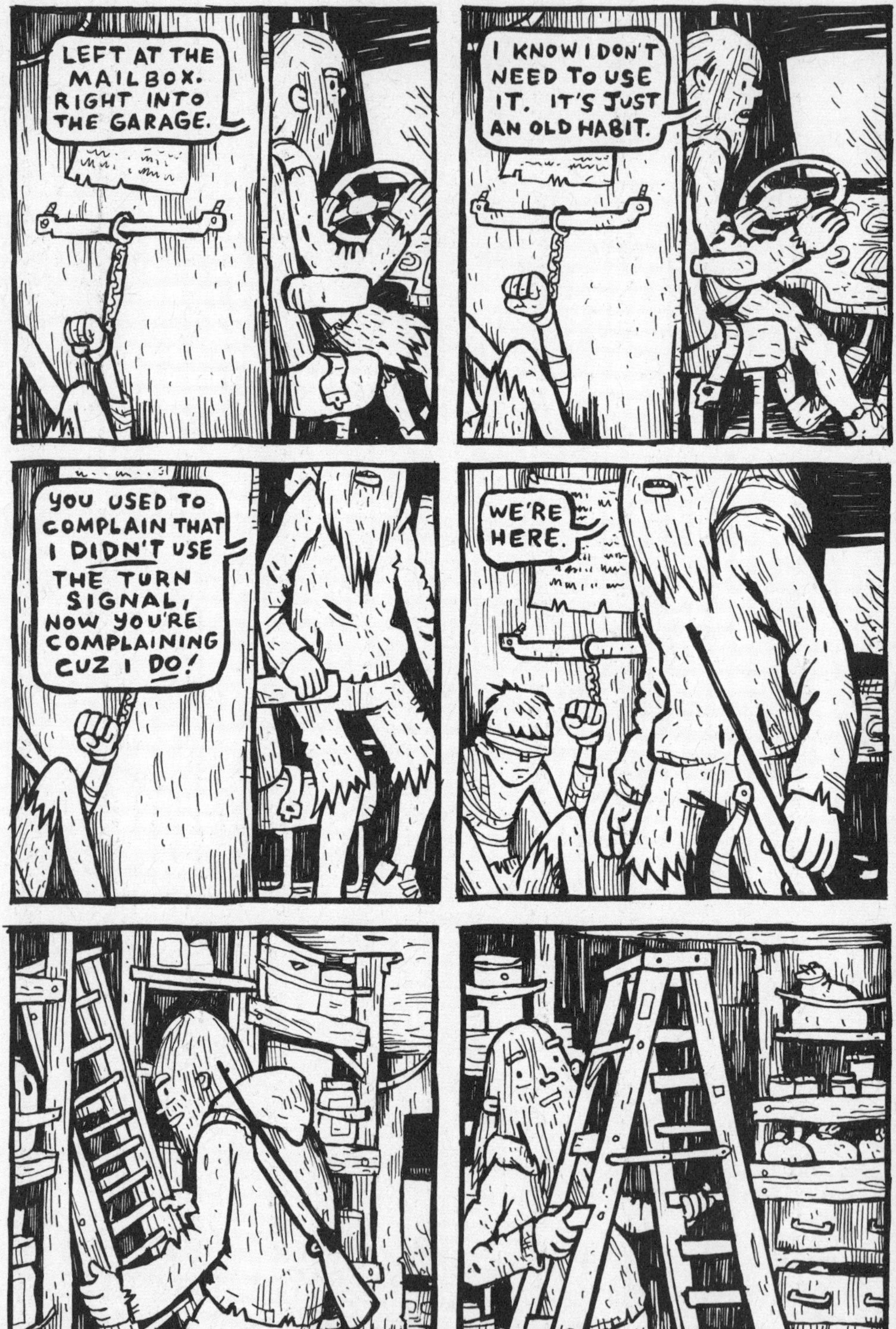
LEFT AT THE MAILBOX. RIGHT INTO THE GARAGE.
I KNOW I DON'T NEED TO USE IT. IT'S JUST AN OLD HABIT.
YOU USED TO COMPLAIN THAT I DIDN'T USE THE TURN SIGNAL, NOW YOU'RE COMPLAINING CUZ I DO!
WE'RE HERE.

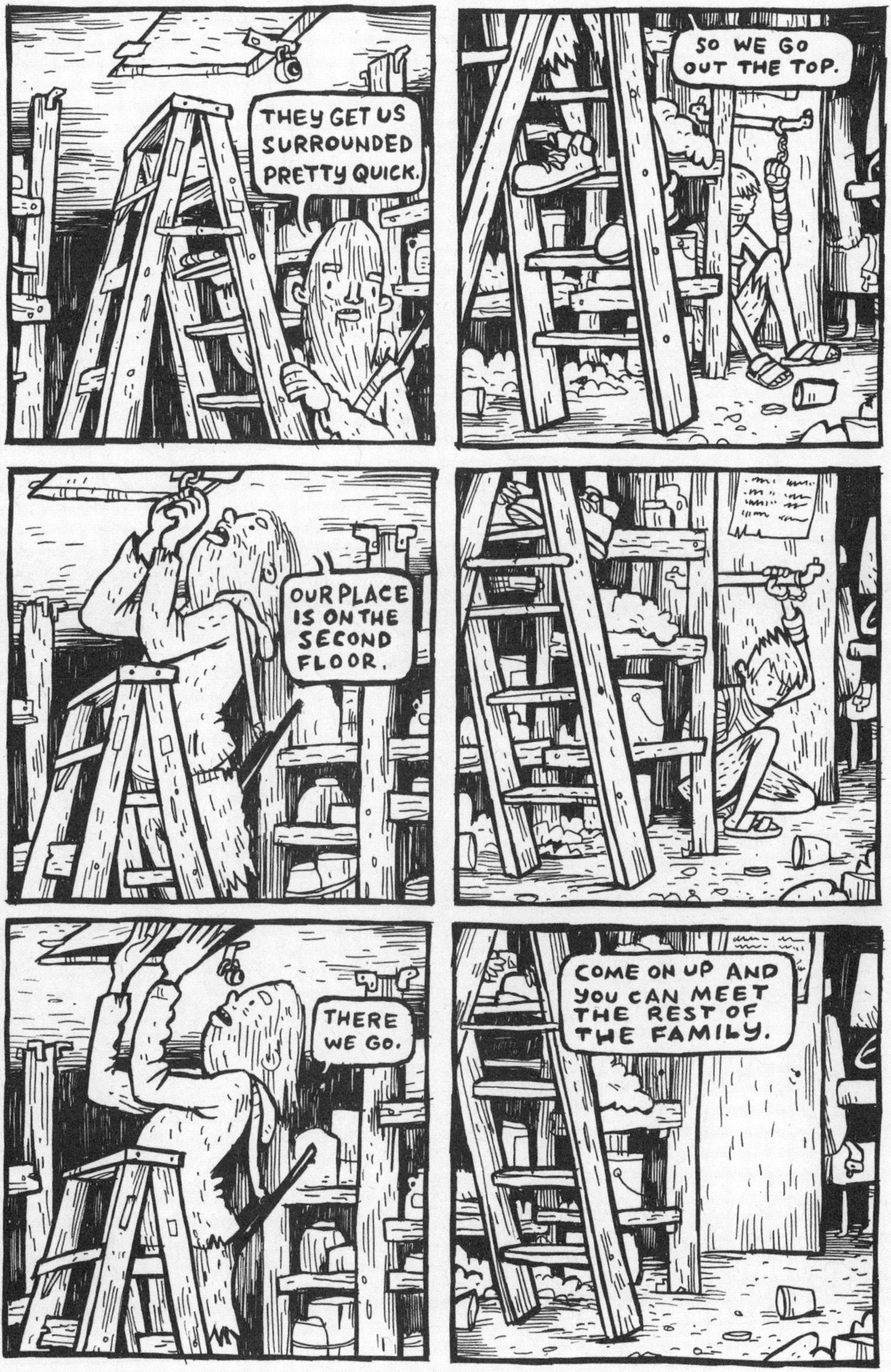
THEY GET US SURROUNDED PRETTY QUICK.
SO WE GO OUT THE TOP.
OUR PLACE IS ON THE SECOND FLOOR.
THERE WE GO.
COME ON UP AND YOU CAN MEET THE REST OF THE FAMILY.

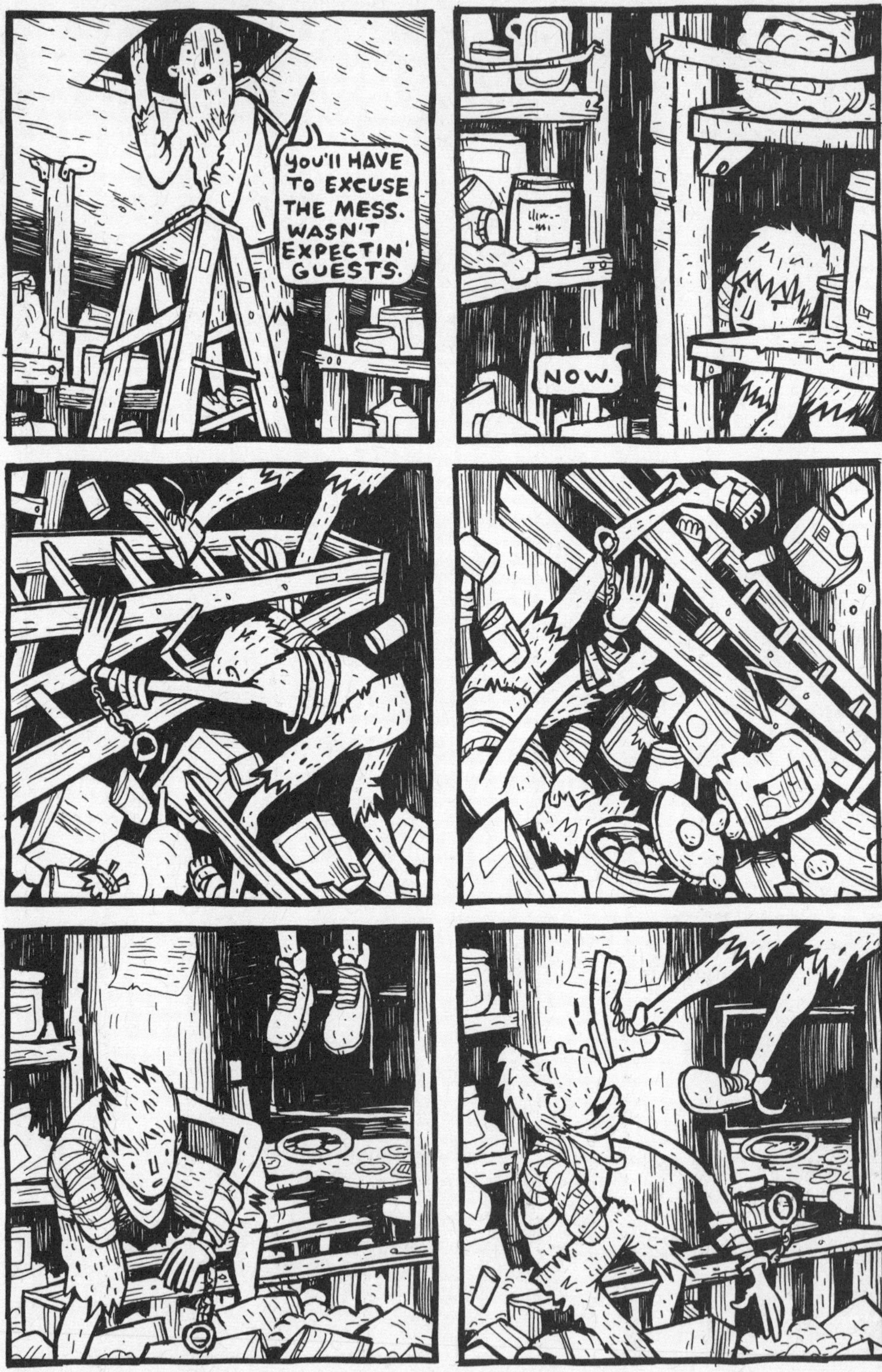
YOU'LL HAVE TO EXCUSE THE MESS. WASN'T EXPECTIN' GUESTS.
NOW.

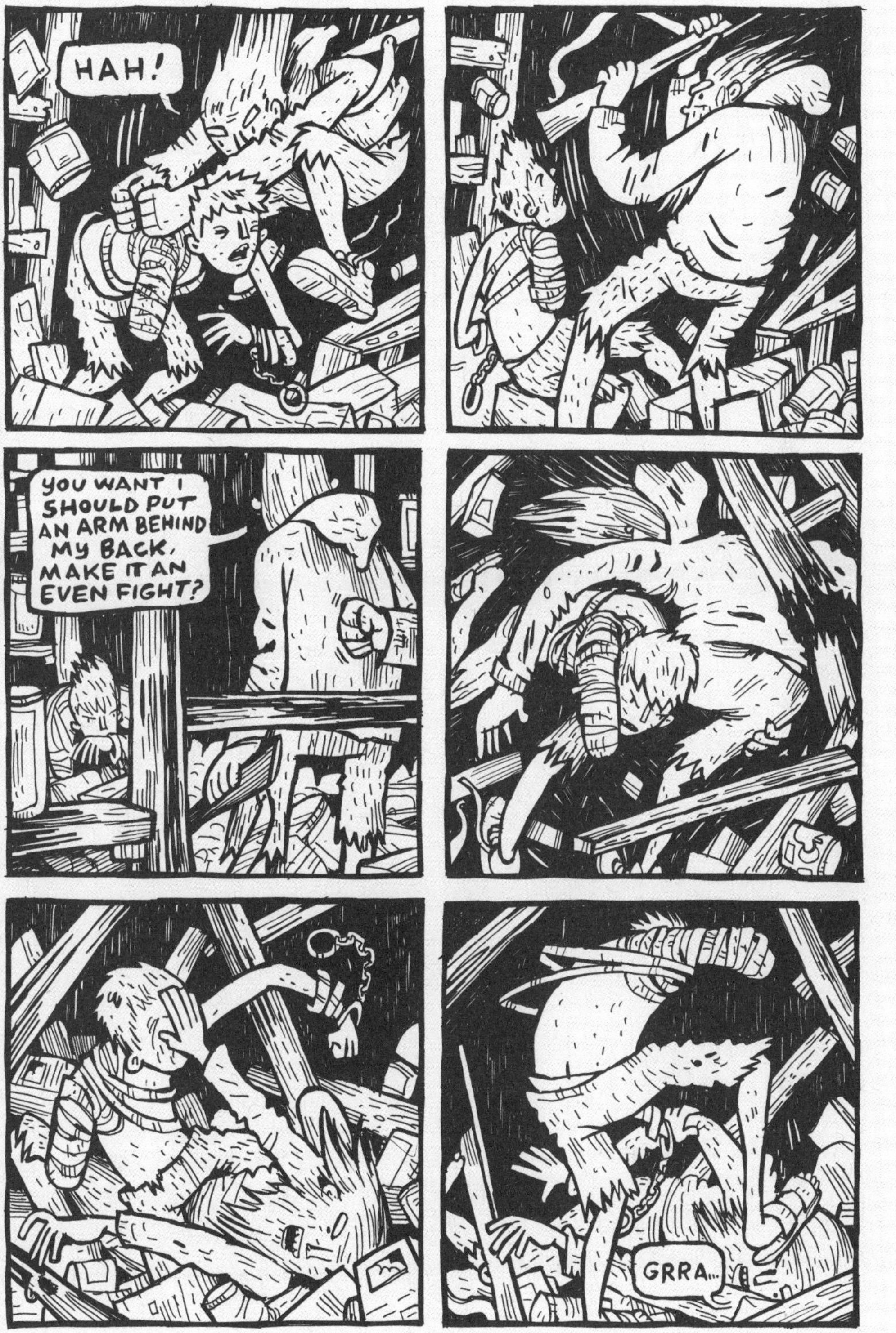
HAH!
YOU WANT I SHOULD PUT AN ARM BEHIND MY BACK, MAKE IT AN EVEN FIGHT?
GRRA...

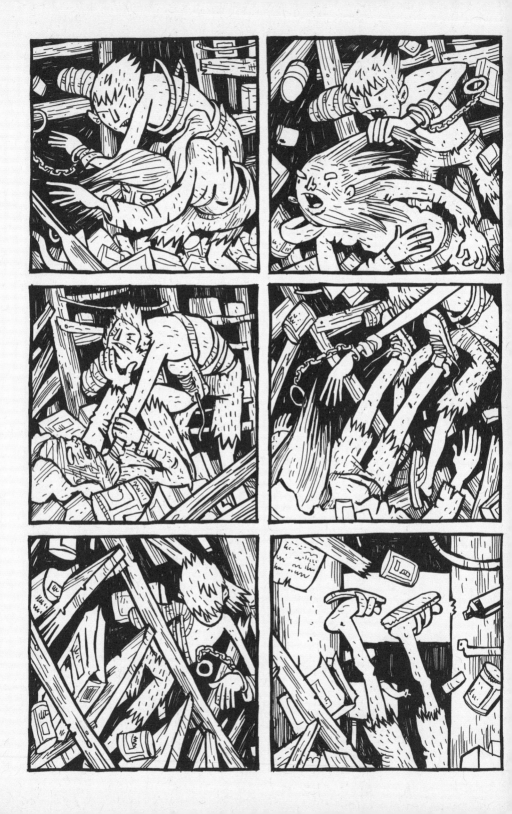

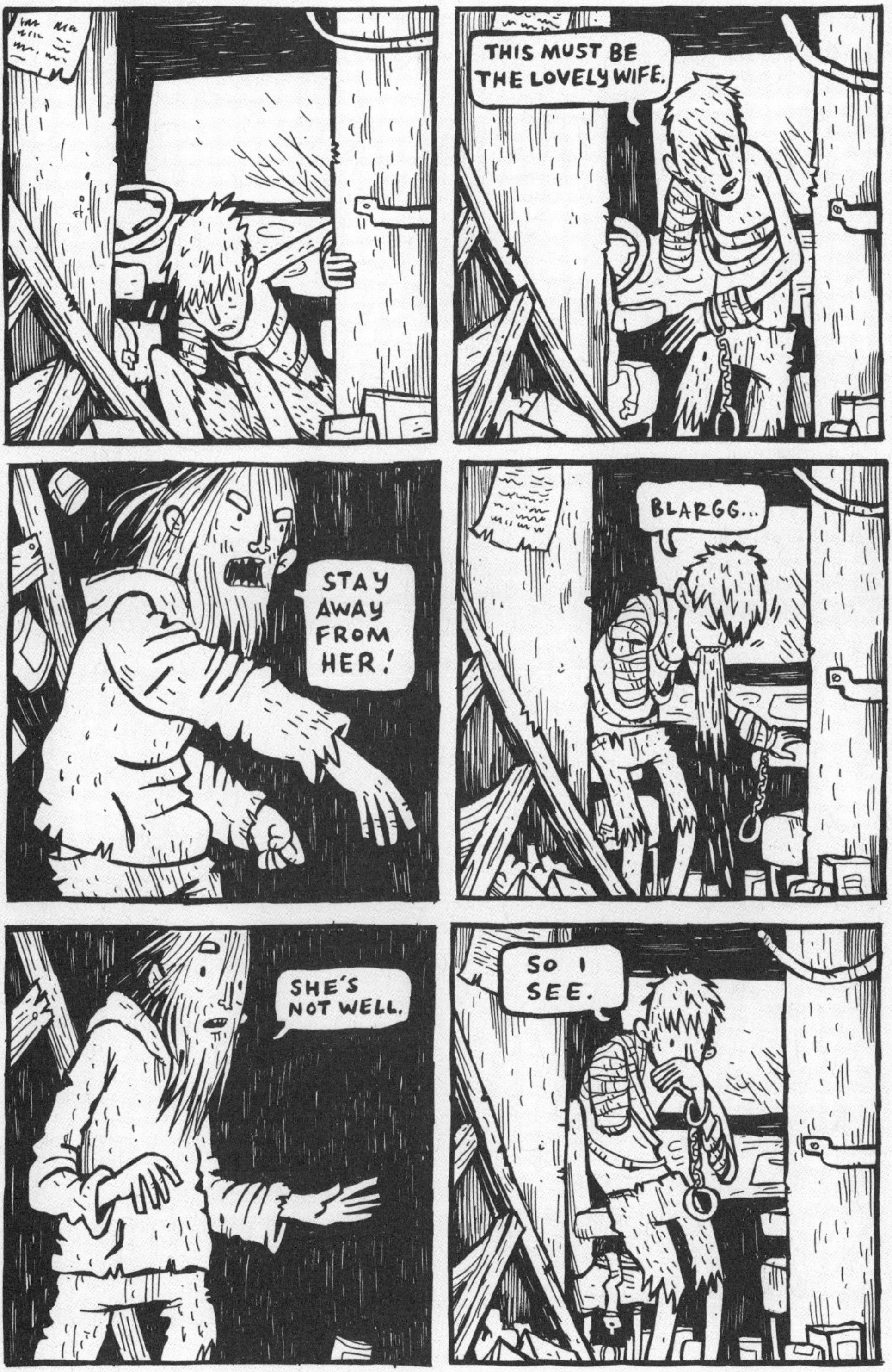
THIS MUST BE THE LOVELY WIFE.
STAY AWAY FROM HER!
BLARGG...
SHE'S NOT WELL.
SO I SEE.

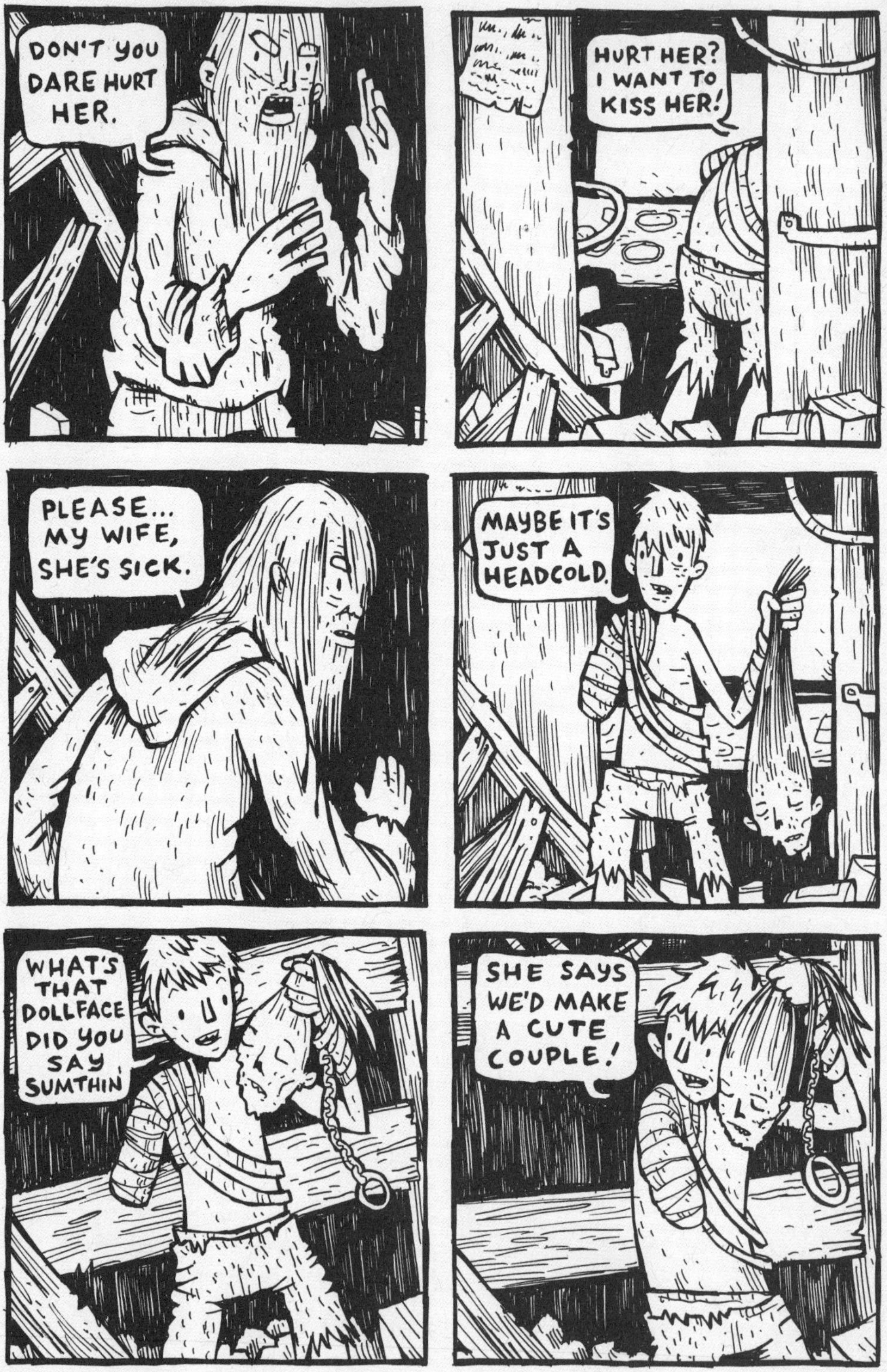
DON'T YOU DARE HURT HER.
HURT HER? I WANT TO KISS HER!
PLEASE... MY WIFE, SHE'S SICK.
MAYBE IT'S JUST A HEADCOLD.
WHAT'S THAT DOLLFACE DID YOU SAY SUMTHIN
SHE SAYS WE'D MAKE A CUTE COUPLE!

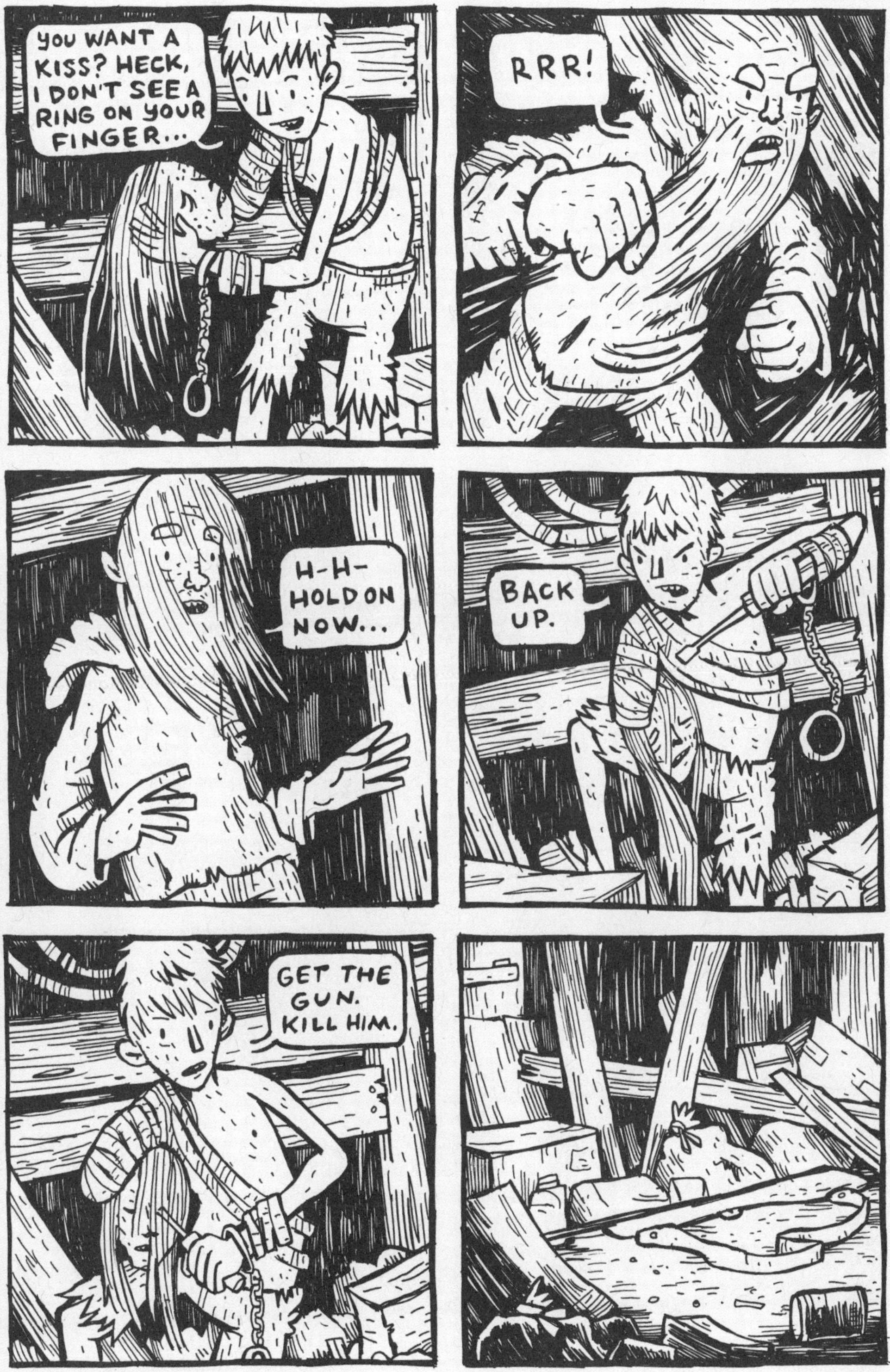
YOU WANT A KISS? HECK, I DON'T SEE A RING ON YOUR FINGER...
RRR!
H-H-HOLD ON NOW...
BACK UP.
GET THE GUN. KILL HIM.

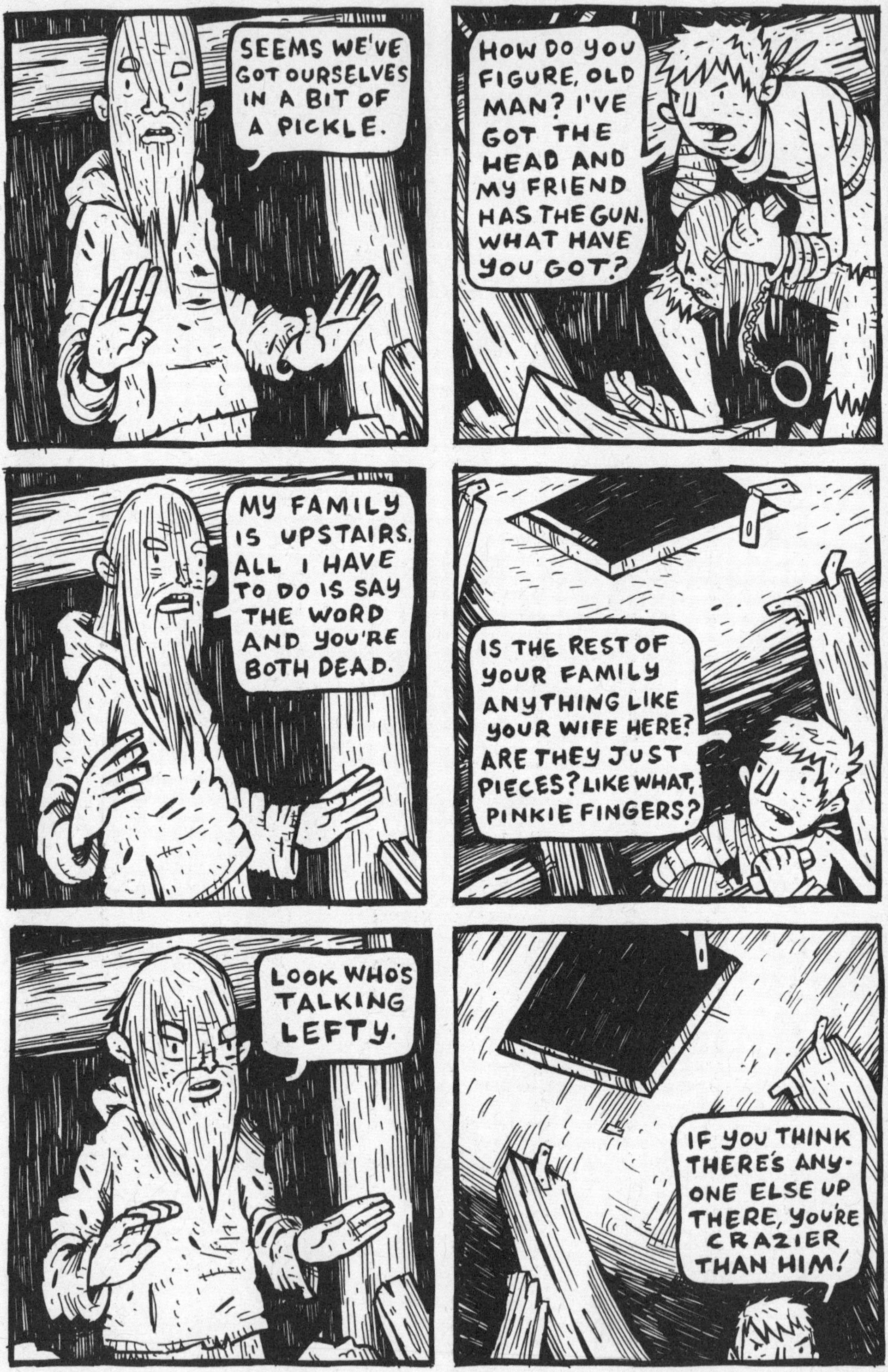
SEEMS WE'VE GOT OURSELVES IN A BIT OF A PICKLE.
HOW DO YOU FIGURE, OLD MAN? I'VE GOT THE HEAD AND MY FRIEND HAS THE GUN. WHAT HAVE YOU GOT?
MY FAMILY IS UPSTAIRS. ALL I HAVE TO DO IS SAY THE WORD AND YOU'RE BOTH DEAD.
IS THE REST OF YOUR FAMILY ANYTHING LIKE YOUR WIFE HERE? ARE THEY JUST PIECES? LIKE WHAT, PINKIE FINGERS?
LOOK WHO'S TALKING LEFTY.
IF YOU THINK THERE'S ANYONE ELSE UP THERE, YOU'RE CRAZIER THAN HIM!

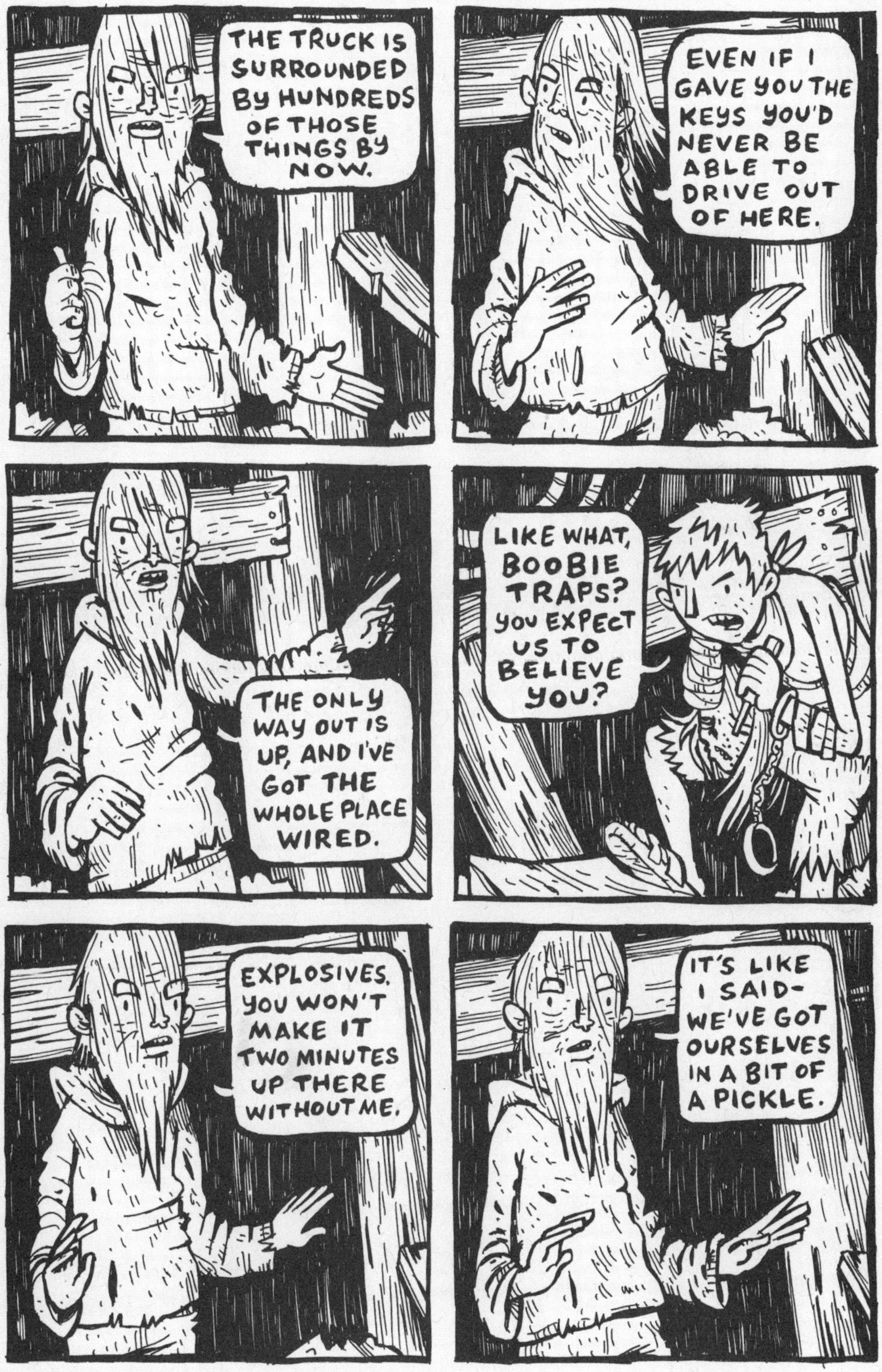
THE TRUCK IS SURROUNDED BY HUNDREDS OF THOSE THINGS BY NOW.
EVEN IF I GAVE YOU THE KEYS YOU'D NEVER BE ABLE TO DRIVE OUT OF HERE.
THE ONLY WAY OUT IS UP, AND I'VE GOT THE WHOLE PLACE WIRED.
LIKE WHAT, BOOBIE TRAPS? YOU EXPECT US TO BELIEVE YOU?
EXPLOSIVES. YOU WON'T MAKE IT TWO MINUTES UP THERE WITHOUT ME.
IT'S LIKE I SAID- WE'VE GOT OURSELVES IN A BIT OF A PICKLE.

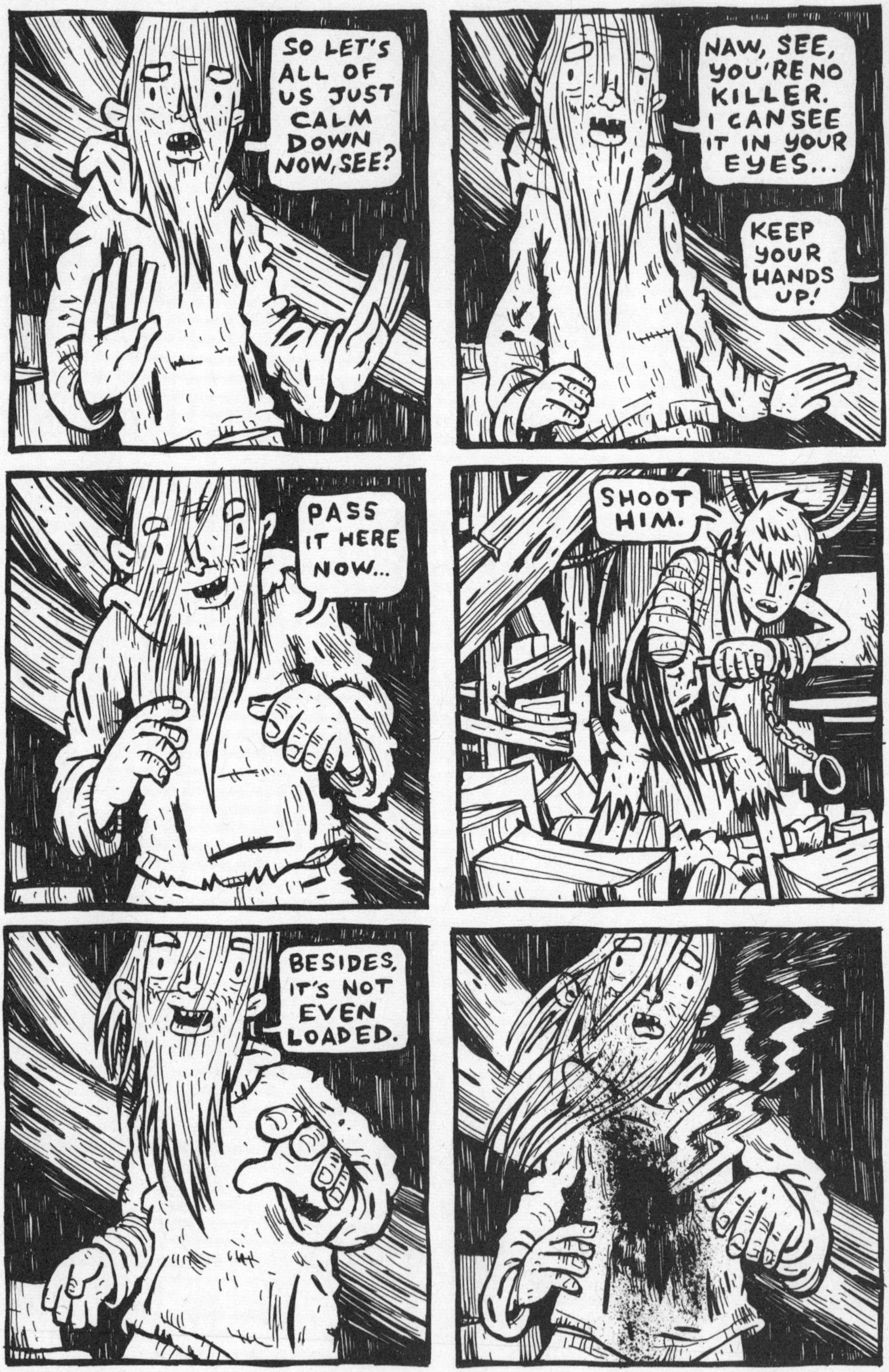
SO LET'S ALL OF US JUST CALM DOWN NOW, SEE?
NAW, SEE, YOU'RE NO KILLER. I CAN SEE IT IN YOUR EYES...
KEEP YOUR HANDS UP!
PASS IT HERE NOW...
SHOOT HIM.
BESIDES, IT'S NOT EVEN LOADED.

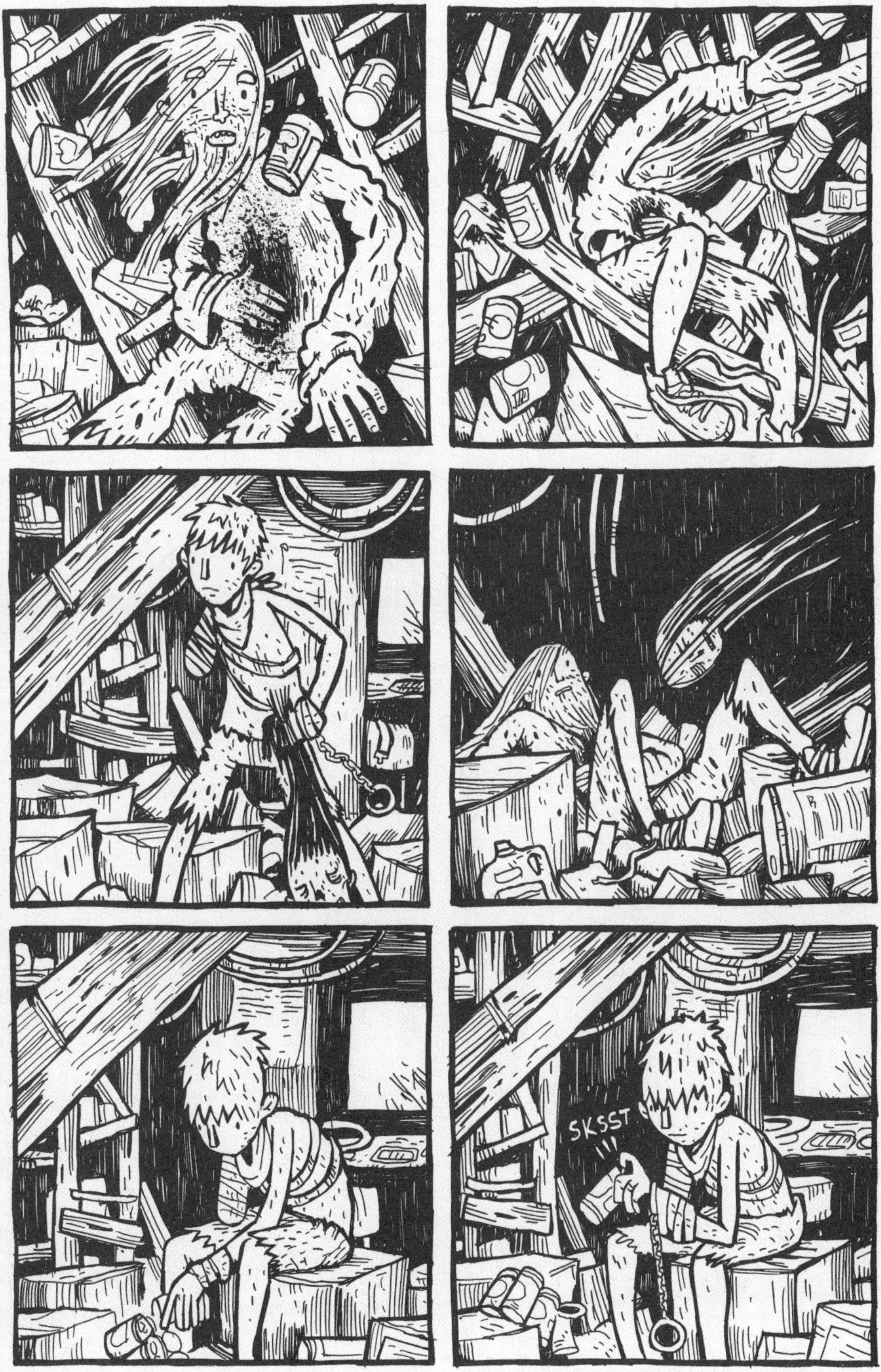
SKSST

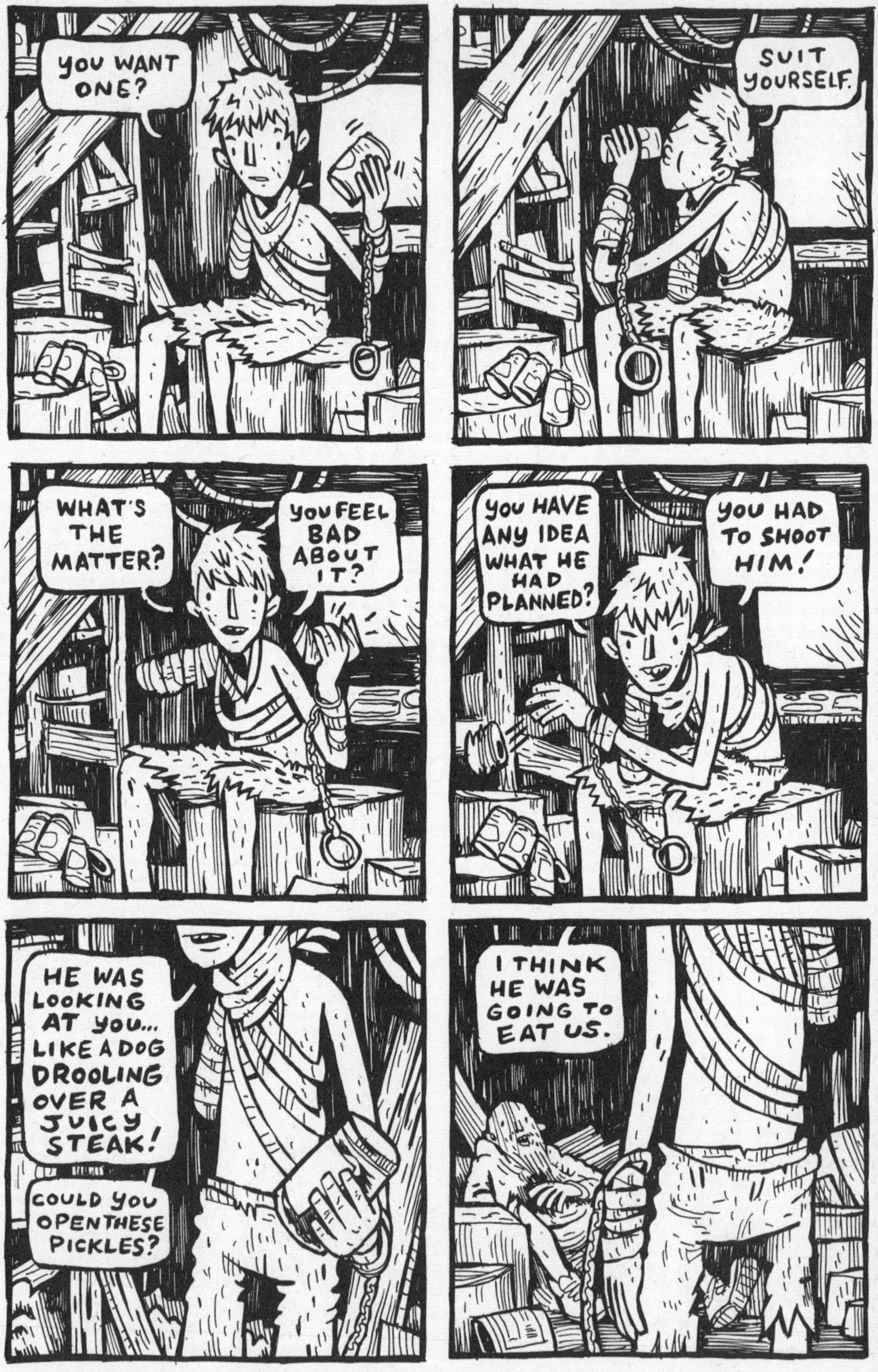
YOU WANT ONE?
SUIT YOURSELF.
WHAT'S THE MATTER?
YOU FEEL BAD ABOUT IT?
YOU HAVE ANY IDEA WHAT HE HAD PLANNED?
YOU HAD TO SHOOT HIM!
HE WAS LOOKING AT YOU... LIKE A DOG DROOLING OVER A JUICY STEAK!
COULD YOU OPEN THESE PICKLES?
I THINK HE WAS GOING TO EAT US.

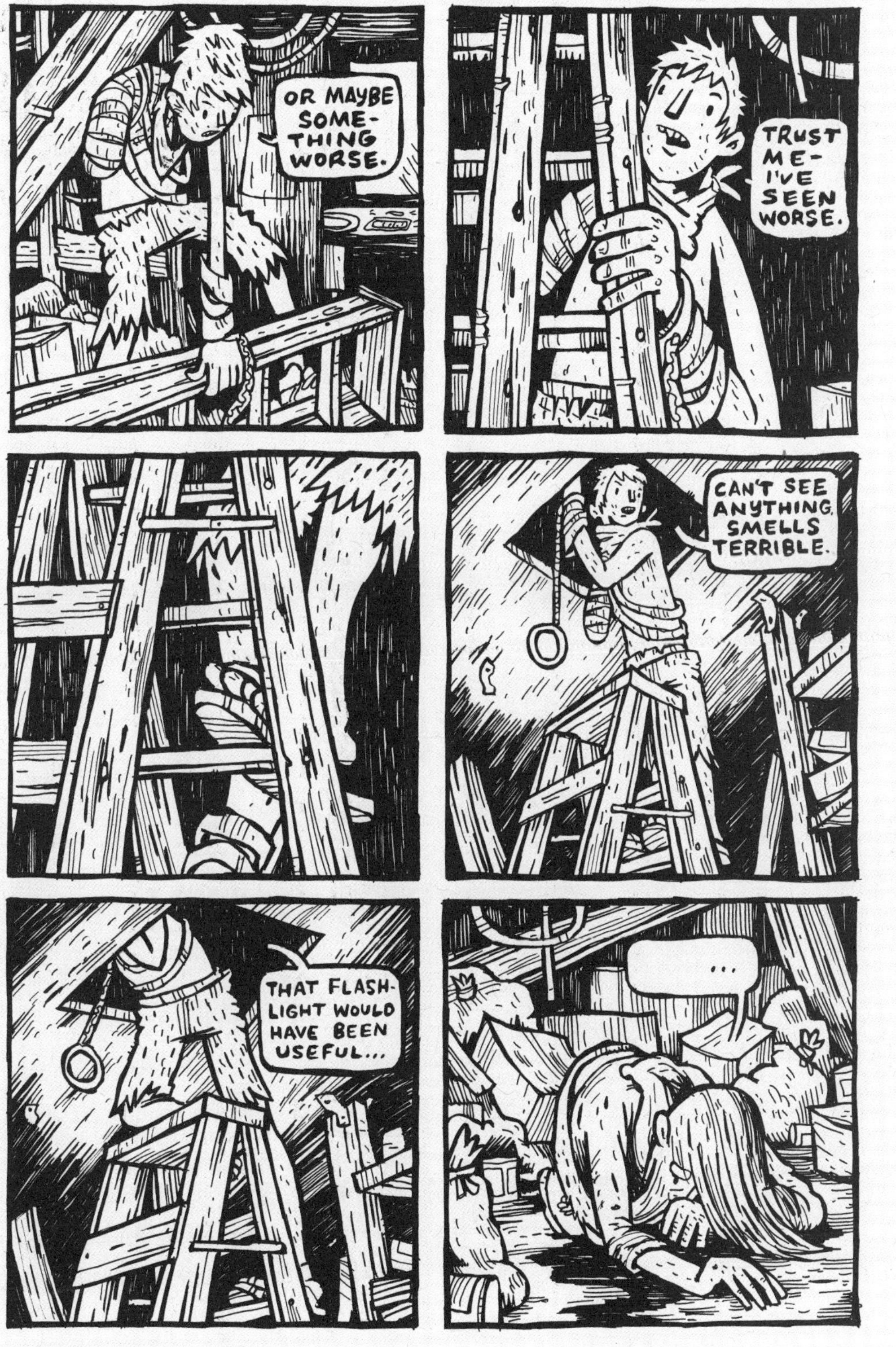
OR MAYBE SOME-THING WORSE.
TRUST ME- I'VE SEEN WORSE.
CAN'T SEE ANYTHING, SMELLS TERRIBLE.
THAT FLASH-LIGHT WOULD HAVE BEEN USEFUL...
...

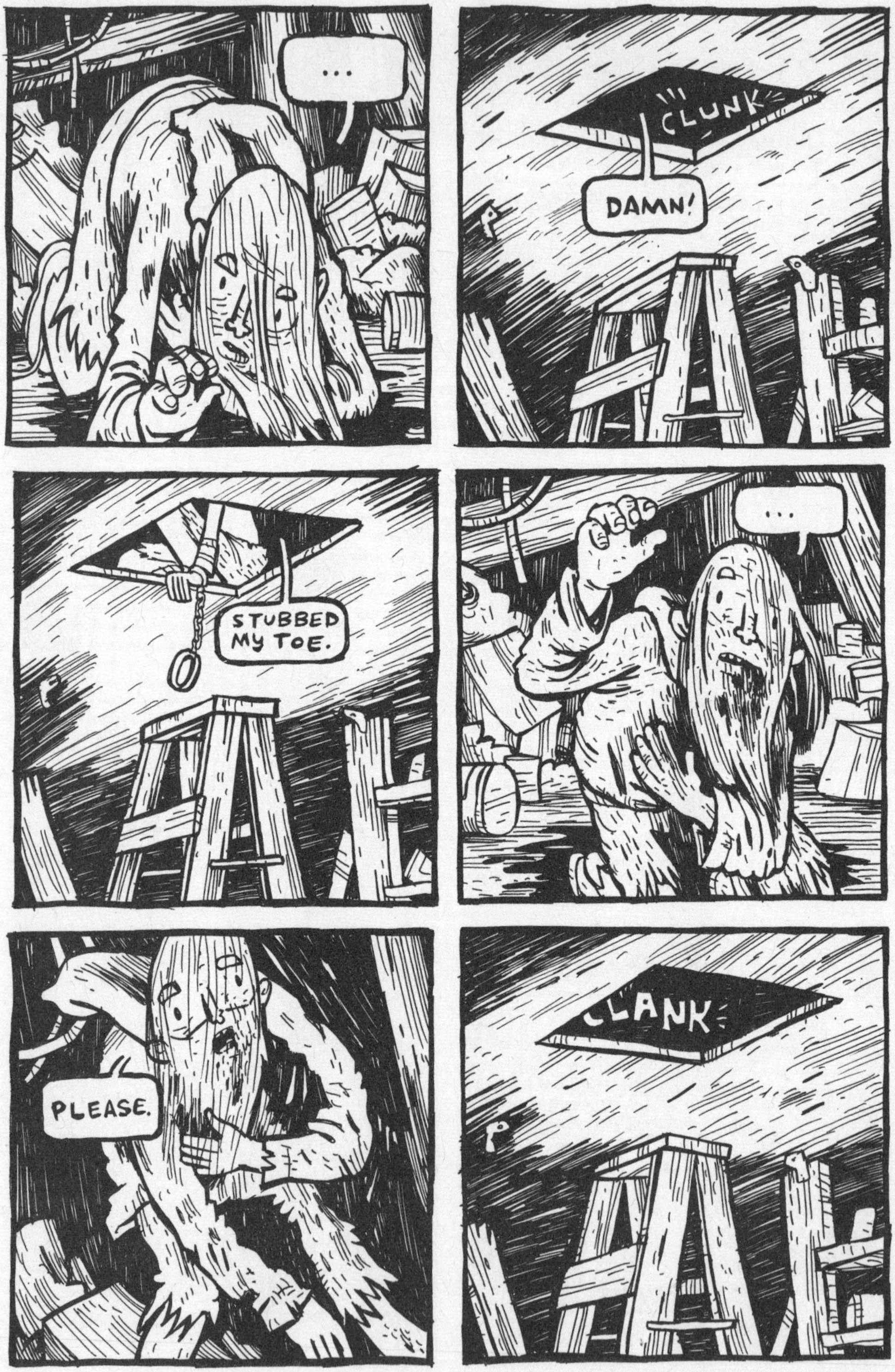
...
CLUNK
DAMN!
STUBBED MY TOE.
...
PLEASE.
CLANK

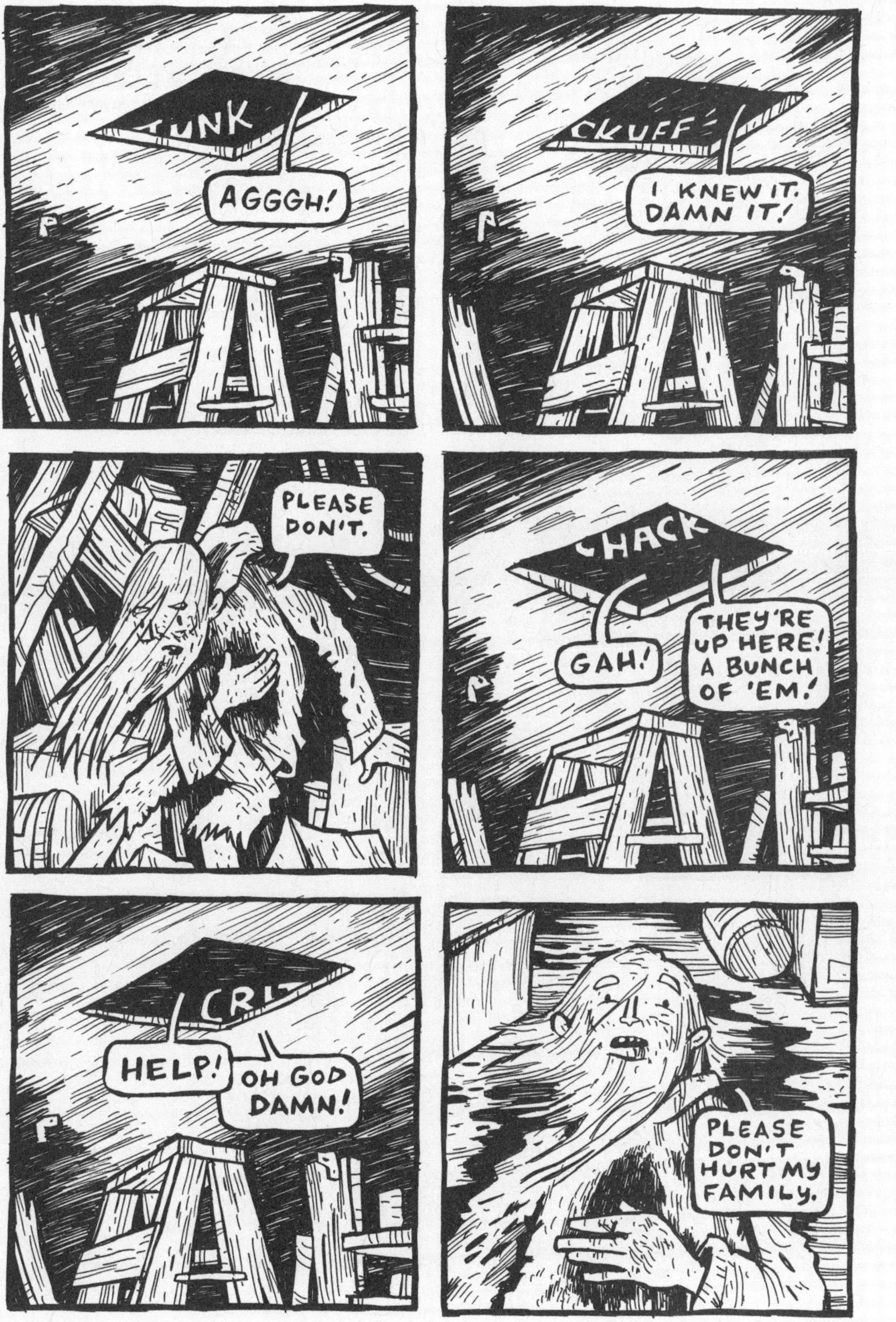
TUNK
AGGGH!
CKUFF
I KNEW IT. DAMN IT!
PLEASE DON'T.
CHACK
GAH!
THEY'RE UP HERE! A BUNCH OF 'EM!
CRI
HELP!
OH GOD DAMN!
PLEASE DON'T HURT MY FAMILY.

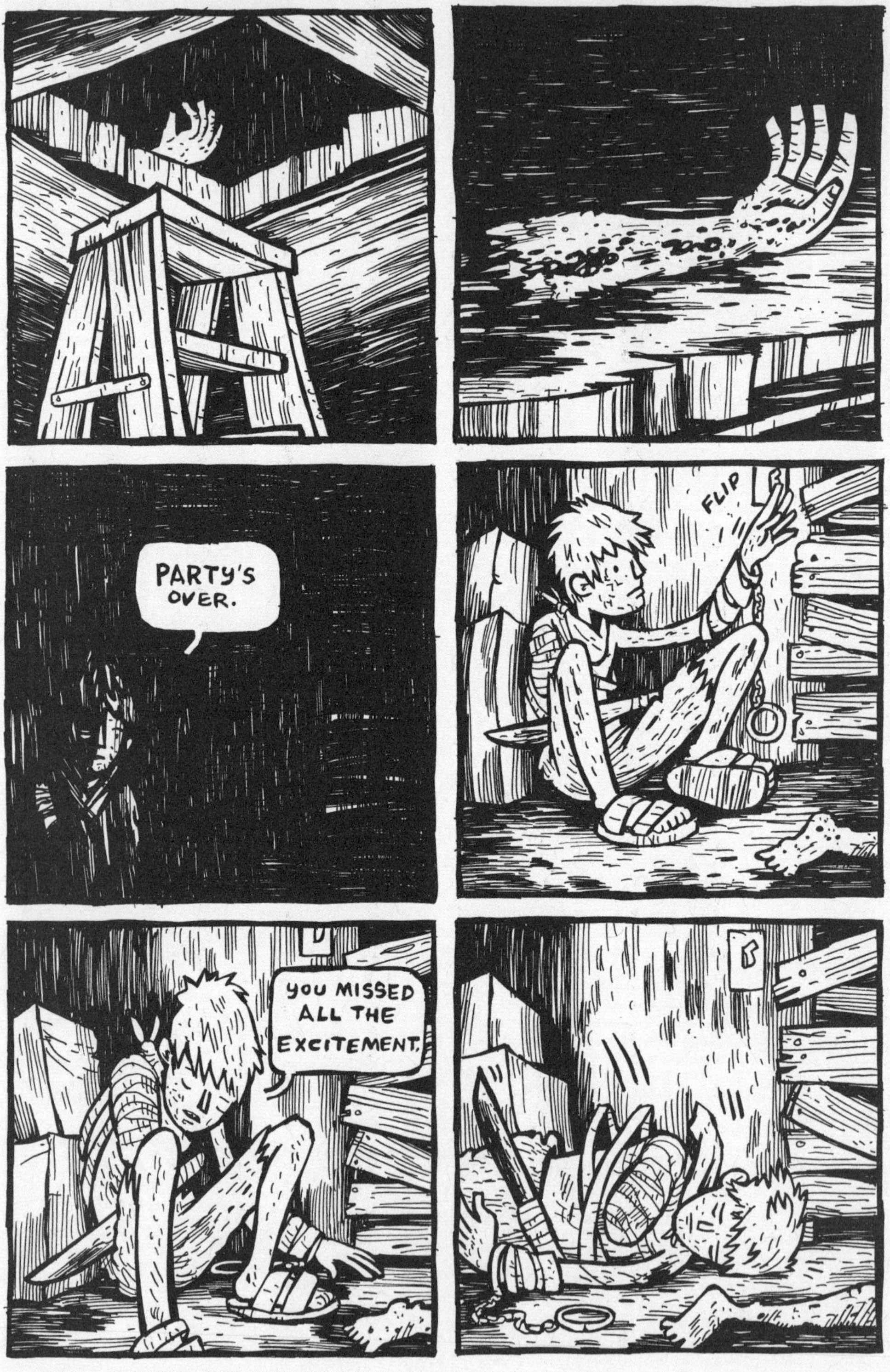
PARTY'S OVER.
FLIP
YOU MISSED ALL THE EXCITEMENT.

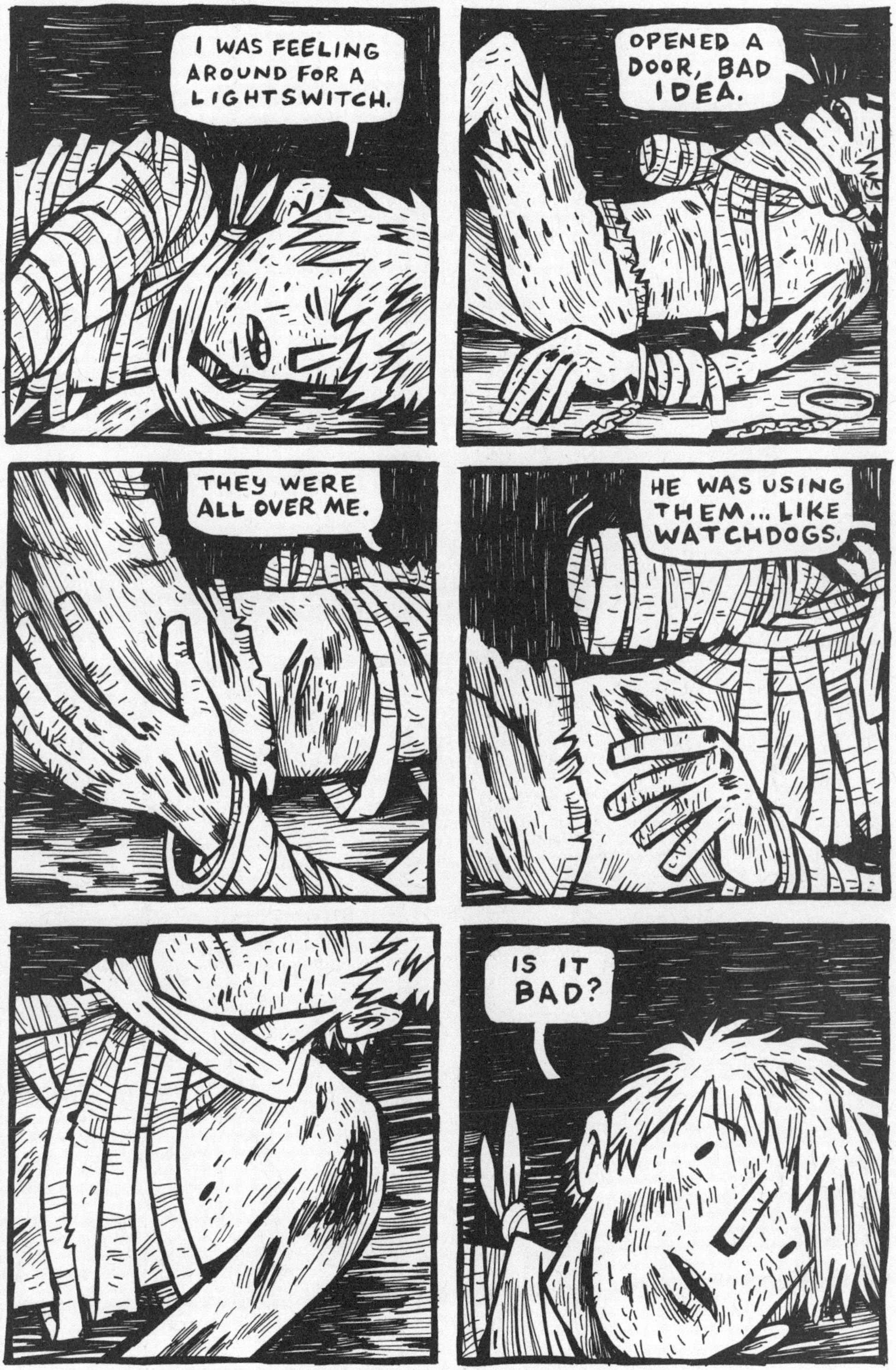
I WAS FEELING AROUND FOR A LIGHTSWITCH.
OPENED A DOOR, BAD IDEA.
THEY WERE ALL OVER ME.
HE WAS USING THEM... LIKE WATCHDOGS.
IS IT BAD?

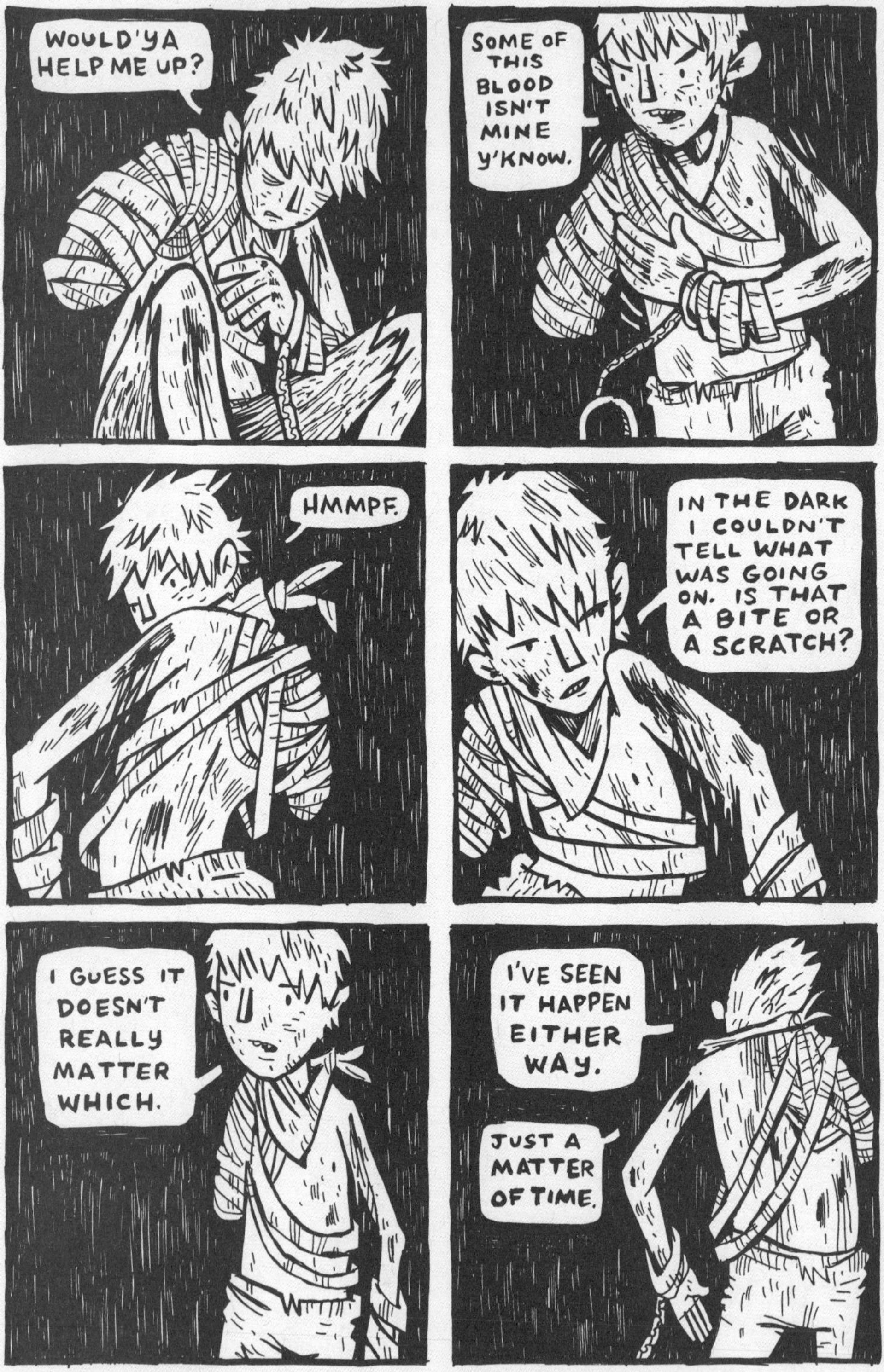
WOULD'YA HELP ME UP?
SOME OF THIS BLOOD ISN'T MINE Y'KNOW.
HMMPF.
IN THE DARK I COULDN'T TELL WHAT WAS GOING ON. IS THAT A BITE OR A SCRATCH?
I GUESS IT DOESN'T REALLY MATTER WHICH.
I'VE SEEN IT HAPPEN EITHER WAY.
JUST A MATTER OF TIME.

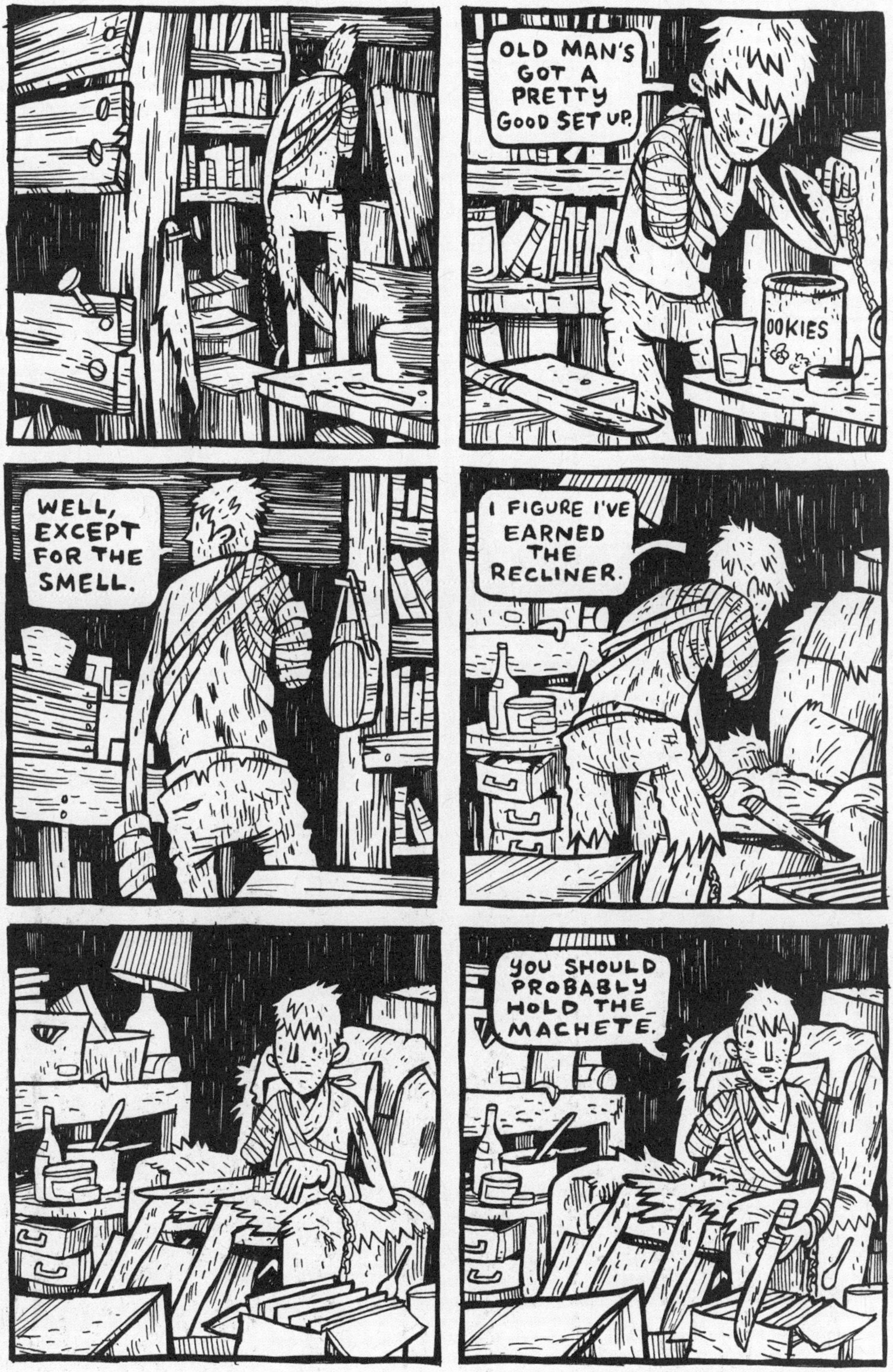
OLD MAN'S GOT A PRETTY GOOD SET UP.
OOKIES
WELL, EXCEPT FOR THE SMELL.
I FIGURE I'VE EARNED THE RECLINER.
YOU SHOULD PROBABLY HOLD THE MACHETE.

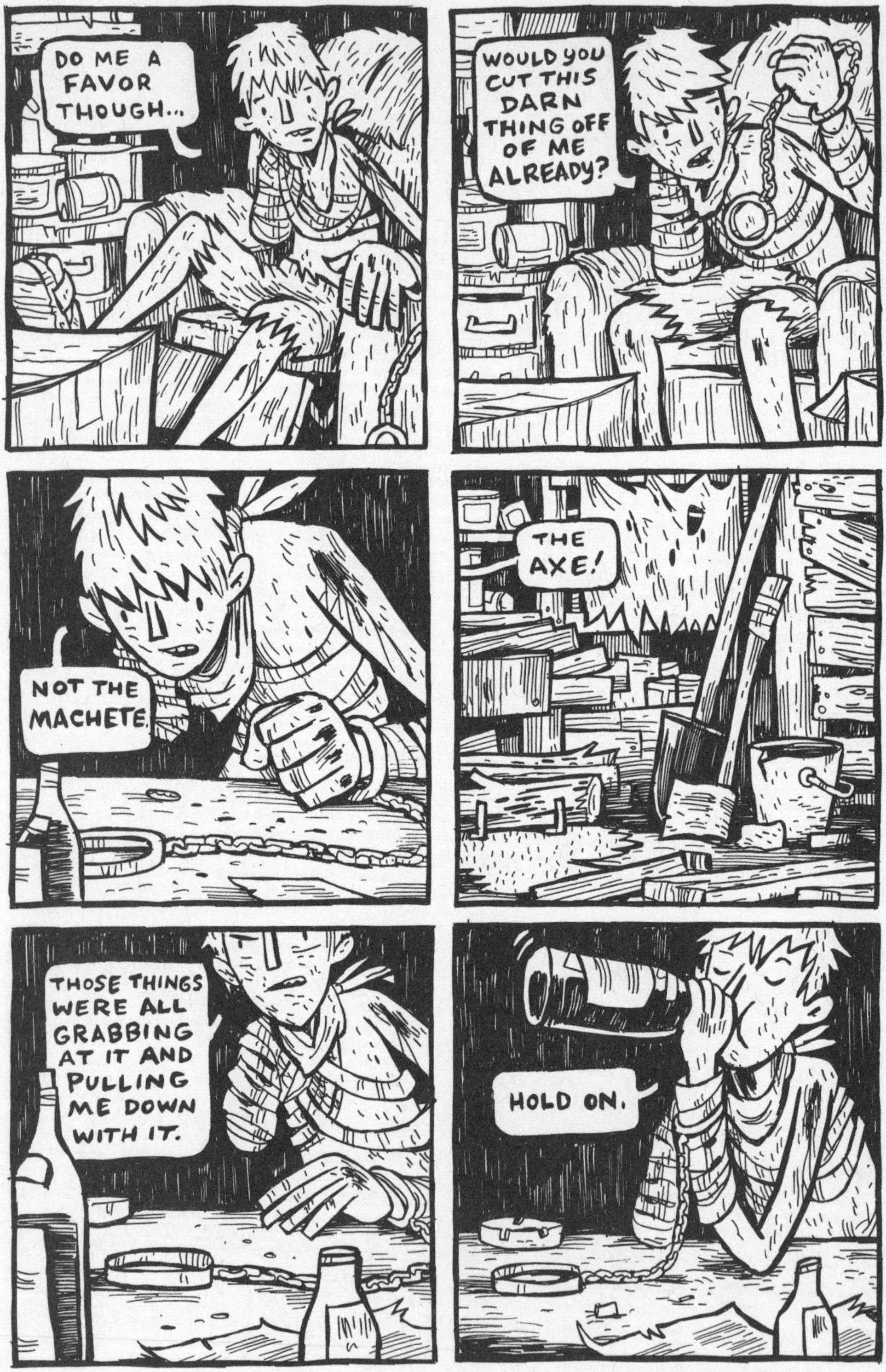
DO ME A FAVOR THOUGH...
WOULD YOU CUT THIS DARN THING OFF OF ME ALREADY?
NOT THE MACHETE.
THE AXE!
THOSE THINGS WERE ALL GRABBING AT IT AND PULLING ME DOWN WITH IT.
HOLD ON.

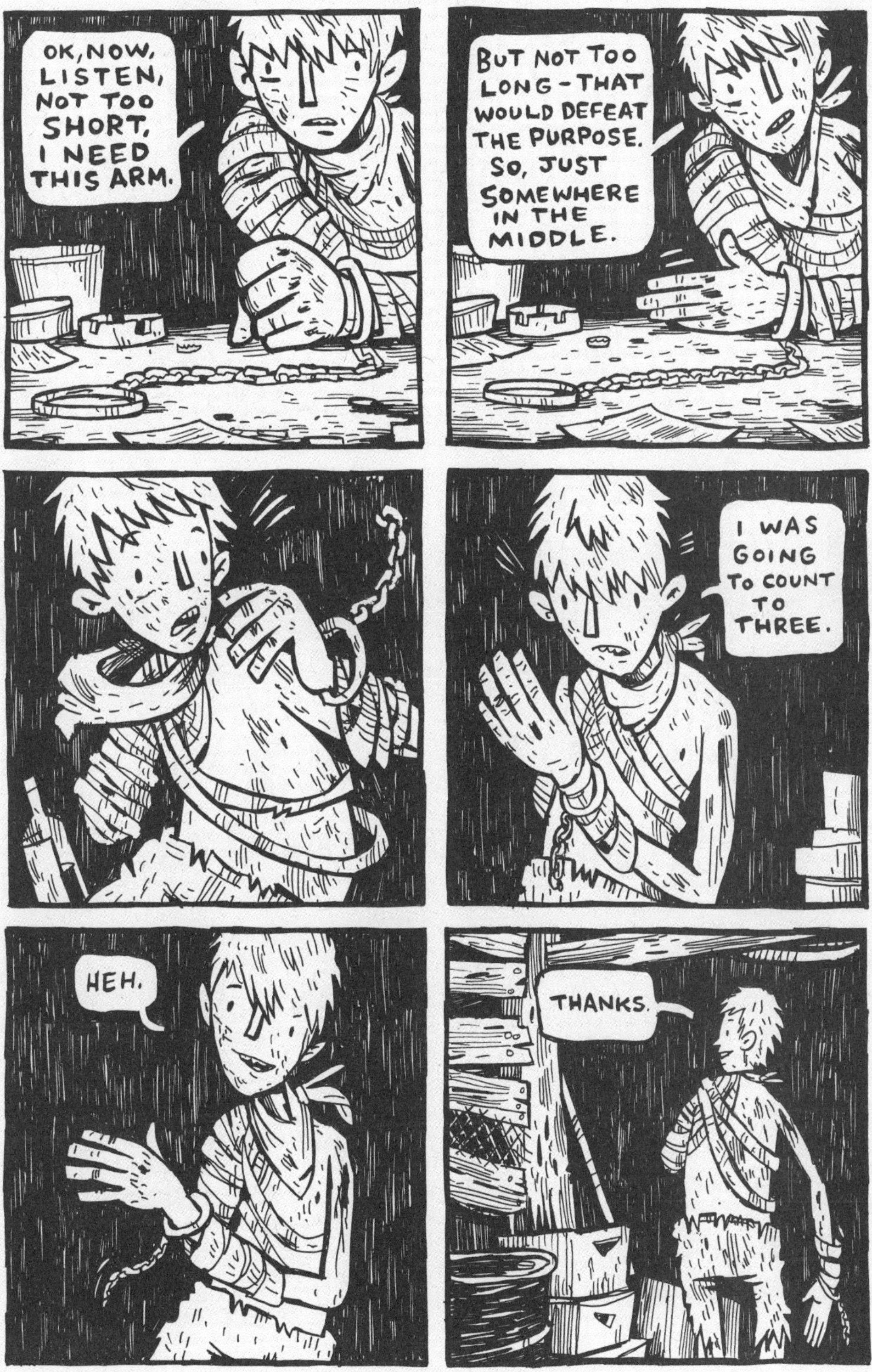
OK, NOW, LISTEN, NOT TOO SHORT, I NEED THIS ARM.
BUT NOT TOO LONG - THAT WOULD DEFEAT THE PURPOSE. SO, JUST SOMEWHERE IN THE MIDDLE.
I WAS GOING TO COUNT TO THREE.
HEH.
THANKS.

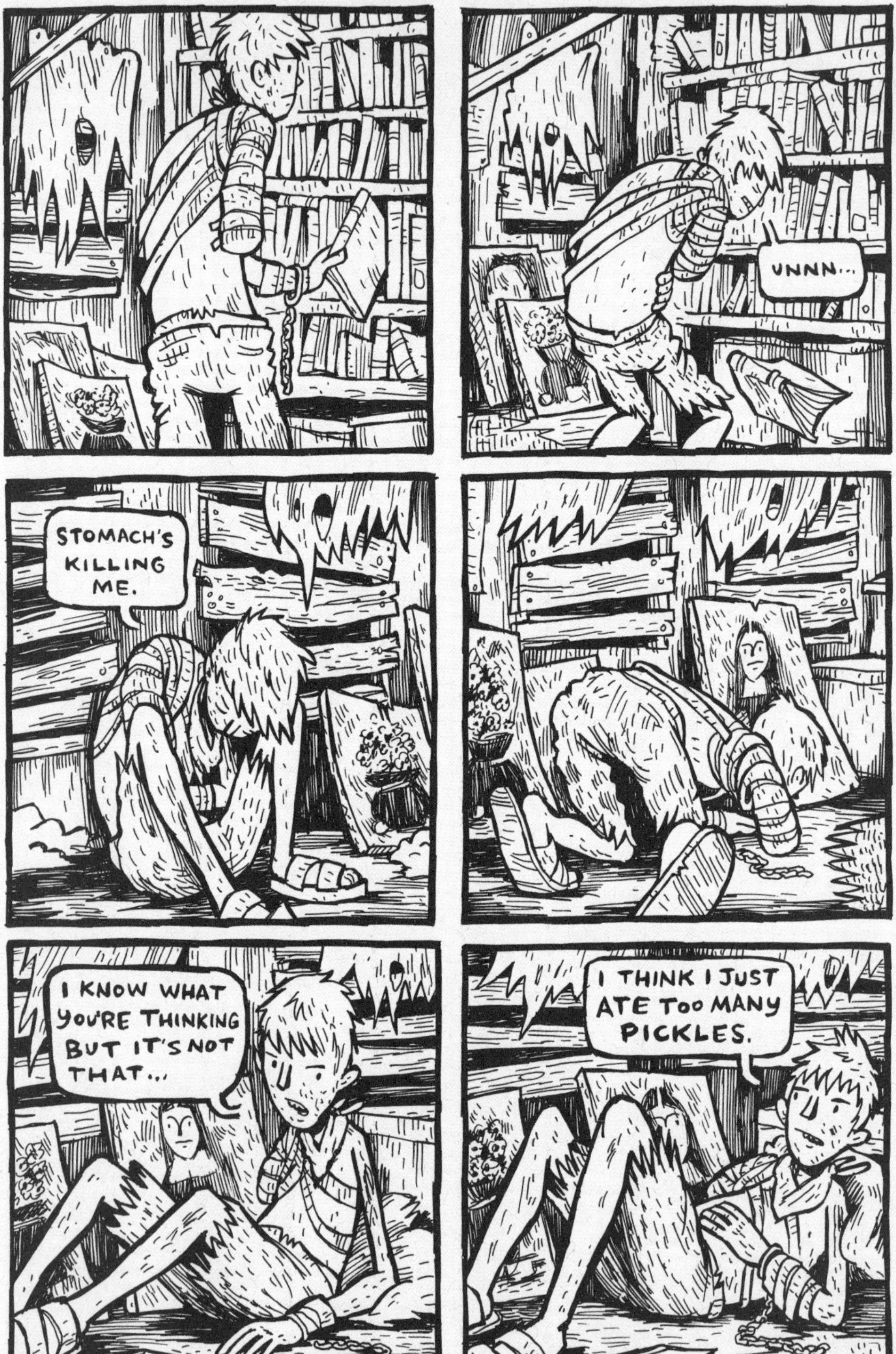
UNNN...
STOMACH'S KILLING ME.
I KNOW WHAT YOU'RE THINKING BUT IT'S NOT THAT...
I THINK I JUST ATE TOO MANY PICKLES.

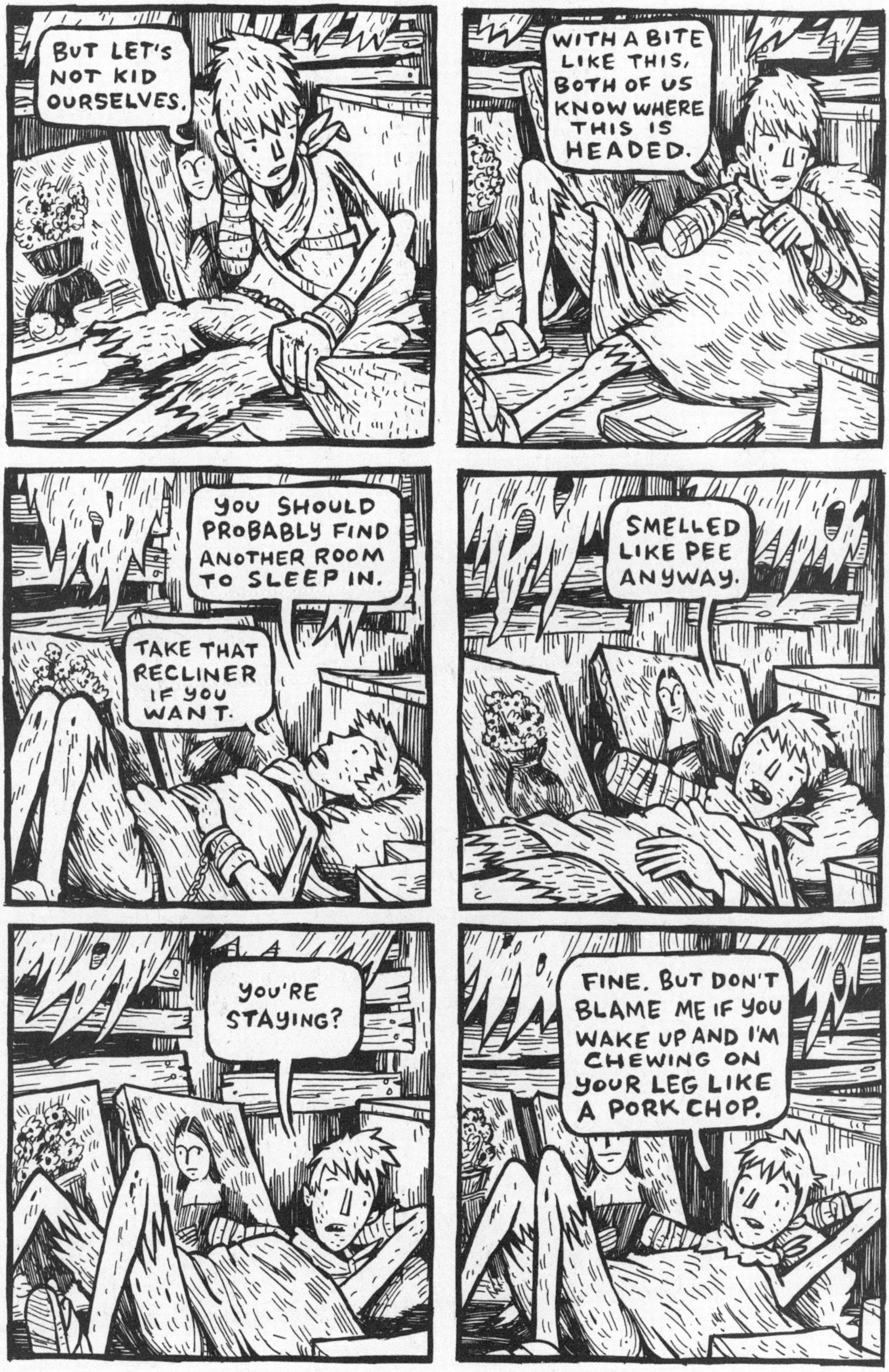

BUT LET'S NOT KID OURSELVES.
WITH A BITE LIKE THIS, BOTH OF US KNOW WHERE THIS IS HEADED.
YOU SHOULD PROBABLY FIND ANOTHER ROOM TO SLEEP IN.
TAKE THAT RECLINER IF YOU WANT.
SMELLED LIKE PEE ANYWAY.
YOU'RE STAYING?
FINE. BUT DON'T BLAME ME IF YOU WAKE UP AND I'M CHEWING ON YOUR LEG LIKE A PORK CHOP.

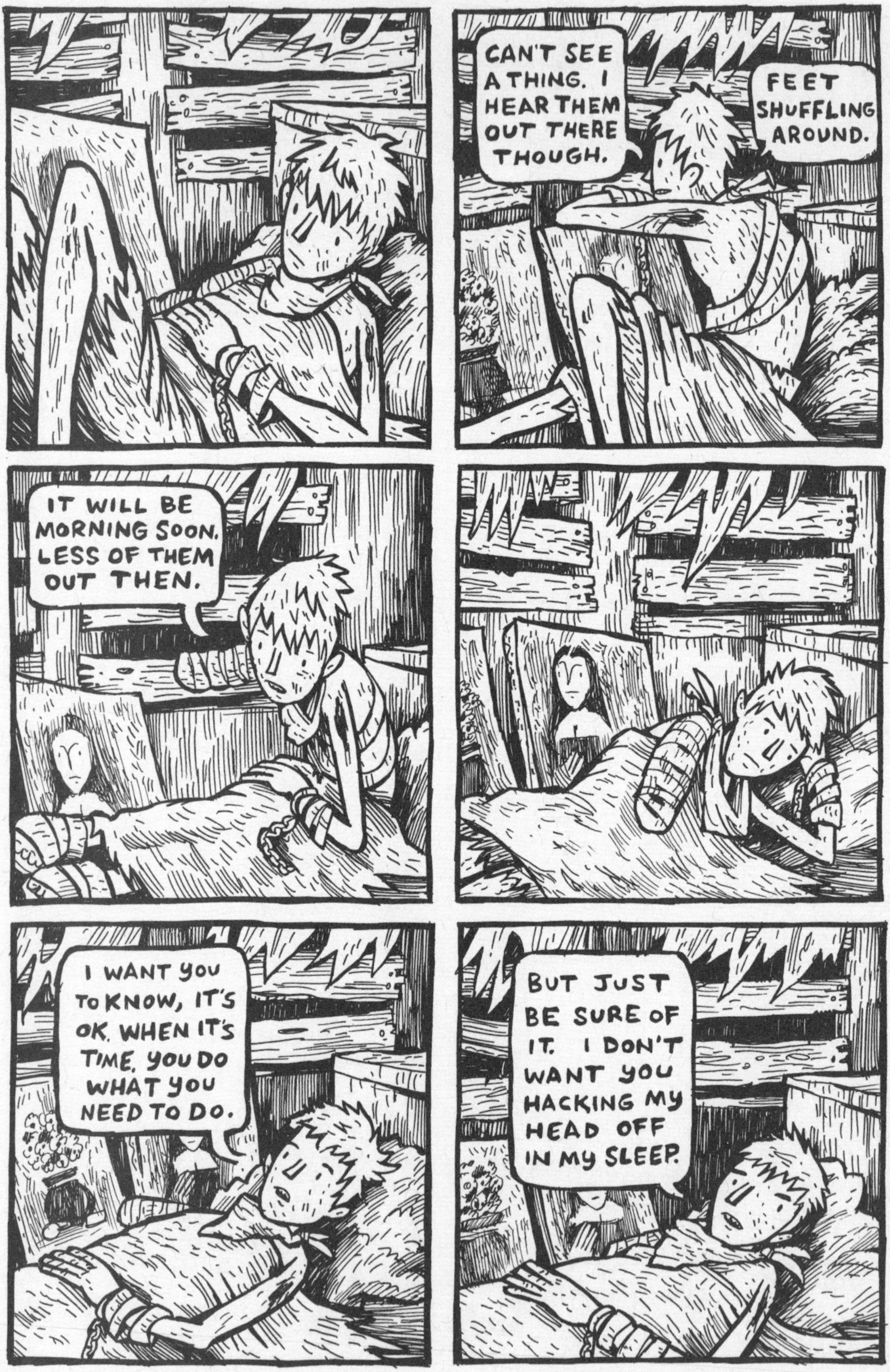
CAN'T SEE A THING. I HEAR THEM OUT THERE THOUGH.
FEET SHUFFLING AROUND.
IT WILL BE MORNING SOON. LESS OF THEM OUT THEN.
I WANT YOU TO KNOW, IT'S OK. WHEN IT'S TIME, YOU DO WHAT YOU NEED TO DO.
BUT JUST BE SURE OF IT. I DON'T WANT YOU HACKING MY HEAD OFF IN MY SLEEP.

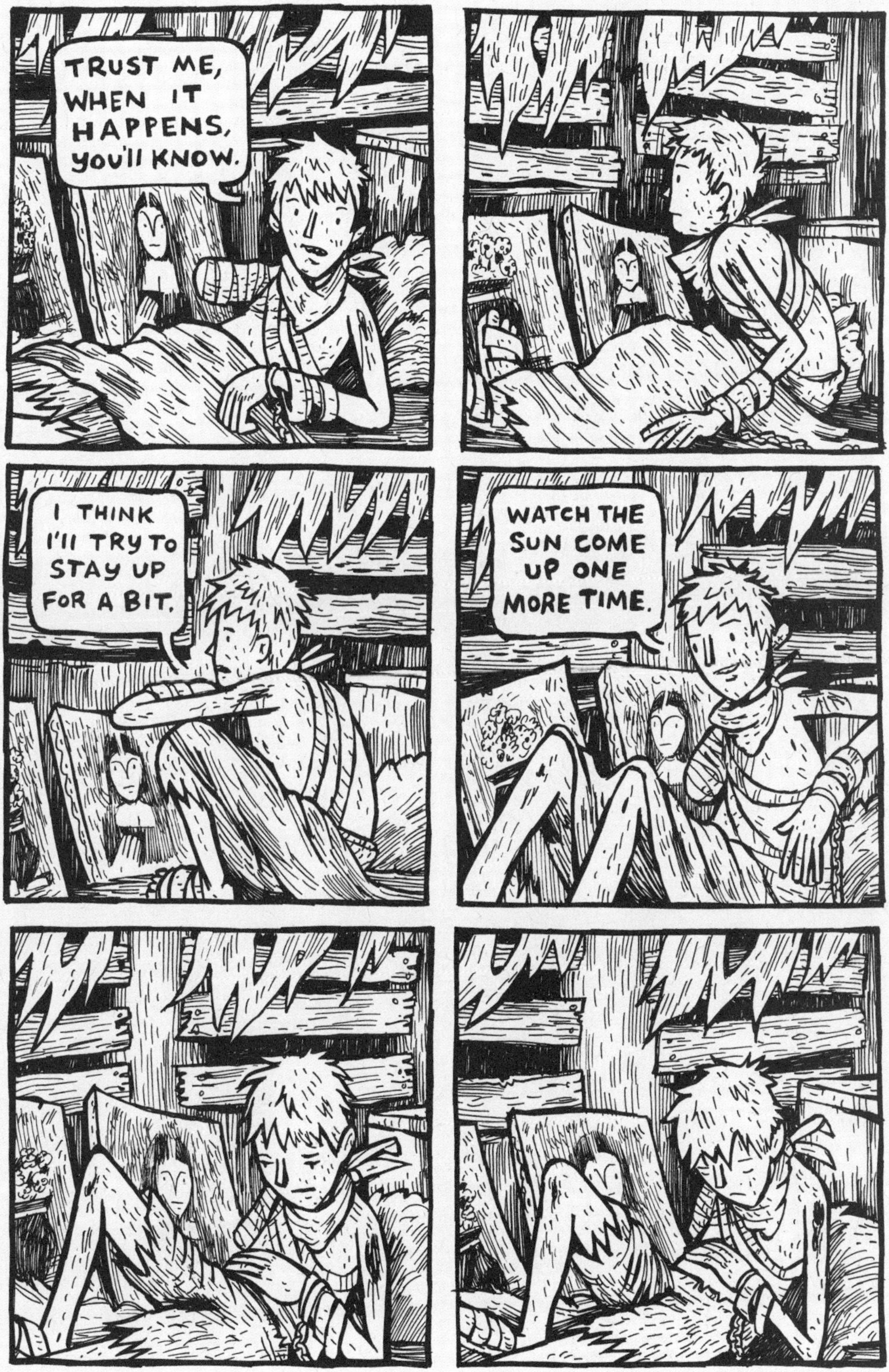
TRUST ME, WHEN IT HAPPENS, you'll KNOW.
I THINK I'll TRY TO STAY UP FOR A BIT.
WATCH THE SUN COME UP ONE MORE TIME.

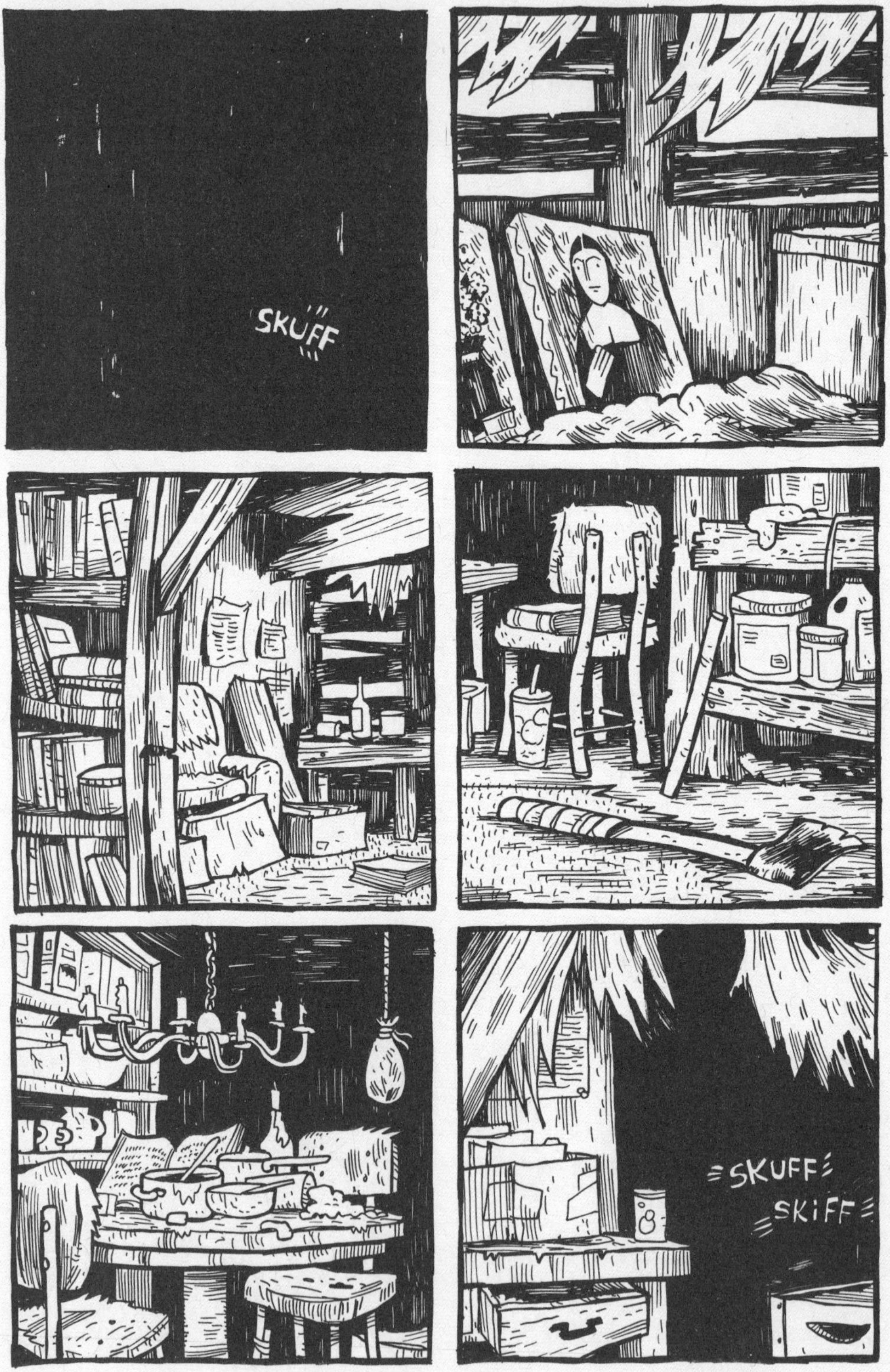
SKUFF
SKUFF
SKIFF

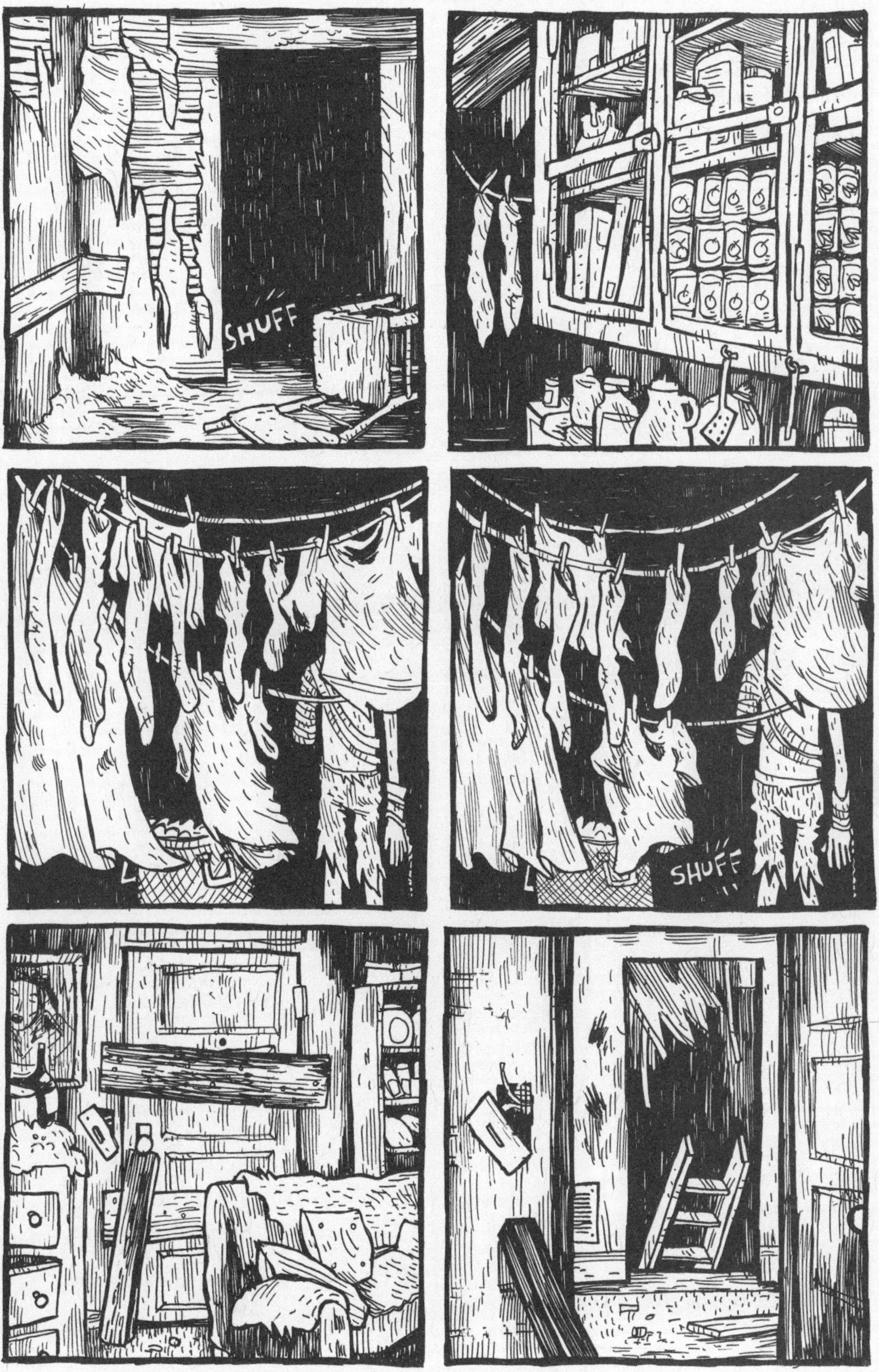
SHUFF
SHUFF

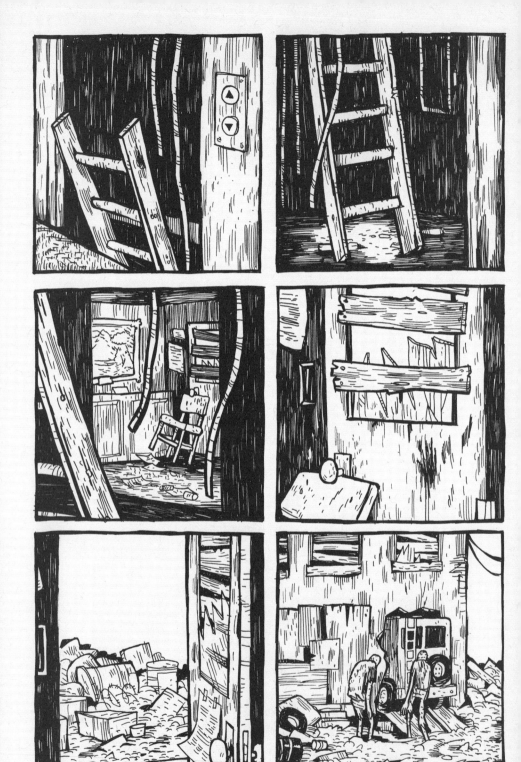

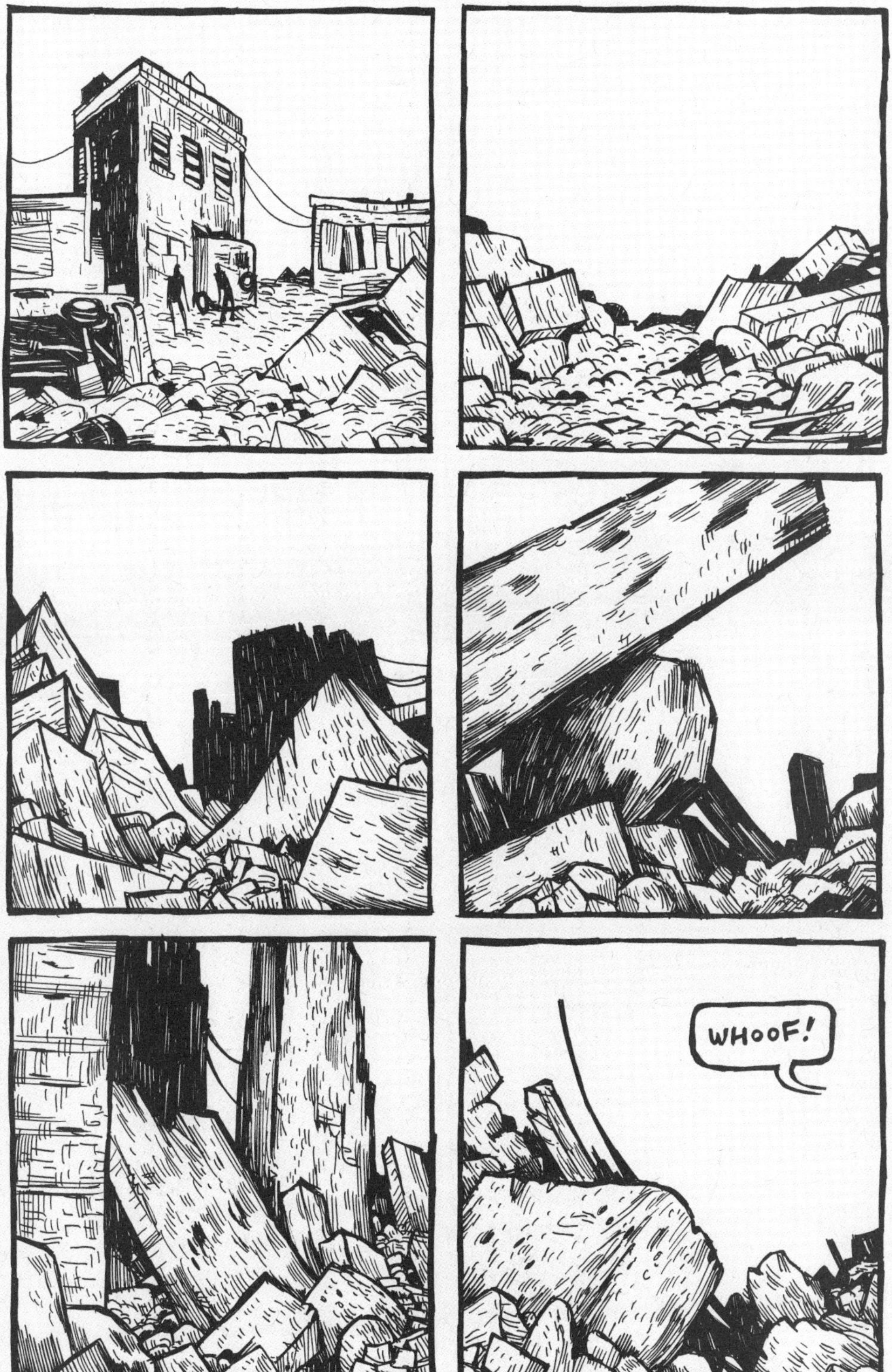
WHOOF!

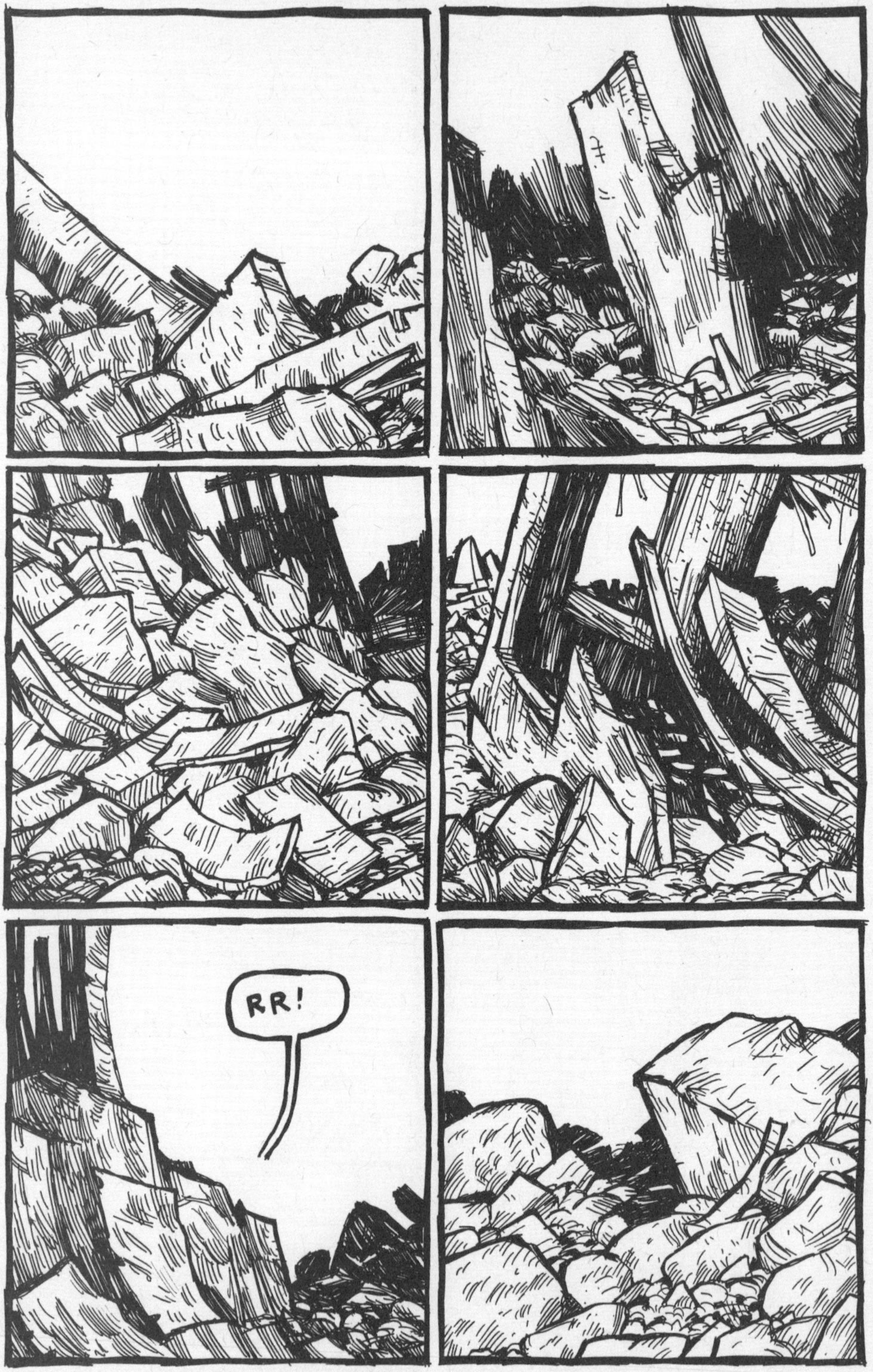
RR!

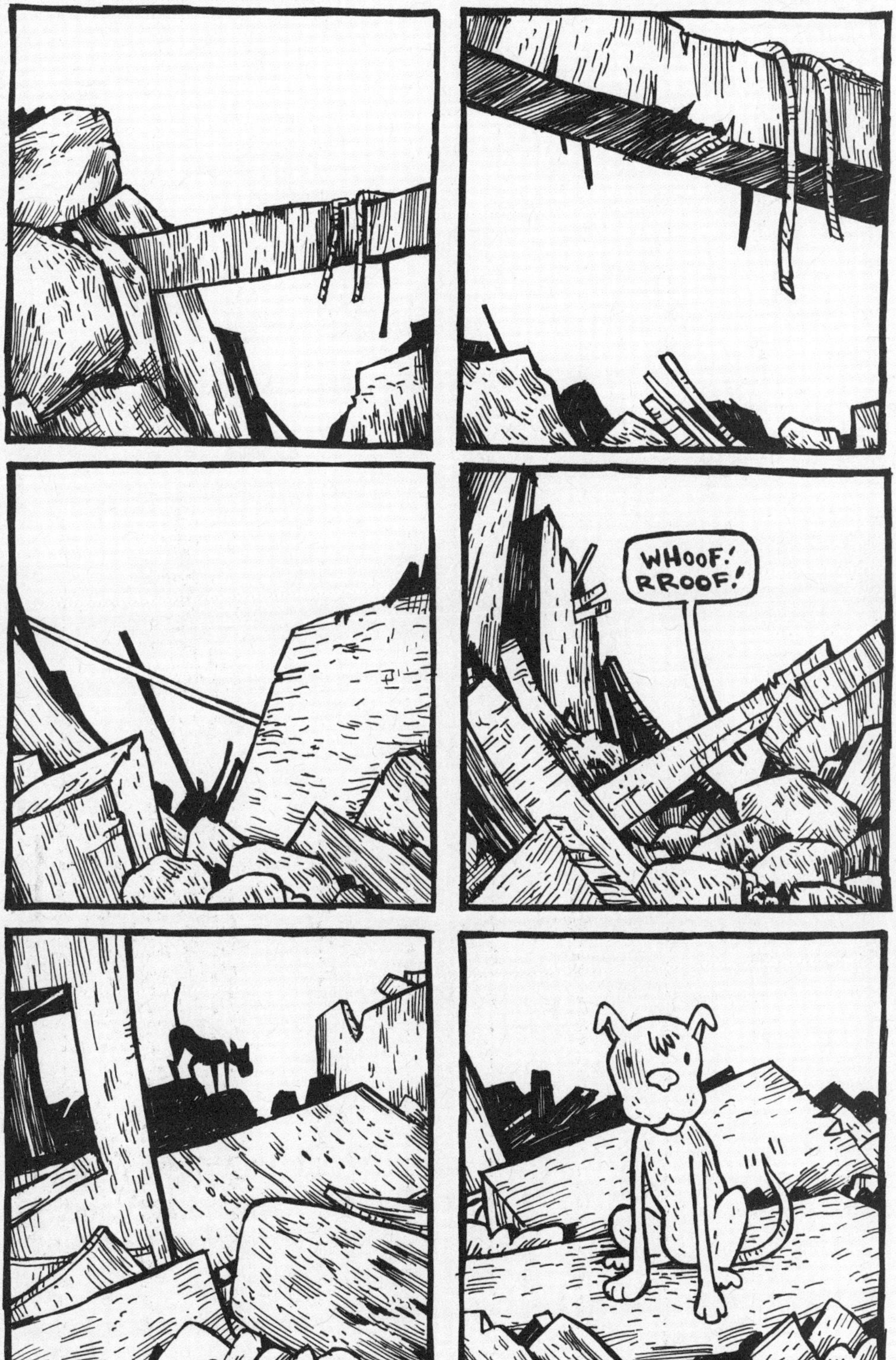
WHOOF! RROOF!

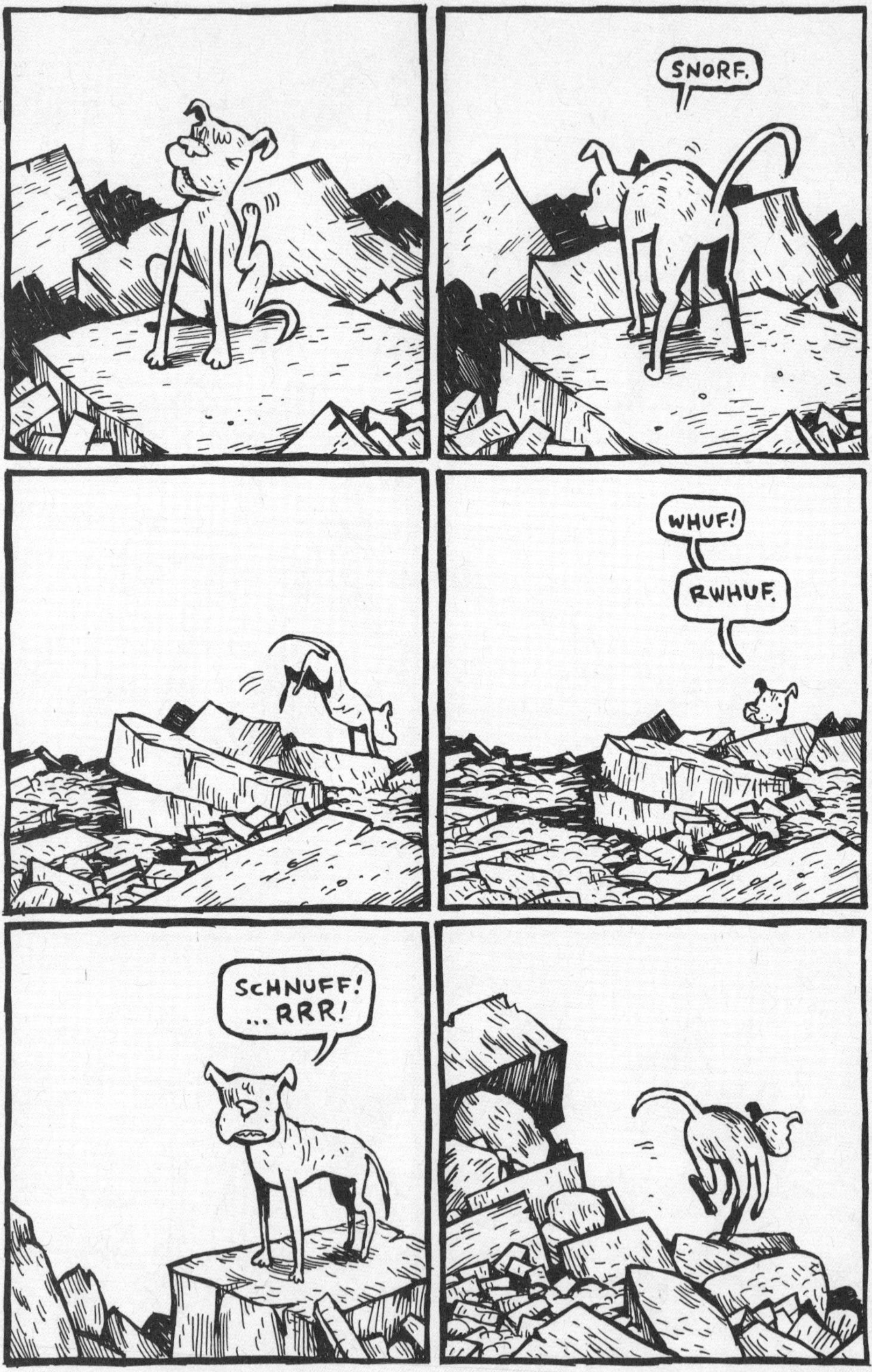
SNORF.
WHUF!
RWHUF.
SCHNUFF! ...RRR!

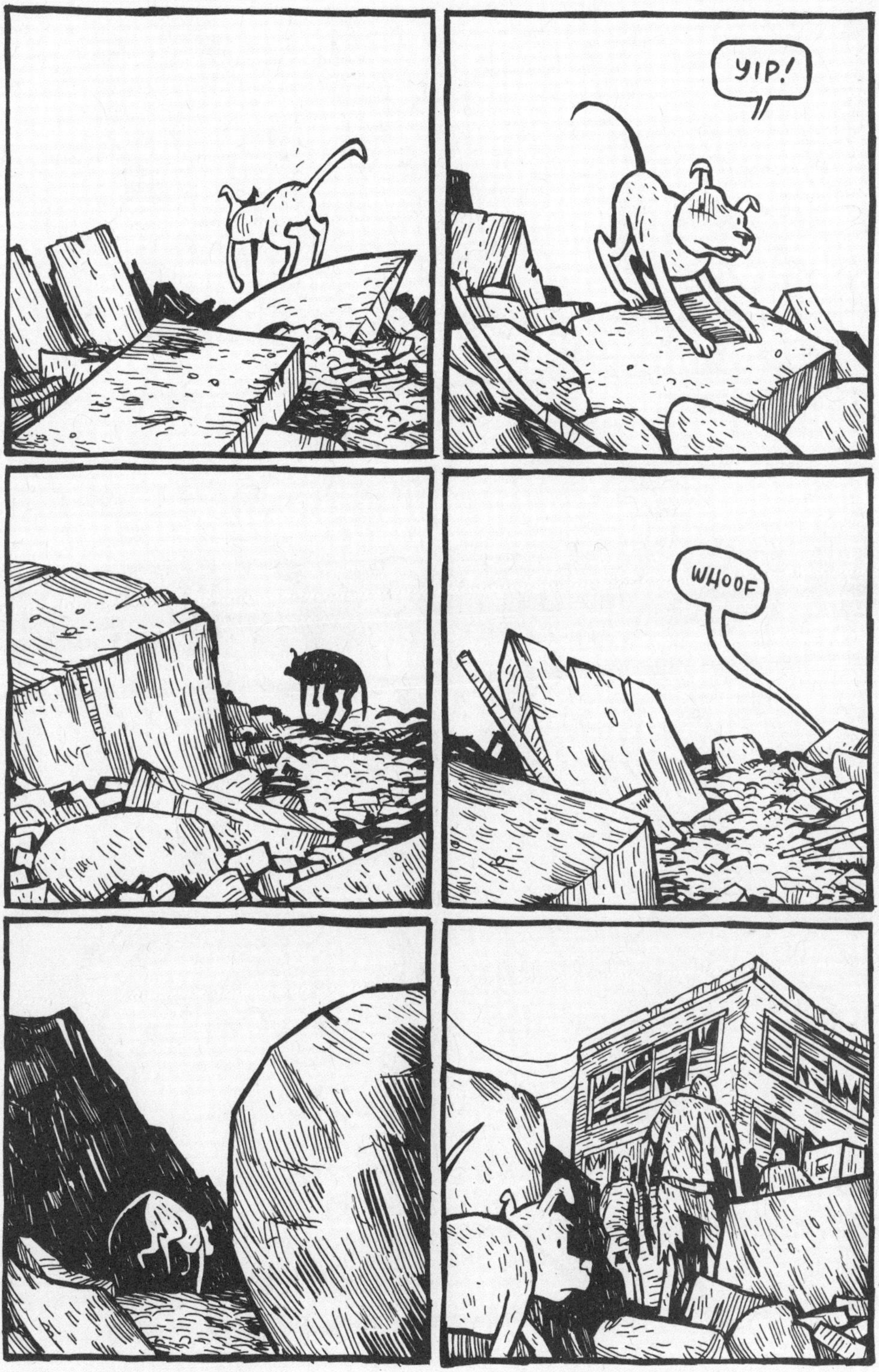
YIP!
WHOOF

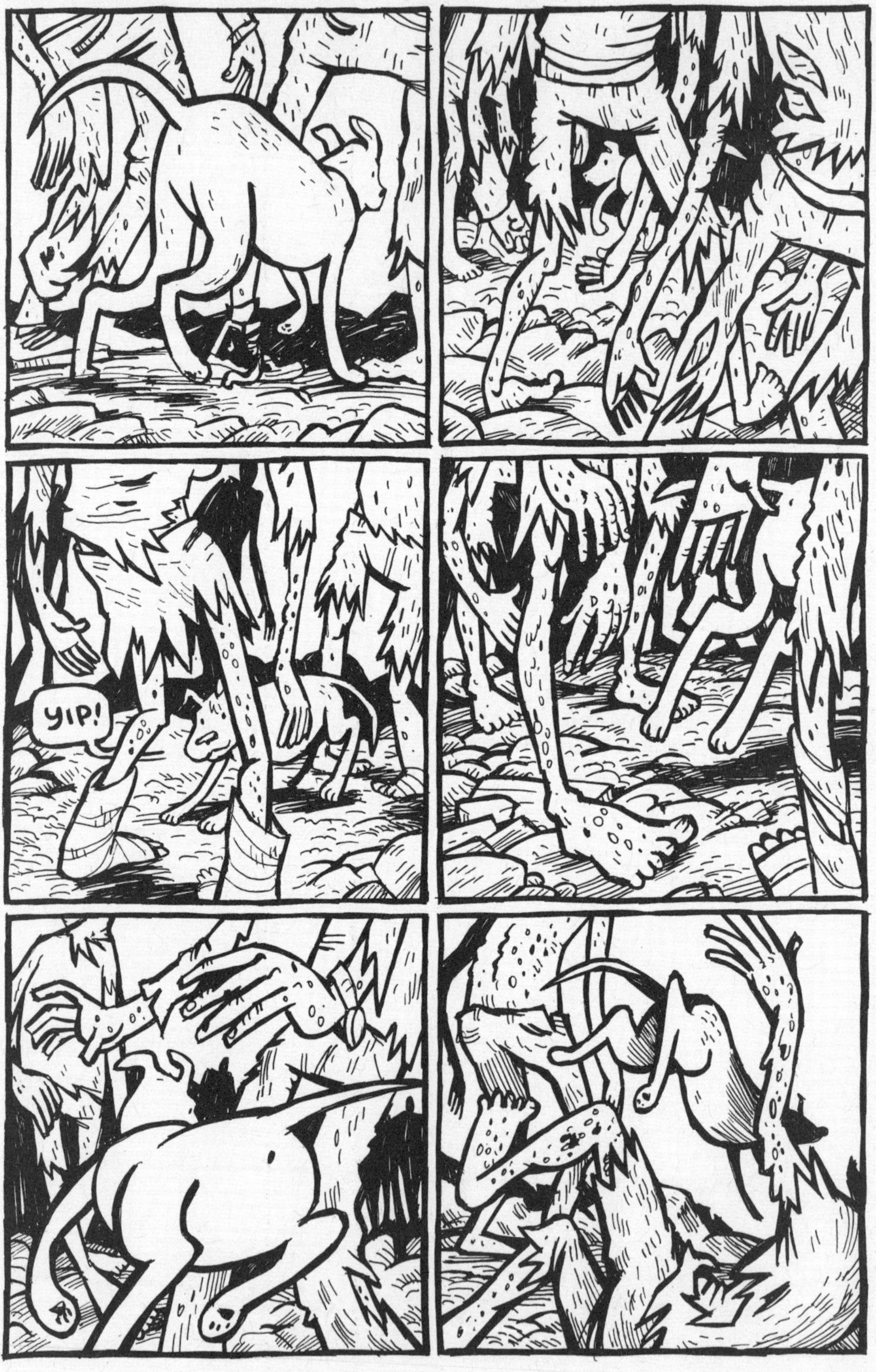
YIP!

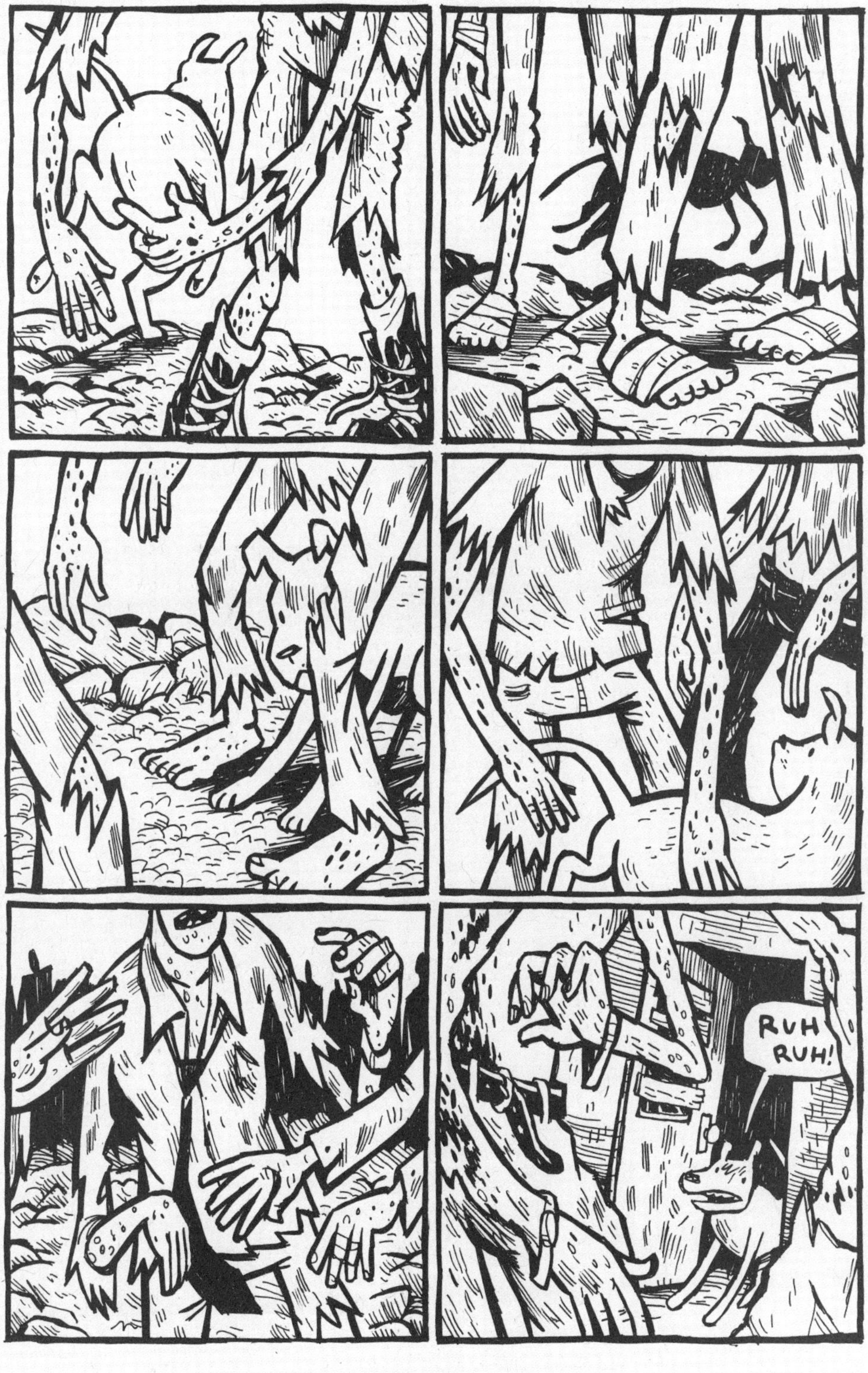
RUH RUH!

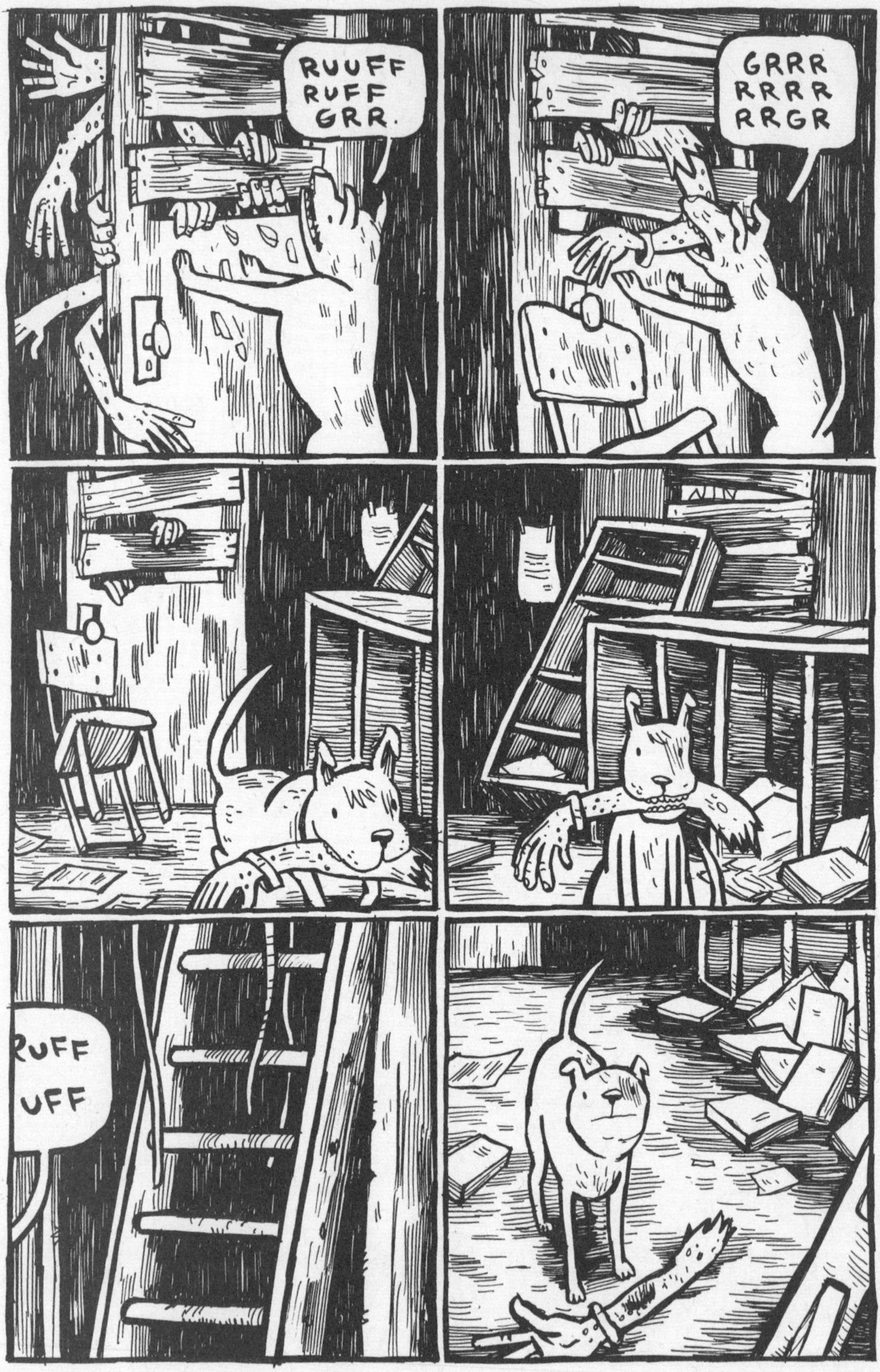
RUUFF
RUFF
GRR.
GRRR
RRRR
RRGR
RUFF
UFF

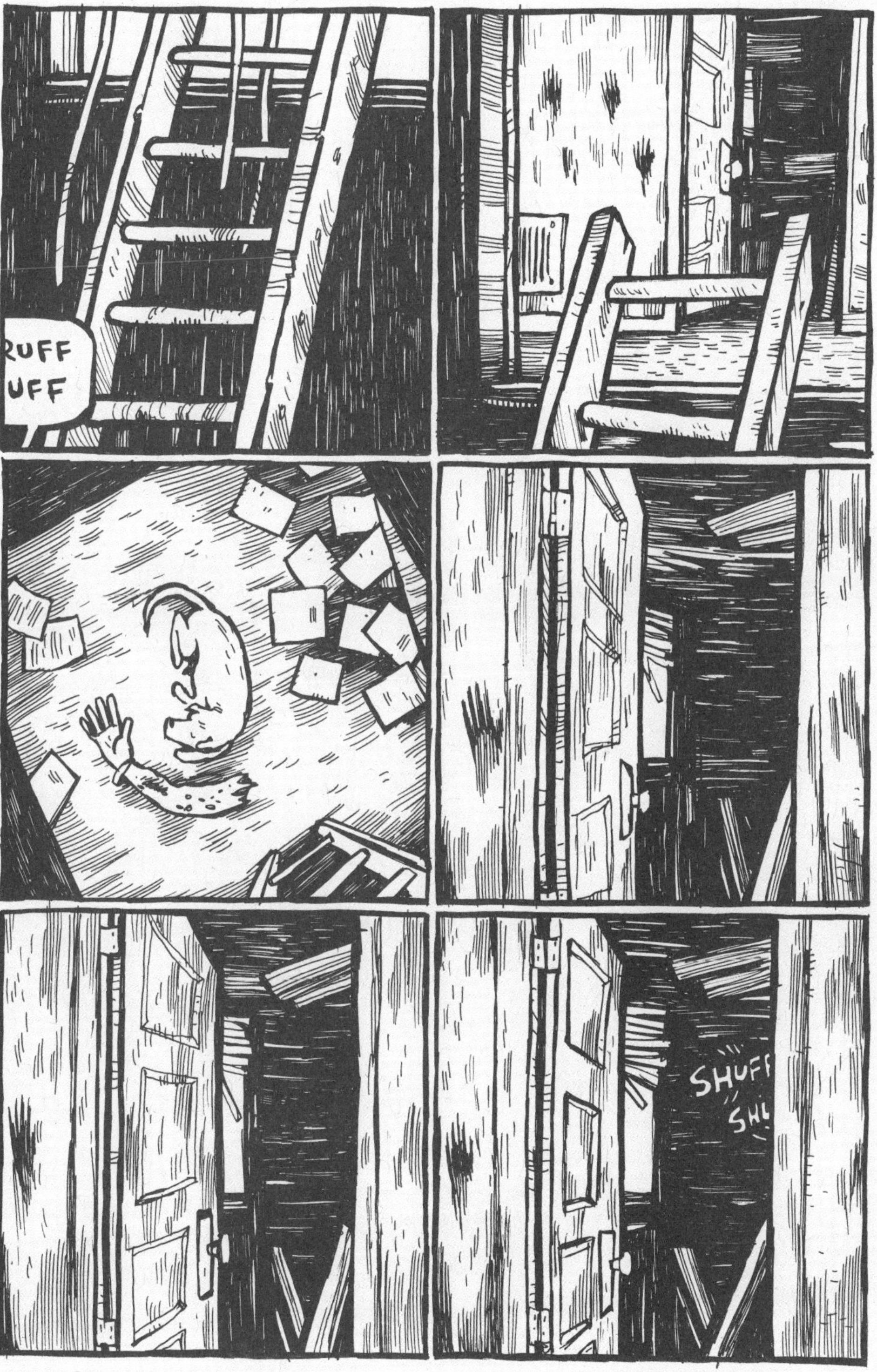
RUFF
UFF
SHUFF
SHU

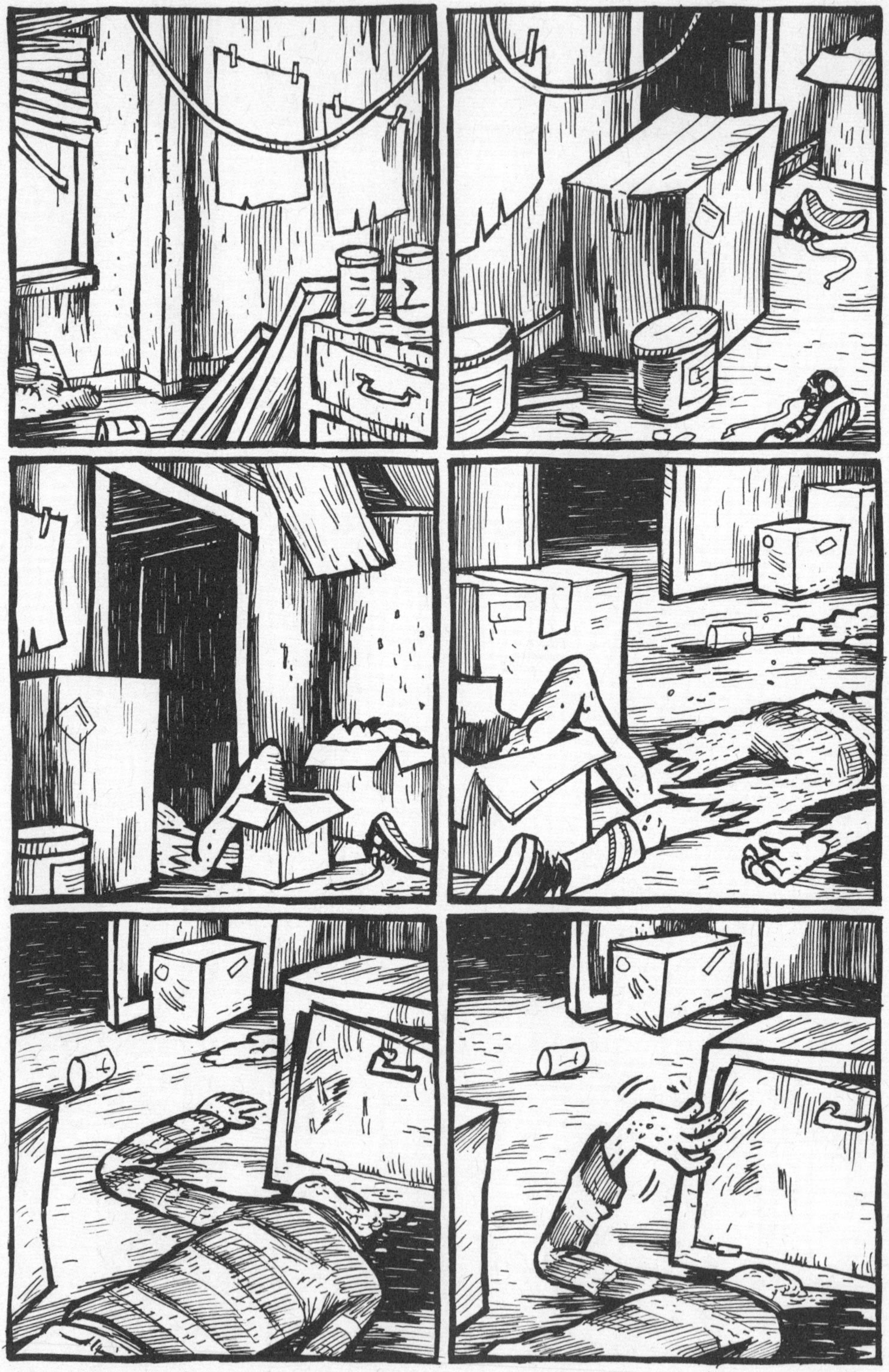

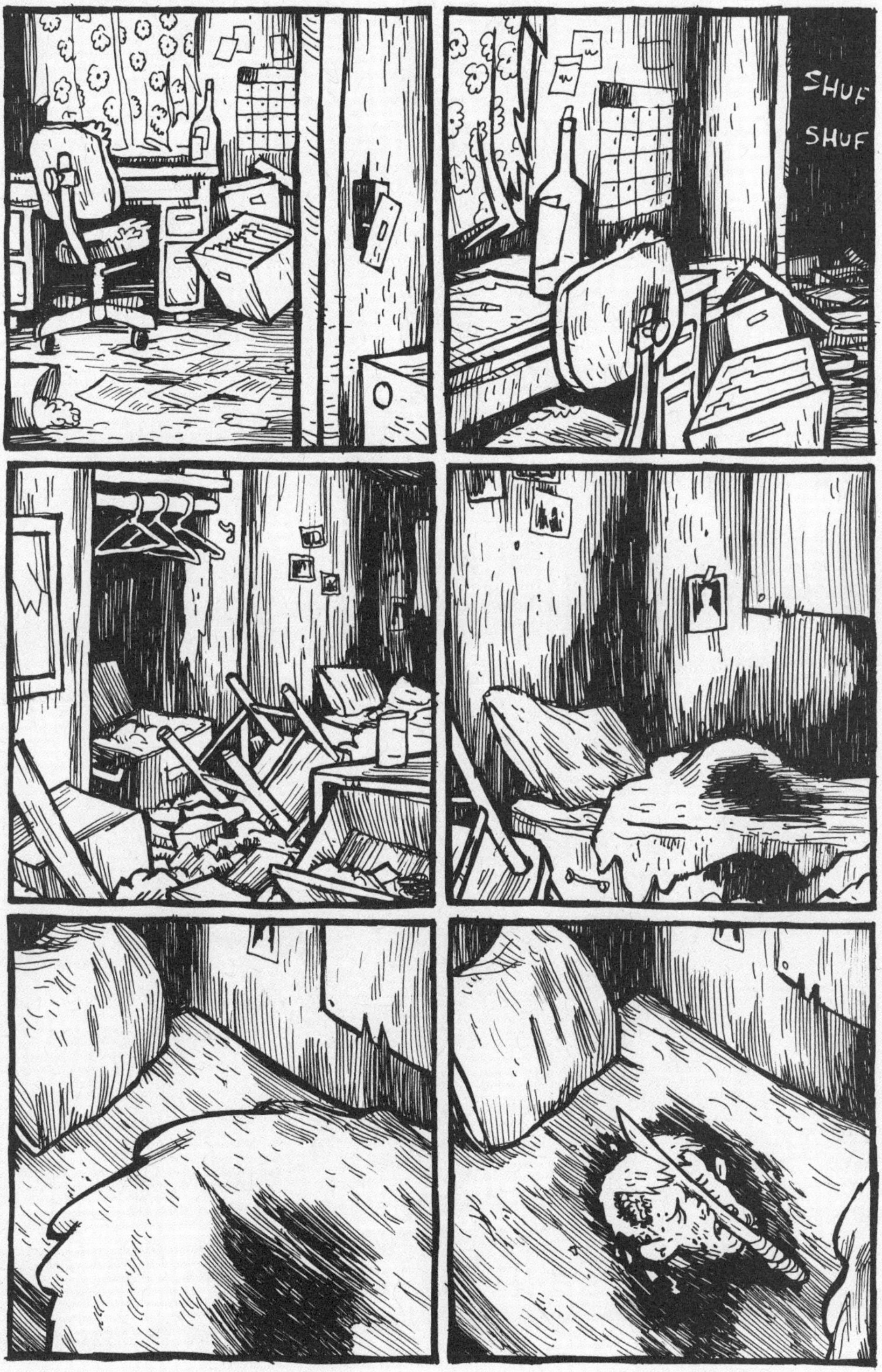
SHUF
SHUF

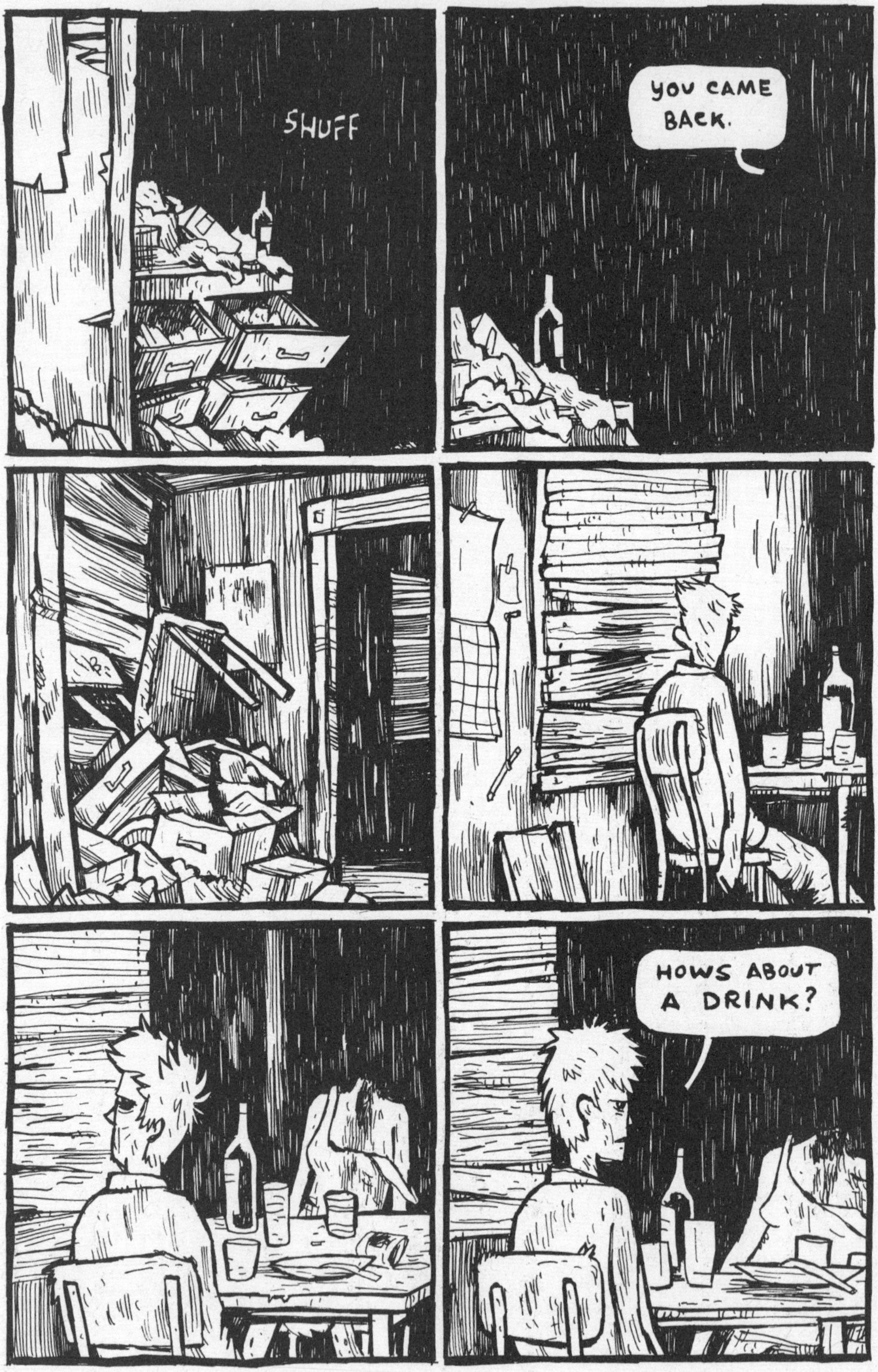
SHUFF
YOU CAME BACK.
HOWS ABOUT A DRINK?

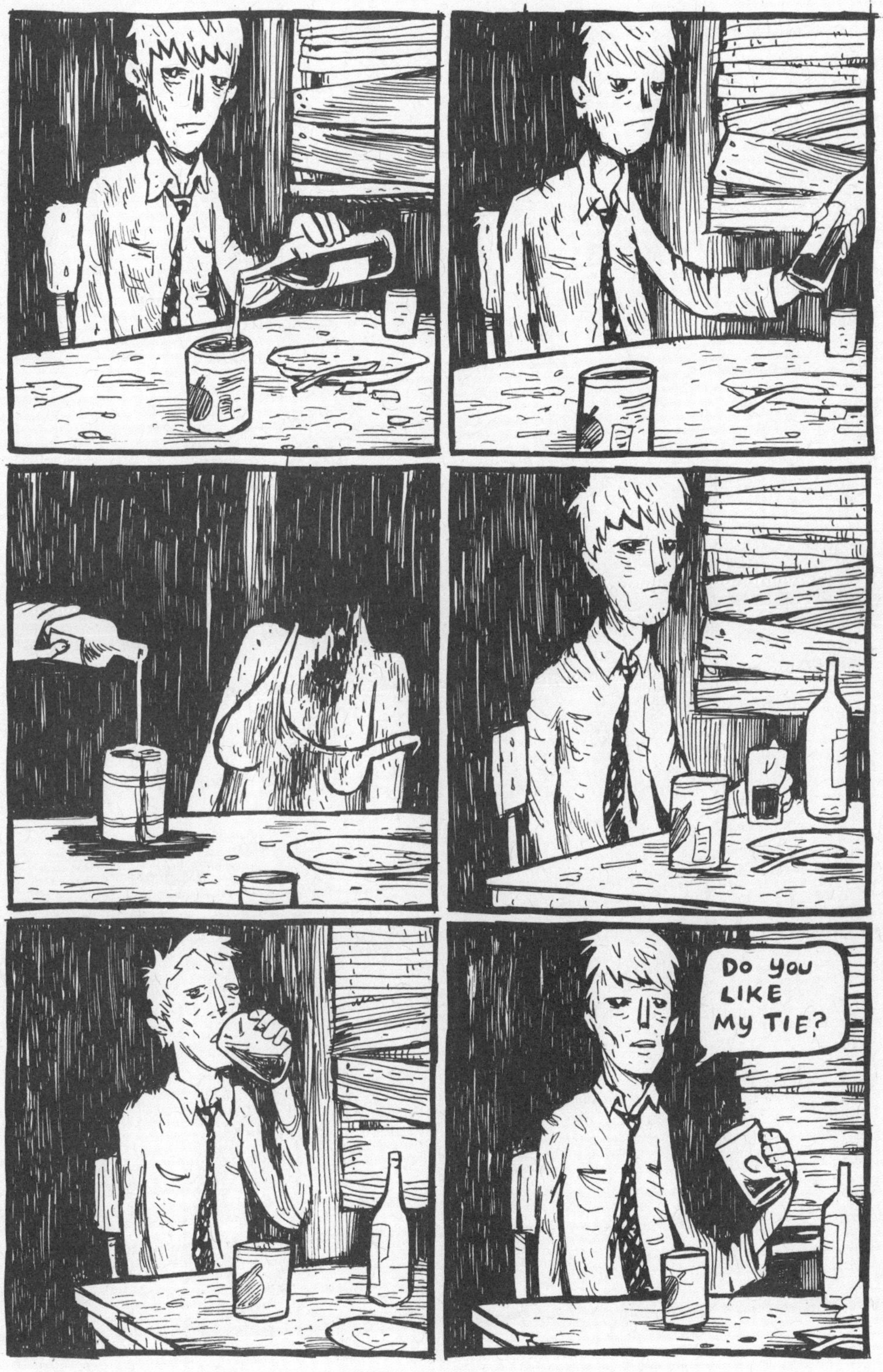
DO YOU LIKE MY TIE?

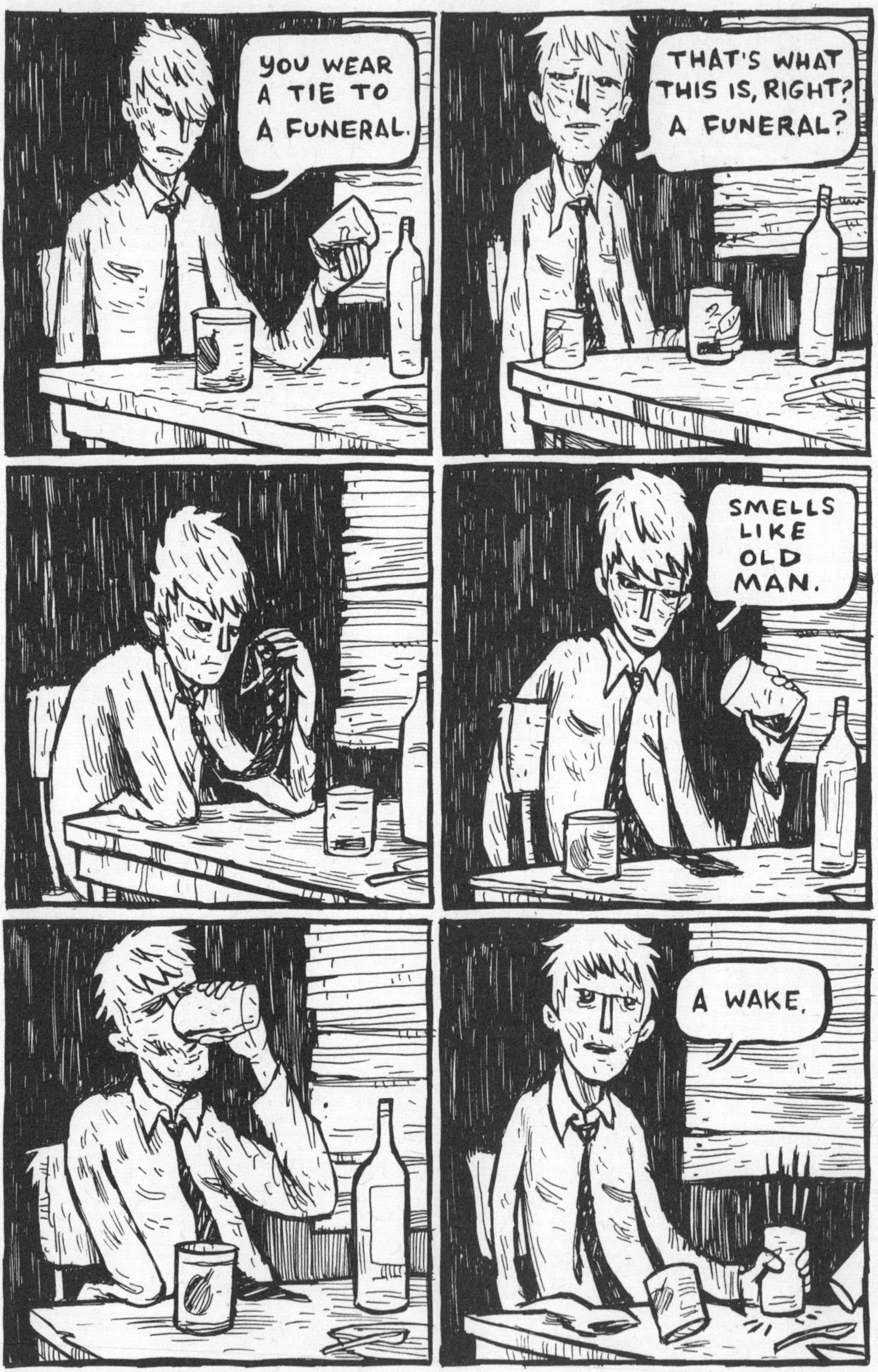
YOU WEAR A TIE TO A FUNERAL.
THAT'S WHAT THIS IS, RIGHT? A FUNERAL?
SMELLS LIKE OLD MAN.
A WAKE.

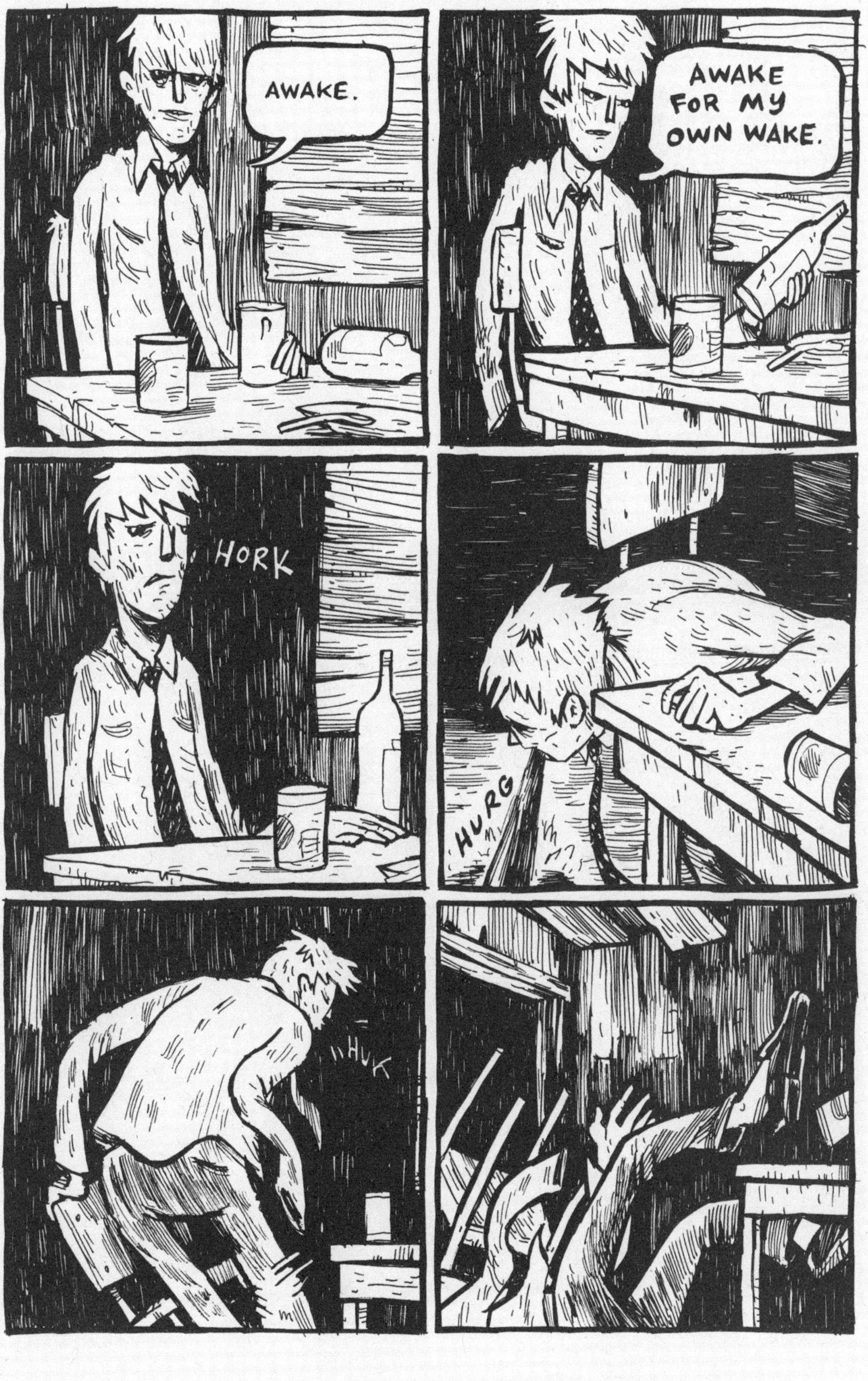
AWAKE.
AWAKE FOR MY OWN WAKE.
HORK
HURG
HUK

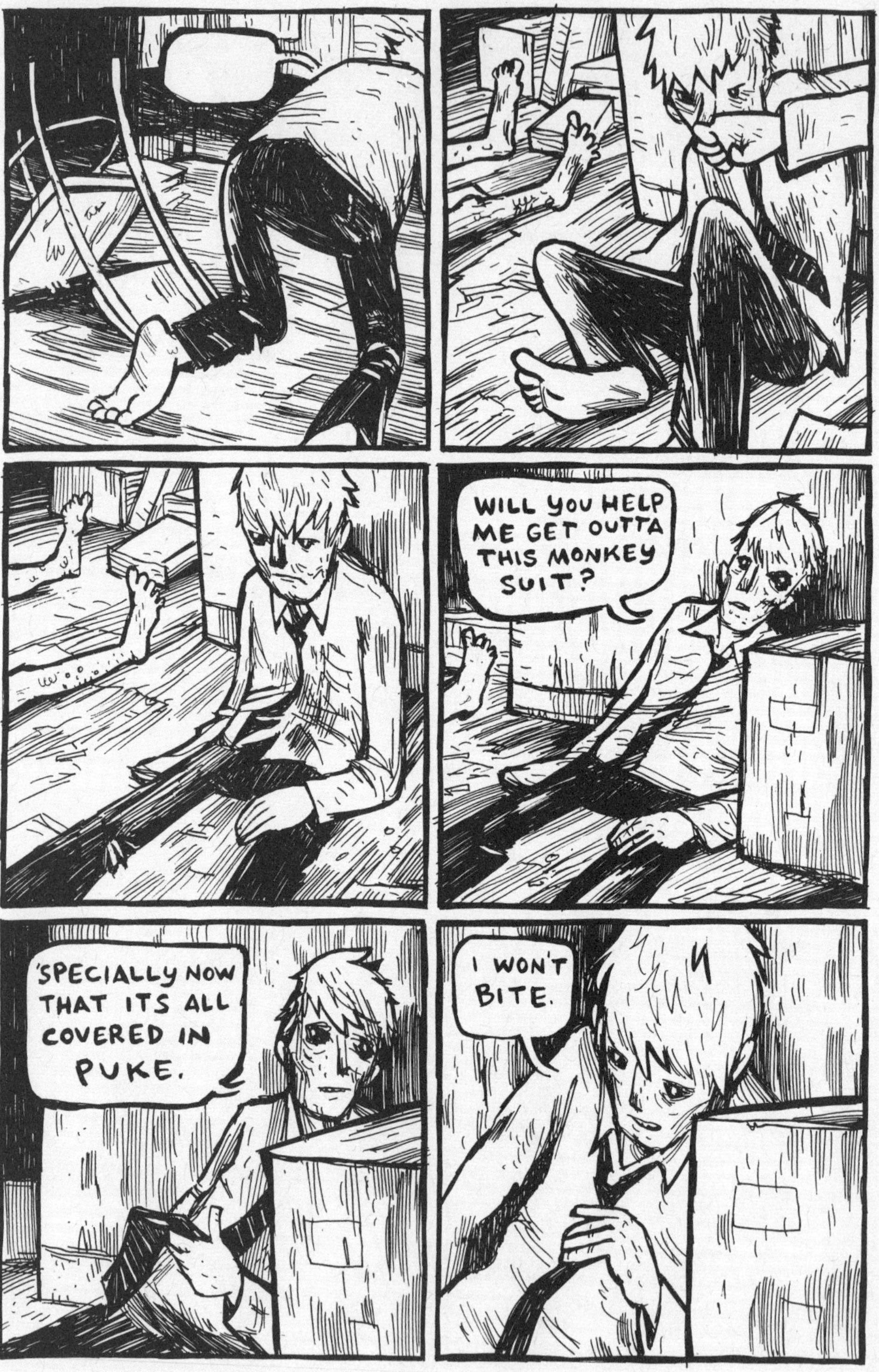
WILL YOU HELP ME GET OUTTA THIS MONKEY SUIT?
'SPECIALLY NOW THAT ITS ALL COVERED IN PUKE.
I WON'T BITE.

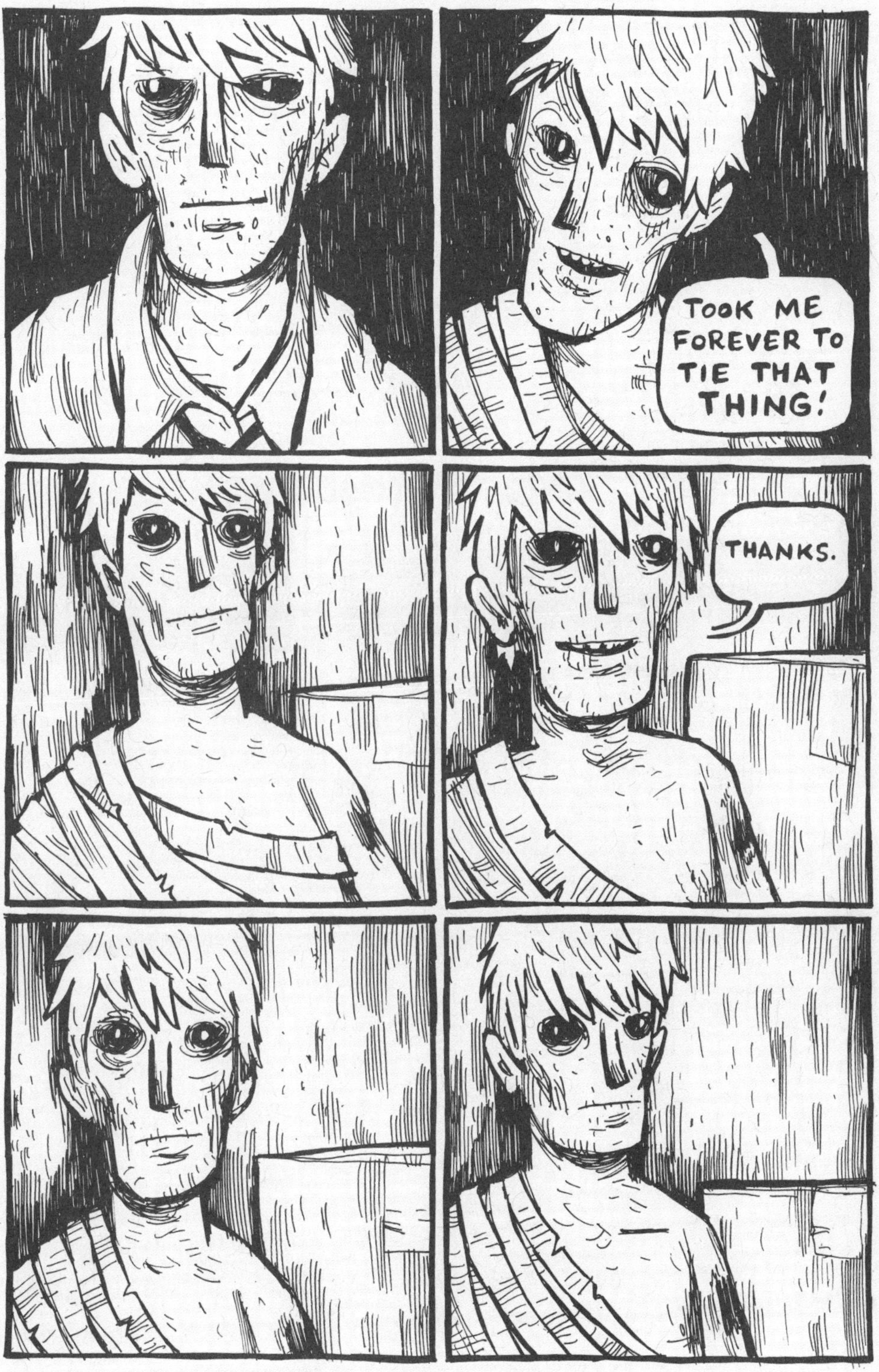
TOOK ME FOREVER TO TIE THAT THING!
THANKS.

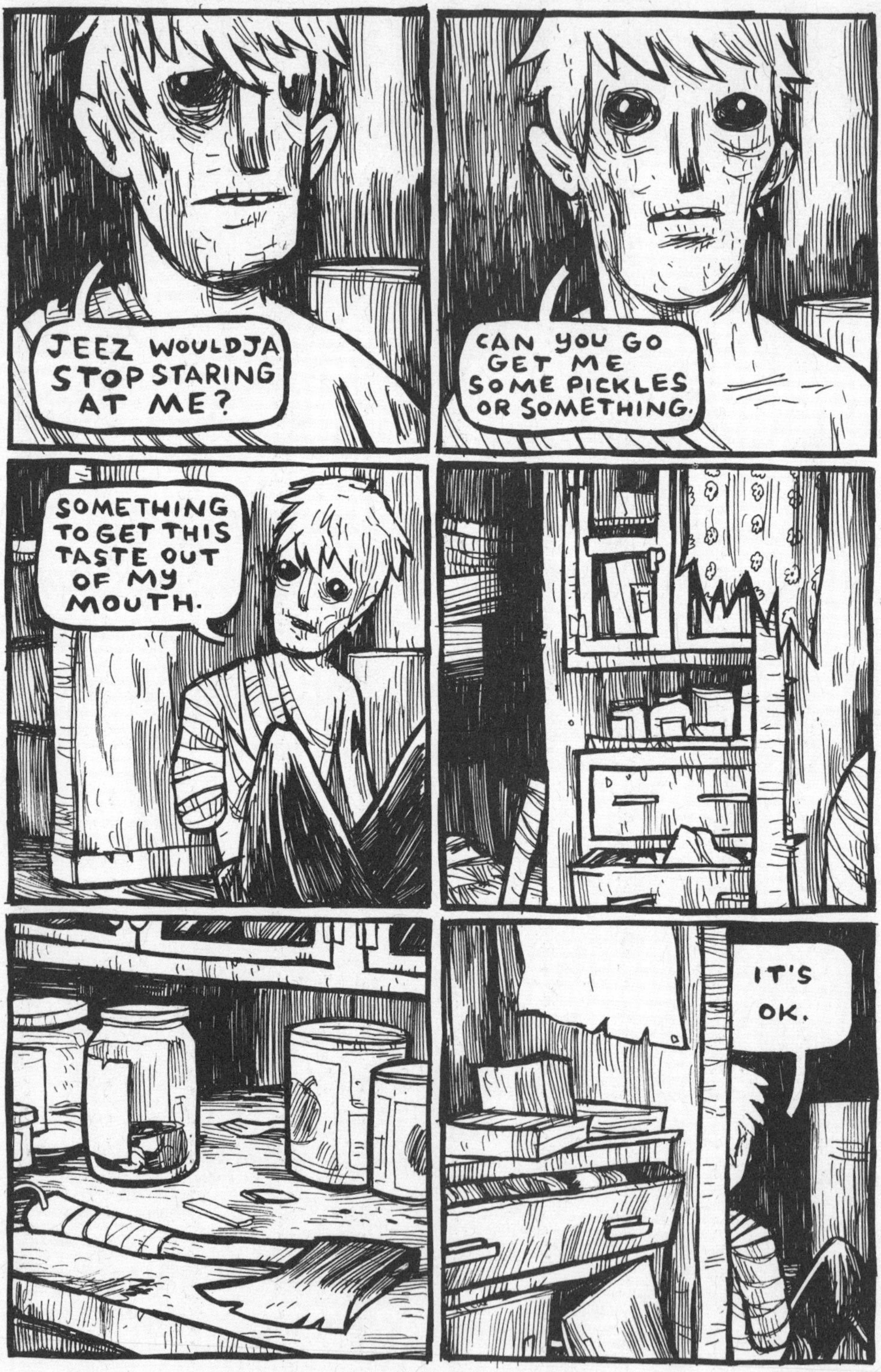
JEEZ WOULDJA STOP STARING AT ME?
CAN YOU GO GET ME SOME PICKLES OR SOMETHING.
SOMETHING TO GET THIS TASTE OUT OF MY MOUTH.
IT'S OK.

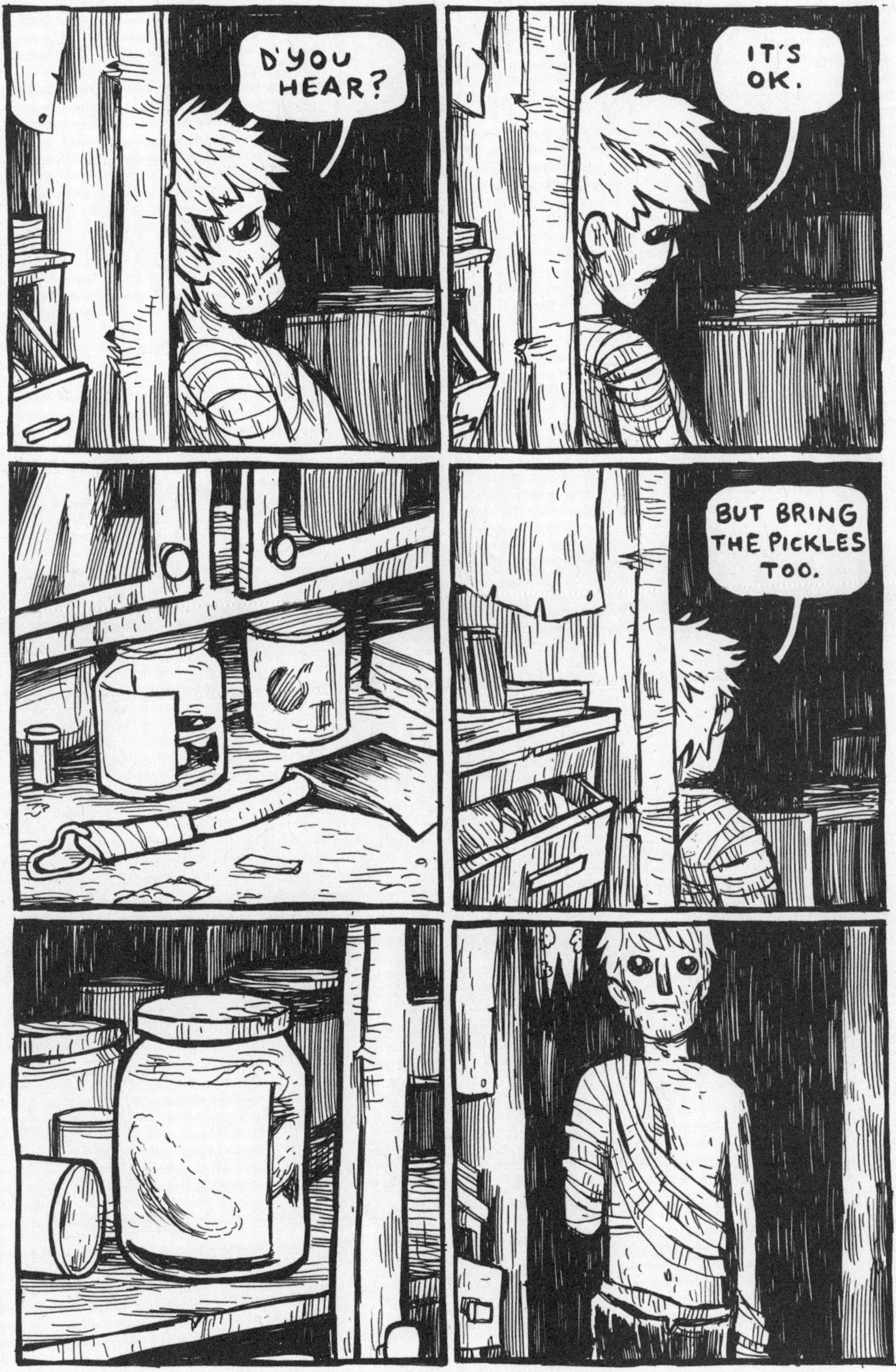
D'YOU HEAR?
IT'S OK.
BUT BRING THE PICKLES TOO.

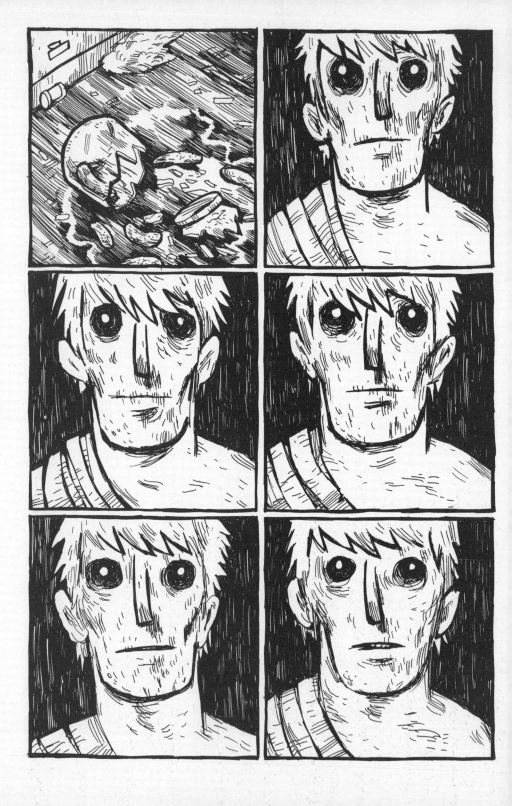

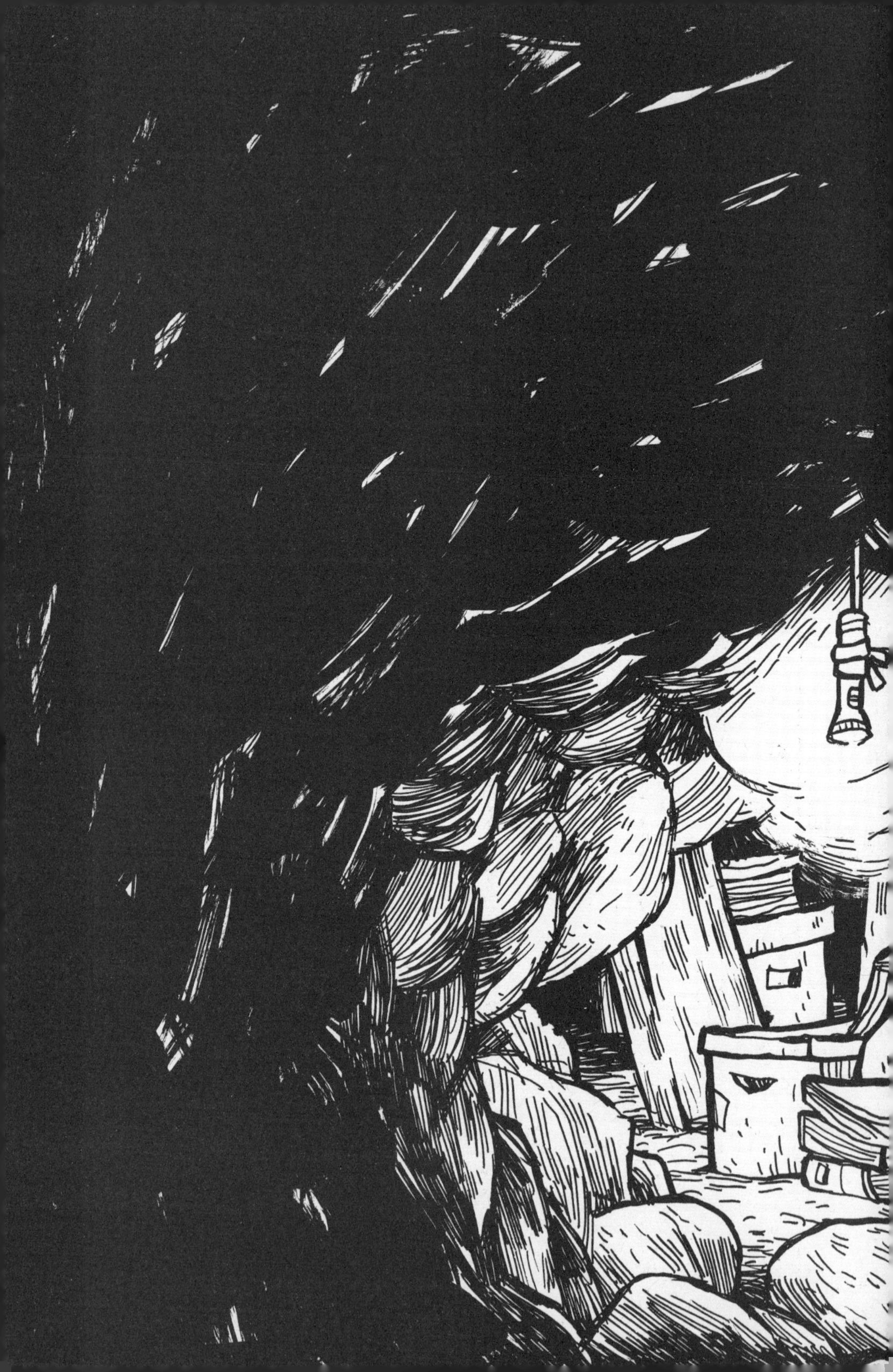